American Identity

OTHER WORKS BY B. KUMARAVADIVELU

Beyond Methods: Macrostrategies for Language Teaching (Yale University
 Press, 2003)
Understanding Language Teaching: From Method to Postmethod (Routledge, 2006)
Cultural Globalization and Language Education (Yale University Press, 2008)
Language Teacher Education for a Global Society (Routledge, 2012)

Three of the above books have been translated into Chinese and one into Japanese.

American Identity

Myth and Reality

B. Kumaravadivelu

HAMILTON BOOKS
an imprint of
Rowman & Littlefield
Lanham • Boulder • New York • London

Published by Hamilton Books
An imprint of The Rowman & Littlefield Publishing Group, Inc.
4501 Forbes Boulevard, Suite 200, Lanham, Maryland 20706
www.rowman.com

86-90 Paul Street, London EC2A 4NE, United Kingdom

British Library Cataloguing in Publication Information Available

Library of Congress Cataloging-in-Publication Data Available

ISBN 978-0-7618-7452-2 (paper) | ISBN 978-0-7618-7453-9 (ebook)

∞™ The paper used in this publication meets the minimum requirements of American
National Standard for Information Sciences—Permanence of Paper for Printed Library
Materials, ANSI/NISO Z39.48-1992.

To the memory of my father

Contents

Preface

It was W. E. B. Du Bois who, at the dawn of the previous century, predicted that "the problem of the Twentieth Century is the problem of color-line."[1]

Channeling him, it is reasonable to suggest that the problem of the twenty-first century is the problem of identity.

Identity has become a watchword everywhere. It crystallizes the anxieties, fears, conflicts, and tensions witnessed in many parts of our globalized and globalizing world. Several nations, communities, and peoples are confronted with real or perceived threats to their religious, cultural, and linguistic identity, and are fiercely engaged in preserving and protecting them.

"Demand for recognition of one's identity," as Francis Fukuyama points out, "is a master concept that unifies much of what is going on in world politics today."[2]

In Europe, the birthplace of Enlightenment, there has recently been a surge in right-wing political parties that are successfully exploiting matters of identity for political gains. Independence Party in Britain, National Front in France, Alternative for Germany (AfD) in Germany, Freedom Party in Austria, Party for Freedom (PVV) in the Netherlands, Golden Dawn in Greece, Fratelli d'Italia in Italy, Fidesz in Hungary, United Right in Poland— just to name a few.

Recent British Prime Ministers have been struggling with the aftermath of Brexit which was, in part, attributed to Britain's identity crisis. Chancellor Angela Merkel lost her majority in the Bundestag because her immigration policies were seen as a threat to German identity. In seeking French Presidency for a second term, Emmanuel Macron had to face a fierce challenger in the far-right leader Marine Le Pen who, promising to restore French identity, captured 33% of the popular vote.

In China, President Xi Jinping has been highlighting Chinese identity as he laid out the details of what he called the "Chinese Dream." In India, Prime Minister Narendra Modi's ruling party has been successfully campaigning about Hindutva, a nationalist version of Indian identity. In

Myanmar, the ongoing Rohingya problem is rooted in the perceived threat to Burmese identity.

America[3] is no exception. It is churning politically, socially, religiously, culturally. A root cause is the problem of identity.

The hitherto veiled discourse on identity and identity politics came to the fore before, during and after the 2016 presidential election. During that period, a perceived threat to White American identity propelled an unlikely candidate to the White House. Not to lag behind, many progressive politicians and pundits accentuated the identities of ethnic communities as well as those of LGBTQ+ communities. The trend continues unabated.

The storming of the U.S. Capitol on January 6, 2021, has raised the public discourse to a potentially treacherous level. Justifiably or not, some Americans lament that the America they grew up with is unrecognizable now. They see threats to their religious, cultural, and linguistic identity, and are determined to protect them. They raise nativist slogans. They doubt the very Americanness of minorities, legal immigrants, and naturalized citizens. In doing so, some of them deliberately blend the distinction between information and disinformation, ideas and ideologies, myth and reality.

The time, therefore, is ripe to take a fresh look at who we really are. That is precisely what I have attempted to do in this book.

My central goal is to critically re-examine the changing nature of American identity—primarily its creedal identity, religious identity, cultural identity, and linguistic identity—and do so within a broader perspective informed by national as well as a global network of connections.

More specifically, I explore several questions including but not limited to: How do common Americans, living in a pluralistic society, engage in a meaningful negotiation of differences between the culture they inherited by birth and the culture they learned through their lived experience? How do they succeed in re-defining and re-designing their religious, ethnic, cultural, and linguistic identity while at the same time honoring core American ideals? How do they defy religious, political, and ideological elites in order to shape and reshape their individual identities?

In attempting to tease out these and other related questions, I am informed by four contemporary realities as I see them: (a) the global reality that is shaping creative as well as chaotic forms of interconnections among nations, economies, cultures, ideas, and peoples; (b) the national reality that is nurturing a robust (and, sometimes, militant) nationalism on the one hand and a relative weakening of nation-states on the other hand; (c) the social reality that is mostly created and sustained by ethnic organizations that foster shared values and beliefs among the members of their ethnic communities; and (d) the individual reality in which individuals, caught in a microscopic mesh in an intricate sociocultural web, try to navigate Self and society.

Clearly, the global, national, social, and individual realities interweave and interact with each other in a synergistic relationship resulting in a cultural whole that is greater than the sum of the parts. The impact of such a relationship may vary among individuals, and within an individual at different times, places, and situations. It is this daunting dialectical relationship that is now influencing, if not determining, identity formation in America and elsewhere.

In light of the above, it is not difficult to notice that neither the melting pot nor the salad bowl satisfactorily explains the contours of American identity in a global society. Instead, what seems to shape and reshape American identity is a nuanced form of cultural realism that is sensitive to the demands of contemporary realities.

I have persuaded myself that my lived experience as a naturalized citizen, my learned knowledge as a scholar, and more than a quarter century of teaching culturally and linguistically diverse university students in California—have all prepared me to take a critical look at American identity.

The concept of identity, being multidisciplinary and multifaceted, warrants that I draw insights from scholarly work straddling a spectrum of Humanities and Social Sciences, from surveys by recognized agencies like the Pew Research Center, from the practice of everyday American life, and from other relevant sources.

The discourse about American identity is as old as the Republic itself. Our Founding Fathers started it all. Ever since, it has been a subject of interest for numerous thought leaders—past and present. Many authors have continued to explore and to explain what part of American identity constitutes the core and what part the periphery.

Perched on their shoulders, I venture to present my perspective synthesizing the professional, the political, and the personal. As I do it, I am fully aware that what I am getting into, to quote anthropologist Clifford Geertz, is not "an experimental science in search of law but an interpretive one in search of meaning."[4]

Searching for meaning is rendered even more challenging when dealing with a concept like identity which is malleable and constantly evolving. There is no fixed, frozen finality about it. Therefore, every generation has to re-examine and rediscover their and their nation's identity on a continual basis.

And as such, the scrutiny of American identity—or any identity for that matter—will always remain contemporary. One that is revisited from time to time. One that is renewed from time to time.

The journey must continue.

Acknowledgments

This challenging yet rewarding project has been made possible because of the goodwill of many colleagues and friends.

My greatest debt is to Julian Edge of Manchester University, England. He read almost the entire manuscript giving me critical and constructive feedback on the style and substance of the book. I did not agree with all his suggestions, but his friendly intervention made this book much more reasoned and much more readable. He was selfless in spending an enormous amount of time even though he was busy with his own creative writing at that time. Thank you, Julian.

I am thankful to many professional colleagues whose conversations helped me clear some of the conceptual cobwebs and terminological bedbugs that I came across in the complex narratives about the concept of identity. Too many to name them all here. But there are a few I must highlight: Salwa Mrabet Abid at the University of Carthage, Tunisia; Rosemary Henze at San José State University; Adrian Holliday at Canterbury Christ Church University, England; Andy Kirkpatrick at Griffith University, Australia; Sandra McKay at San Francisco State University; Adriana González Moncada at Universidad de Antioquia, Colombia; and Robert Phillipson at Copenhagen Business School, Denmark.

I have had the pleasure of being invited to give keynote/plenary addresses or guest lectures in various universities around the world on identity, cultural globalization, and related topics. Probing questions from professors and participants helped me in ways that they may not even be aware of. The universities include Peking University, Beijing, China; Canterbury Christ Church University, England; Boğaziçi University, Istanbul, Turkey; University of Wisconsin-Madison, USA; The English and Foreign Languages University, Hyderabad, India; The University of the West Indies, Trinidad & Tobago; Universidad de Antioquia, Colombia; Widya Mandala Catholic University, Surabaya, Indonesia; National Institute of Education, Singapore; and Hong Kong Baptist University, Hong Kong.

I am also thankful to my graduate students at San José State University where I taught several semesters of classes in intercultural communication. Delightful cohorts of American and international students were challenged to put their personal identities to test and, in the process, to confront how they may be considered victims as well as victimizers of cultural stereotypes. All their interesting and intriguing questions and comments opened my eyes to various perspectives which I might have overlooked otherwise.

My thanks are also due to my editor Brooke Bures, my copyeditor Sam Brawand, and other members of the editorial team at Hamilton Books for their help and guidance.

Thanks to Carcanet Press in England for granting permission to reproduce the poem titled "Search for my Tongue" by Sujata Bhatt.

As usual, my gratitude goes to my wife Revathi. Amid her own professorial preoccupation, she graciously shielded me from the onslaught of daily chores. With her innovative thoughts about Deep Humanities and with her insatiable thirst for good-natured arguments, she often provided helpful counterpoints to my ideas. She has always been a valuable personal and professional companion.

Finally, my affectionate thanks to our millennial children Chandrika Kumar and Anand Kumar who, through a sliver of an opening, let me peep into their intractable cultural multiverse, thereby injecting a dose of worldly wisdom in me.

PART I

Understanding the Complexity of Identity

Chapter 1

Identity Matters

I came to America in 1984, the year made infamous by George Orwell. It did not take me long to recognize that "the home of the brave" is also a house of cards. ID cards, that is. When I landed at the Detroit airport on a freezing January day to start my PhD program at the University of Michigan, Ann Arbor, I had no plastic card on me. I had only my Indian passport and a student visa.

On the opening day of school, the first thing I was asked to do in a hurry was to get my student ID card, and also my Social Security card so that I could be hired as a Teaching Assistant right away.

Ever since, Uncle Sam has been deciding how to identify me from time to time. My own preferences about how I wish to be identified do not seem to matter. I was first labelled a *non-resident alien*, holding a non-immigrant visa that allowed me to pursue my higher education. Even though I was called a non-resident, believe me, I was not non-residing. I was very much living and breathing here in America. The best part of being a non-resident alien was that I did not have to pay taxes for the money I was paid as a Teaching Assistant. Right there, I saw the humane side of Uncle Sam—spare the starving students from taxation.

After I completed my studies and became a Doctor—Doctor of Philosophy, that is—and started teaching in a university as a regular faculty, the Immigration and Naturalization Service of the U.S. Department of Justice (there was no Department of Homeland Security then) thought it fit to respect my new status and to drop the negative prefix *non* in *non-resident alien* and to elevate me to a higher level—a *resident alien*.

After a lengthy and cumbersome legal process, I was given what is popularly called a *green card* which was actually pink; only recently, somebody thought it sensible to make the green card, well, green. The card labelled me as a *resident alien* with a nine-digit identification number prefixed with a big, bold letter A. I assured myself that it had nothing to do with the scandalous Scarlet Letter. Although I was amused by the label *alien*—a label associated with funny-looking fictional creatures from the outer world—I had grown to feel comfortable with it particularly after watching heroic as well as hilarious deeds of aliens romanticized in popular movies ranging from George Lucas's *Star Wars* to Mel Brooks's spoof of them.

The practice of legalistic labelling of me finally ended (or, did it?) on the 13th of February 2002, when the Commissioner of Immigration and Naturalization Service certified that I was "entitled to be admitted to citizenship." Of course, I made myself "entitled" by spending more than the required number of years as a well-behaving, law-abiding, tax-paying, civic-minded resident, and also by proving my knowledge of basic American history and functional English. On that day, along with I do not remember how many, I raised my right hand and took the Oath of Allegiance in a solemn naturalization ceremony conducted at the U.S. District Court in San José, California. With that rite of passage, I am no longer considered an alien, at least not legally. Uncle Sam now calls me *a naturalized citizen.*

As I said earlier, I never had a plastic ID card as long as I lived, studied, and taught in India. Even schools and colleges never issued student or faculty plastic ID cards at that time (things have since changed). Now, my wallet is bulging with ID cards. Each of them declaring my affiliation to something or the other.

Anybody who raids my wallet will instantly know that I am associated with a University in California. I drive around with DMV's approval. I use two credit cards to enjoy the blessings and suffer the curse of consumerism. I deposit my money in a bank that has been conveniently called too big to fail. I visit a hospital run by the largest HMO. I call AAA whenever my car breaks down. I go to a local fitness center to work out, and more. Some of these cards, like my driver license, reveal my age and my residential address, against my will.

I often get cautionary notifications from my bank, credit card companies, Internet providers, and others that I should protect my ID cards as well as my passwords against "identity theft." Sometimes, I come across friendly reminders in unexpected places. A big, eye-catching poster inside my neighborhood post office, picturing a man with a menacing look, benignly asks: "IDENTITY THEFT. Has someone taken over your good name?" So far, no one has found my name good enough to take over.

The U.S. Federal Trade Commission has a dedicated website offering "one-stop resource for identity theft victims."[1] Free service from our friendly government.

In addition, several companies have sprouted to save me from those wicked identity thieves. They promise to protect my identity for a cost of $8.99 a month, sometimes with a 10% discount.

"Start Monitoring Your Identity Today"—implores Costco, the largest members-only wholesale corporation in the United States that sells a wide range of merchandise. One of their recent additions is what they call *Premium Identity Protection* for an affordable cost of (yes, you guessed it) $8.99 per month for its executive members. A colorful, glossy promo flier from the corporation shows a bunch of credit cards safely secured with a large, black, combination lock promising to protect "you and your family from identity theft."

Identity theft? Seriously?

I never thought that by stealing my ID cards or my passwords, one could steal my identity. Let's be clear: the cards stacked up in my wallet and my passwords floating in cyberspace are not my *identity* markers; they are my *identification* markers. It is true, thieves can steal my identification; but they cannot steal my identity. Sadly, the mix up between these two closely related words—identity and identification—is quite common among the public, in the government, in the industry, in the media, and elsewhere.

What my ID cards do is to identify me in terms of my name, number, affiliation, etc. What they do not do is to reveal the core of my identity, the essence of my being. The criminals who steal my cards may deplete my bank balance, forge my driver license, misuse my Social Security number, and do other illegal activities. But they can never ever steal the religion I follow, the culture I practice, the languages I speak, the knowledge I possess, the values I cherish, the hopes I nurture, the fears I hide, the struggles I wage, the pain I endure, or the pleasures I enjoy. These are some of the things that constitute my identity. And, that is true of your identity as well.

My identity, and yours, cannot be miniaturized and plasticized into a $3\frac{3}{8}'' \times 2\frac{1}{8}''$ card with a coded magnetic strip. My ID cards cannot be used or abused to strip me of that which makes me, me. Clearly, the use of the term *identity* in the ubiquitous phrase *identity theft* is a misleading simplification. Let's not be fooled by this common mistake. It trivializes the concept of identity which is by any measure deep and dense.

The word *identity*, according to historian Philip Gleason, has been used in the English language since the sixteenth century, although its usage became widespread only by World War II. And then it rapidly became a much used and misused term. Gleason notes: "By the mid-1960s, the word *identity* was used so widely and so loosely that to determine its provenance in every context would be impossible."[2] Because of its widespread use, many of us may be familiar with the word *identity* but we have only a superficial understanding of what it actually means. The globalized and digitalized world we all live in has only intensified and complicated the use of the term, as we will see in the next chapter.

It is not as if scholars have not been wrestling with the complexity of identity or identity formation. In fact, it has been explored for a long time in as varied academic disciplines as sociology, anthropology, psychology, philosophy, political science, history, cultural studies, linguistics, and literature. You would imagine that with such exalted and extended scrutiny, scholars would have reached a consensus about what constitutes identity, or how it is shaped and reshaped. That is just not the case.

Identity continues to be, as the Australian sociologist Anthony Elliott laments, "one of the most vexing and vexed topics in the social sciences and humanities."[3] Vexing or not, we must try to grasp the meaning of identity. The meaning of *our* identity. So that we can have a sense of being alive. So that we can know who we are.

WHO ACTUALLY ARE WE?

We cannot even begin to address that perennial and puzzling question without a clear understanding of our sense of Self.[4] That's why the concept of Self has captured the imagination of saints and sages down the ages. The Greek philosophers who laid the foundation for Western civilization thought it fit to inscribe the maxim *Know Thyself* at the entry of the sacred Temple of Apollo at Delphi. They had the wisdom to see an invisible and inviolable connection between our microcosmic Self and the macrocosmic forces above and beyond us. Similarly, ancient Indian scriptures such as the Bhagavad Gita stressed the connection between the Supreme Being and individual Self. As the Indian philosopher-President Sarvepalli Radhakrishnan explained: "The seers see the Supreme in the self, and not in images."[5]

Self-identity is commonly associated with the question *who am I?* The question is so simple. And yet, so profound. It requires a considerable degree of critical self-reflection on our part to explore it, analyze it, understand it. Pause here for a moment if you will. Ask yourself the question: *who am I?*

If you think about the question seriously, you will find that it masks the complex nature of your identity. However hard you think, you may not be able to come up with a true and complete profile of your Self. You might even conclude that the question itself is not pertinent. Or that it is too vague or too elusive to make sense. If you do, you are in good company.

The celebrated American psychologist Erik H. Erikson, for instance, registers "a certain impatience" with people who equate the term identity with the question *who am I?* "Nobody asks this question," he admonishes, "except in a morbid state or a creative self-confrontation." According to him, the pertinent question would be "what do I want to make of myself and what do I have to work with?"[6] Similarly, Canadian philosopher Charles Taylor tells us that the question *who am I?* "can't necessarily be answered by giving name and genealogy. What does answer this question for us is an understanding of what is of crucial importance to us."[7]

What do I want to make of myself? What do I have to work with? What is crucially important to me?

Each of us will answer these questions differently. And, we will also answer them differently at different stages in our life.

If we are serious about seeking answers to these questions, we must first understand the *concept* of identity.

The term *identity* stems from the Latin root *idem*, meaning *the same*. Broadly speaking, our identity entails membership in one or more categories such as nation, ethnicity, race, religion, class, profession, or gender. Each of these categories relates us in some way to other members of the same category because people in a particular category are generally expected to share some characteristics in common. Being a white American Christian female, for instance, connects a person with shared aspects of whiteness, Americanness, Christianness, and femaleness—however we choose to define them.

We inherit some identities (for example, ethnic identity), acquire some (for example, professional identity), and some others are ascribed to us (for example, Asian American). Some of the identity markers are so common that we all use them as convenient short-hand labels to position ourselves in the practice of everyday life. Our identity labels also create certain expectations in others, certain stereotypes about others, using which they measure us up, though superficially. The moment I am introduced as a professor, people may automatically and stereotypically associate me with who they think an academic is, such as, someone who is a loony left, or someone who gives long and boring lectures, or someone who writes unreadable prose with babble of jargons.

Although sameness is a crucial element of identity, it is difference that often stands out in proclaiming and projecting our identity. In fact, identity presupposes difference, as the French philosopher Étienne Balibar argues. "A self-identity," he says, "is maintained, or better, reiterated through difference."[8] Most often we characterize somebody's identity in terms of how different somebody is from somebody else. Each of us can justifiably say: "I am not you because I am me" or, in the words of French writer Amin Maalouf, "my identity is what prevents me from being identical to anybody else."[9] We may closely align ourselves to a particular community based on ethnic, religious, or other affiliations, but still we strive to maintain our own individual identity by differentiating ourselves from others within that community. Even within a family, siblings maintain separate identities, separate persona. That includes identical twins as well.

Much has been written about identity and continues to be written. Variously. In various times. By various people. That is largely because the concept of identity itself varies from time to time. One way of understanding it is to look at it through the prism of the sociological narratives about self-identity associated with three broad periods of time in human history—premodern (a period prior to mid-seventeenth century), modern (roughly from mid-seventeenth to late twentieth century), and postmodern (roughly from late twentieth century onward).[10]

A brief note on the philosophical systems of premodernism, modernism, and postmodernism, as prevailed in Western intellectual thought, is helpful in order to put the formation and re-formation of an individual's self-identity in proper historical perspective.

PREMODERNISM, MODERNISM, AND POSTMODERNISM

Broadly speaking, the three "isms" define and describe significant phases of growth and development in Western civilization as reflected in science and humanities, in politics and religion, as well as in art and architecture. An important purpose of these "isms" is to shed light on the expanding knowledge about natural, physical, and biological phenomena, ultimately leading us to a better and deeper understanding of the human condition itself.

During the premodern times (that is, before the mid-seventeenth century), scientific temper was hardly recognized. A theological worldview predominated. Faith prevailed over reason. The supernatural triumphed over the natural. It was believed that knowledge about Ultimate Truth was obtainable only through divine revelation coming from a God or gods. Sacred texts such as the Bible were treated as the authentic and authoritative sources of knowledge. Leaders among the clergy were considered to be the sole custodians, interpreters, and purveyors of that knowledge. Recall how in 1633, Galileo was placed under house arrest until his death in 1643 because the highest ecclesiastical council in his country disapproved his claim that the earth revolves around the sun. The clergy wielded enormous power and influence over the ruling class (mostly kings and feudal lords) as well as the common people. For these and other reasons, the premodern period has been characterized as medieval or feudal. It took a very long time—centuries, actually—for a different worldview to evolve. To a large extent, the slow and gradual evolution was the cause as well as the consequence of modernity.

The modern period (roughly from mid-seventeenth to late twentieth century) witnessed fundamental transformations in almost all walks of life, triggered by developments in two major areas of human activity: science and religion. Experimental science based on newly developed scientific methods led to a treasure house of empirically verifiable knowledge systems. It was during the early decades of the modern period that scientists discovered new knowledge on an unprecedented scale and in major branches of science— Galileo Galilei in astronomy, Isaac Newton in physics, Carl Linnaeus in biology, and Antoine Lavoisier in chemistry, just to name a few. Applications of newly produced scientific knowledge led to the creation of technologies that enhanced productivity and prosperity, the Industrial Revolution being a prime example.

The scientific theories of the early modern period, particularly in the seventeenth and eighteenth centuries, along with the importance given to logic and reason contributed significantly to the weakening of the power and influence church leaders enjoyed during the premodern period. In fact, progress in science accelerated and strengthened the challenge to the authority of the church that began a little earlier when, during the mid-sixteenth century, Martin Luther ignited the Protestant Reformation movement.

The church leaders could not ignore the scientific methods introduced during this period and felt compelled to use them to reinterpret and reformulate certain aspects of Christian theology. They also could no longer claim to be the sole source of Ultimate Truth. As a result, the church had to grudgingly concede some of its intellectual authority to scholars in universities and some of its political authority to the rulers of the time.

The emphasis on logic and reason that marked the scientific temper of the early modern period was also nurtured by another parallel movement: Enlightenment. Also dubbed the Age of Reason, European Enlightenment (1685–1815) generated lofty ideas such as liberty, fraternity, equality, tolerance, individualism, liberalism, and, most importantly, separation of church and state. These ideas severely undermined the authority of the monarchy and of the church, sowing the seeds for two prominent sociopolitical revolutions in the West: the American Revolution (1775–1783) and the French Revolution (1789–1799) both of which opened up the flood gates of liberal democracy and individual freedom.

In sum, the early modern period saw scientific objectivism supersede religious dogmatism, reason supersede faith. Further scientific developments and technological innovations during the later part of the modern period solidified the modern way of life. Unquestionably, the modern period launched and celebrated the ideals of liberal democracy, free market economy, individual liberty, and human rights.

But it has another side, a darker side.

The same period witnessed colonialism and imperialism that oppressed a vast number of countries and peoples in Asia, Africa, and South America. The scourge of major wars—World War I and II, the Korean War, the Vietnam

War, the Gulf War, the Afghan War—and the scars they left, caused untold human misery. The same period also witnessed abject poverty, economic inequality, racial conflicts, and gender discrimination on a large scale. The failure of modernity to ensure freedom and equality, peace, and prosperity for all caused widespread disillusionment. It eventually resulted in the denunciation of some of the modernist thoughts and in the emergence of postmodernist views.

The postmodern period (that is, late twentieth century onward) is still in its infancy. And yet, it has shaken the world like an earthquake. It has already experienced sociopolitical aftershocks arising out of people's deep resentment about the modernist project that has, in large part, contributed to the creation of the one-percent-versus-the ninety-nine-percent syndrome. The massive socioeconomic inequality seems to be reaching a crisis point in liberal democracies of the West. Popular resentments, expressed loudly and clearly through the ballot box during the year 2016, are a major reason behind the eventual exiting of Britain from the European Union, and the hoisting of an unlikely Presidential candidate in the White House.

Both these events occurring simultaneously in the two capitalistic countries across the Atlantic can be seen as a direct result of neoliberal economic policies that relied excessively, some would say obsessively, on privatization, deregulation, and free trade. They can also be seen as a repudiation of the Western political establishment and of the professional pundits who failed to foresee popular peaceful revolt, and some of them are still trying to come to grips with it. But, postmodernist social theorists, led by the celebrated trio of French thinkers—Michel Foucault, Jean-François Lyotard, and Jacques Derrida—predicted several of the ill-effects of modernism quite a while ago.

For these and other European postmodern theorists, "the postmodern is the realization of the *hubris* of modernity."[11] They foregrounded the precepts and practices of modernism that, in their view, left much to be desired. They saw disconnections between the laudable goals of modernism and the deplorable outcomes it generated. More specifically, they cautioned against the excesses of capitalism that benefited the elites and trampled upon the lives of the working-class men and women. They admonished governmental policies that directly or indirectly subordinated the citizens to higher political, industrial, and religious authorities. They chided the hypocrisy of liberal democracies that buttressed oppressive regimes around the world to safeguard their own selfish national interests. They lamented the jingoistic voices of nationalism that impeded harmonious relationship between nations and peoples. They alerted individuals, communities, and nations to emerging globalization and digitalization that demand concerted and coordinated actions by them in spite of their diverse ways of knowing and seeing, thinking and acting, believing and behaving.

That, in brief, is how Western intellectual thought unfolded.

A note of caution is in order here: although there are three easily identifiable developmental phases with an approximate time period attached to each of them, it is not as if one period neatly ends before the next one begins. Besides, not all the societies, not all the communities within a society, march ceremoniously from one period to another in a lockstep manner. In the twenty-first century, we can easily come across some of the salient features of each of the "isms" overlapping and coexisting within a nation or within a community. Societies and cultures tend to privilege one or the other for different purposes and at different times. America is no exception.

American society today bears most of the characteristics of modernism. Individualism, a cardinal tenet of modernism, is also America's core value. Its liberal democracy, its free market economy, its religious freedom, its scientific temper, its technological prowess, and its constitutional separation of church and state—all testify to its modernist credentials.

We also witness in America clear signs of postmodernist outlook. The heightened awareness about income inequality that permeated the 2016 and 2020 presidential and the 2018, 2020, and 2022 Congressional elections; the greater acceptance of gay rights that culminated in the 2015 Supreme Court decision to declare same-sex marriage a constitutional right; the increased recognition of ethnic group consciousness that expresses itself in terms of identity politics, the widespread realization about how global issues such as climate change can easily impact our daily life—these are but a few postmodern thoughts enveloping many segments of the American society today.

Arguably, certain premodern traditions, tinged with religious, racial, and gender discriminations, continue to linger even in twenty-first-century America. Consider these: during 1996 through 2015 alone, the country witnessed 4,705 fire incidents at houses of worship—churches, synagogues, temples, and mosques. Fifty-one percent of the fires were ruled intentional.[12] Child marriage is still practiced, with reports showing that between the years 2000 and 2015, more than 200,000 minors got married legally, some as young as thirteen.[13] High school proms in certain counties of the Deep South were racially segregated into "the white-folks prom" and "the black-folks prom."[14] Racial inequality and discrimination is rampant, as the recent nation-wide protests highlighted. Some popular golf clubs systematically excluded women until as recently as 2012.[15] Sexual exploitation in workplaces is extensive, as highlighted by the #Metoo movement. It is still legal in the United States for doctors, if parents requested, to check the hymen of young women, to make sure they are virgins. The historic election of an African American—twice—as President of the United States failed miserably to begin to usher in a post-racial society, as demonstrated dramatically by the ongoing Black Lives Matter movement. These are not isolated examples.

These and other similar occurrences are symptomatic of a prevailing premodern mindset that devalues the merit of the individual in the American society.

Wait a minute, you may wonder: what has all this narrative about the three "isms" to do with identity and identity formation?

A great deal. The central point is that each "ism" is at once the result of and also resulted in certain historical and sociopolitical environment that shaped the concept of identity, and hence the construction of self-identity. Let's peep into each of them once again, this time with particular reference to individual identity.

PREMODERN IDENTITY

In premodern societies, the individual perpetually lived in a state of feudal subordination which determined identity formation. During this period, the freedom enjoyed by the individual to conceive and construct their own identity was so minimal or even non-existent that self-identity was described as "Selfless identity."[16] That is because an individual's identity was tied almost inseparably to affiliation to family and to ethnic community. Individuals were required to strictly follow the prevailing sociocultural beliefs and practices as well as religious rites and rituals, all of which confined them to a religiously-dictated, socially-approved, hierarchically-coded place under the Sun.

Premodern individuals had to assume a communal identity, a collective identity. Deprived of any opportunity to develop their own individualized identity, they had to find personal fulfillment within the boundaries of pre-existing and relatively unchanging societal norms. They had very little meaningful choice outside of clearly specified characteristics of birth such as class, race, religion, gender, or ethnicity. Consequently, as the Scottish sociologist Harvie Ferguson points out, there was no need for them "to reflect on any particular situation, make choices from a range of possibilities, or exercise a sense of inner freedom in projecting a particular self-image."[17] It was all preordained, prescribed, predicted.

In other words, the premodern sense of Self was more externally imposed on individuals than self-constructed by them. More than anything else, it was designed to keep them in their neat little place. The message conveyed to them by their family and their community was as simple as it was stern: You are born there. You belong there. You better stay there. If you try to cross the boundaries, there will be consequences. Such a condition existed for a long time, until a different concept of identity emerged during the modern period.

MODERN IDENTITY

In contrast to the premodern view of identity, the modern view privileges the individual. It bestows on you and me certain fundamental rights to define who we are or who we want to be. It concedes our freedom to exercise our *agency*, that is, our ability, responsibility, and willingness to make the right choice and to take the right action needed for us to shape our own identity. It sees self-identity as something that is actively constructed by us on an ongoing basis. In this never-ending process, we are constantly called upon to make commitments and judgements about our everyday lived experiences. Our commitments and judgements provide, as Charles Taylor points out, "the frame or horizon" for us to determine "from case to case what is good, or valuable, or what ought to be done."[18]

Yet another characteristic feature of modern identity is that it is considered multiple and fragmented. Clearly, all of us have several identities, playing several roles in the practice of our daily life. Each role carries with it a fragment, only a fragment, of who we are, what our beliefs are, and what our attitudes are. Take me for example. What are the identity roles I normally play? I am a son. I am a brother. I am a husband. I am a father. I am a friend. I am a professor. I am an author. And more. Depending on the context, a particular facet of my identity is foregrounded. When I stand in front of my class tutoring my students, it is my professorial identity that comes to the fore. When I accompany my son and cheer him on when he participates in badminton tournaments, it is my parental identity that stands out. When I join my friends for a weekend early morning walk, it is my social identity that is exhibited. When I help my wife with household chores, other aspects of my identity are displayed. Even though each of these identity fragments appears to be separate in its function, all of them are seamlessly connected to me, to my sense of Self, to my sense of who I am. "A person's identity," as Maalouf explains, "is not an assemblage of separate affiliations, nor a kind of loose patchwork; it is like a pattern drawn on the tightly stretched parchment. Touch just one part of it, just one allegiance, and the whole person will react, the whole drum will sound."[19]

Unlike modern identity which marks a drastic departure from premodern identity, postmodern identity is in many ways a continuation of modern identity but with a consequential twist.

POSTMODERN IDENTITY

Postmodern identity accepts the essence of individuality. However, it does not see the individual as the center of the universe. Wary of the excesses of individualism and its tendency to sidetrack the common good, postmodern identity stresses the importance of collectivity, community. It maintains that individuals are not as autonomous as they appear to be or want to be, and hence they can hardly construct any meaningful self-identity without taking into serious consideration the historical, political, social, and economic conditions of the group they belong to. Different groups have different histories, different identities, and different experiences. Group affiliations based on religion, race, class, gender, or sexual or political orientation have become an important aspect of postmodern life.

Group consciousness has grown markedly in early twenty-first-century America. A clear reflection of that can be seen in the kind of identity politics that plays out particularly during election seasons in our country. Remember how in the 2016 and 2020 presidential elections, perhaps more blatantly than before, the Republicans amplified white identity politics while the Democrats amplified the group identities of women, African Americans, Hispanics, Asian Americans, and LGBTQ+ communities.

Although we are past the first two decades of the twenty-first century and are technically in a postmodern era, individuals and communities as well as nations can be found to struggle and straddle between the self-imposed and externally imposed pulls and pressures of premodern, modern, and postmodern identity formation, and do so at different speed, with different priorities, and with different outcomes.

Turning specifically to America, a couple of related questions arise: In a society where individualism is considered a central tenet of living and being, to what extent are you, as an individual, really free to construct your own self-identity? And to what extent the society at large is free to infringe upon your freedom. In other words . . .

"WHO DECIDES WHAT YOUR IDENTITY IS?"

Uncle Sam. Says American historian David A. Hollinger answering his own question. "The United States," he tells us, "has always practiced identity ascription, that is, the ascribing of identity to individuals whatever their own personal preferences may be."[20] Worth repeating: *whatever their own personal preferences may be.* Just as I was given a series of labels on my way to naturalized citizenship. Just as we are all given a pre-fabricated set of options to choose from, for instance, in a Census form.

Clearly, official ascriptions are simple and simplistic. If we strictly go by them, all of us—more than 330 million Americans—belong to no more than five major identity groups: White, Asian American, Hispanic, African American, or American Indian.[21] I am sure you are familiar with the label Uncle Sam has ascribed you. I am dubbed Asian American. Honestly, I don't even know what that means. As the Nobel laureate Amartya Sen says, "classification is certainly cheap, but identity is not."[22]

Official ascriptions have limitations. They are useful and usable mainly for legal, institutional, or governmental purposes. In personal spheres, though, you do have a modicum of agency to act in your special interest.

But, even in the personal sphere, is your agency to form your self-identity absolute? Not at all. Your agency comes with strings attached.

Yes, strings attached. Because, unlike God, society intrudes in not so mysterious ways. Even strangers, as co-members of the society you live in, may claim the right to tell you who you are and who you are not. However much you may resent it or reject it, your identity needs their tacit, sometimes explicit, approval.

Take a case that raised a frenzy in the media, particularly the social media, during the summer of 2015. Rachel Dolezal was President of the Spokane chapter of National Association for the Advancement of Colored People (NAACP). By all accounts, she was a committed activist and was doing her job well. And yet she was forced to resign. The reason: the thirty-seven-year-old blonde-haired blue-eyed white woman changed her looks and pretended to be black for years. She was outed by none other than her own parents who accused her of living a life of lies. They revealed that they are of German and Czech origin.

Some in the social media denounced her for misrepresenting her identity in order to advance her career and to ensure upward social mobility. Some others supported her for her activism and leadership. Putting societal identity ascription in proper perspective, and writing in *Time* magazine, basketball hall of famer turned essayist Kareem Abdul-Jabbar wondered whether it really mattered whether she is black or white. After all, he said, she has been doing "exceptionally well—making America more American."[23]

Arguably, society meted out harsh treatment to Dolezal. Not so to Bruce Jenner, a former Olympic decathlon champion, who, without even a gender-altering surgery, called himself a woman and gave herself a new name, Caitlyn. Unlike Rachel who acted on her free will to portray a particular self-identity, Caitlyn, like other members of the LGBTQ+ community, had a biological imperative to which the American society seems to be much more receptive.

Yet another act of free will in self-identity, and the societal scrutiny it evoked, involves a well-known Republican governor, Bobby Jindal. He was born in Baton Rouge, Louisiana, to Hindu parents from India. They named him Piyush Jindal. When he was four years old, we are told, he decided to change his first name to Bobby. That is the name of a character in the popular TV show, "The Brady Bunch." As a teenager, he converted to Christianity, and was later baptized as a Catholic. He and his wife got married twice, once following Hindu ceremony and another following Catholic one.

During his failed campaign to become Louisiana's governor in 2003, and later during his successful campaign in 2007, Jindal actively sought and got financial, political, and moral support from the Indian American community. Even at that time, there were clear indications that he was distancing himself from his Indian heritage. In 2007, when he was a member of the U.S. House of Representatives, a non-binding resolution was introduced in the House to recognize Diwali, the Hindu festival of lights. An overwhelming number of 358 Christian, Jewish, and members of other Faiths voted in favor of the resolution. Jindal abstained. There were also reports that Indian invitees were asked not to wear Indian clothes for his 2008 gubernatorial inauguration, a report he later disowned. Soon after, he and his wife stopped observing Indian cultural traditions.

It was not until he was forty-four years old, in 2015, that Jindal, as a candidate in the Republican presidential primary, announced that he is simply an American, not a hyphenated Indian American. In a speech delivered in London at the conservative club Henry Jackson Society, he declared: "I do not believe in hyphenated-Americans." Referring to himself and his parents, he said, "If we wanted to be Indians, we would have stayed in India."[24]

Jindal has an "identity crisis," declared Joseph Crowley, the then member of the U.S. House of Representatives from New York. He thought that it was "unfortunate" that Jindal had to say what he said in order to "overly demonstrate the fact that he is an American." He continued: "I am from New York. I am very proud of my Irish roots. . . . I do not apologize where my ancestors came from, I let it shine, I applaud it."[25] Unsurprisingly, Jindal's identity crisis drew severe criticism from a segment of the Indian American community.

Back in India, he was ridiculed as "Bobby McJindal," and was even labeled "a traitor."[26] In one of his newspaper columns, Sashi Tharoor, an Indian parliamentarian and a former Under-Secretary General of the United Nations, politely rebuffed Jindal by telling fellow Indians: "let us not make the mistake of thinking that we should be proud of what he stands for."[27]

Jindal was not the only American politician to have a questionable or questioned identity in recent times. U.S. Senator Elizabeth Warren claimed

Cherokee Indian heritage based on "family stories" heard at the dining table ever since she was "a little girl."[28] The New England Historic Genealogical Society found no proof of her Cherokee descent, nor did the Cherokee Indian Nation ever make her a citizen. Her attempt in October 2018 to provide DNA evidence to support her claim was rebuffed by an official from the Cherokee Nation. She apologized later during her primary campaign for the Democratic nomination for President saying, "I'm sorry for the harm I have caused." U.S. Senator Marco Rubio described himself as the "son of exiles" from Castro's Cuba, although his parents migrated to the United States and became permanent residents nearly three years before Castro's forces took power and started exiling Cuban dissidents. Former Florida Governor Jeb Bush, as a candidate in the 2016 Republican presidential primary, had incorrectly marked "Hispanic" rather than "White, not Hispanic" in his voter registration form. The Bush camp called it an error.

It is fairly common for politicians to try to take on a different persona from time to time. It could possibly be a mark of their cultural growth or political maturation. Or, it could plainly be an indication of their desire to appeal to a particular segment of their electorate at a particular moment in time. Or, it could happen just by oversight. But all that does not prevent their political opponents from accusing them of faking their identity.

Faking one's identity has apparently become much easier and more widespread, thanks to twenty-first-century technological tools. Especially Facebook (now subsumed by Meta).

According to the portal Statista, as the most popular social network in the world, the California-based Meta that has a reported market value of about $730 billion (as of June 2023), has about 3.74 billion global monthly active users (as of June 2023). When it was founded in 2004, the company's original goal was just to help people connect with friends. The company later conceded that users are not merely keeping up with their friends and family, but "they're also building an image and identity for themselves, which in a sense is their brand"[29] according to its CEO and Founder Mark Zuckerberg.

Branding, whether for commercial, political, or personal purposes, does not always respect truth values. In building a brand for themselves, some Facebook users deceptively portray different images of themselves by creating fake profiles with fake accounts. Nobody, not even Facebook, knows the exact number of fake identities. Zuckerberg has repeatedly reminded them that they should have only one Facebook identity, their real identity. Having multiple identity profiles may be considered to reflect a lack of integrity. The fact is, even people who use their real name and create only one Facebook identity do embellish their profile and present an imagined or desired persona which is at variance with who they really are.

Brooke Hauser, in her book about high school students and their use of Facebook, reports about one of her subjects who "changes her name almost as frequently as she changes the color of her contact lenses. Facebook is the perfect place to try on different identities until she finds one that sticks."[30]

Trying on different identities until finding one that sticks, until reaching an impressive tally of "likes" may work for Facebook. But it will not work in reality.

What then are the realities that confront us in our attempt to shape and reshape our identity in this age of globalization and digitalization? I will turn to them next.

Chapter 2

Global Realities and Local Identities

In our globalized and globalizing world, the reality is that whether we "are awake or asleep, scarcely a moment of our daily lives—sipping morning coffee, driving a car, talking on the phone, sending an email, or going to the movies—doesn't involve global supply chains."[1] This is true of individuals as well as corporations.

To start with, take Boeing, for instance.

It is the world's largest aerospace company. For more than a century, it has been the leading manufacturer of commercial jetliners as well as defense, space, and security systems. It supplies and supports airlines and government customers in more than 150 countries. Employing about 140,000 workers in sixty-five countries, it generates tens of billions of dollars' worth of products. When something goes wrong with any of its aerospace products, the result is a tragic loss of lives, and untold misery to loved ones.

Many people consider Boeing a quintessential American company. That includes U.S. Presidents. When Donald Trump visited the company in the very first year of his presidency, he praised the company, its workers, and its products. "We want products," he declared loudly and proudly, "made by our workers, in our factories, stamped with those four magnificent words: Made in the USA."[2]

Made by our workers? In our factories? Not entirely true of companies like Boeing. Whether for its smallest 737 commercial jet or for its largest 787 Dreamliner, Boeing's supply chains that provide the company with essential structural parts extend way beyond the American shores. For instance, some of the parts of its flagship 787–10 Dreamliner, considered to be more fuel efficient, more cost-effective, bigger, lighter and quieter than any other large aircraft, are manufactured by as many as forty-five companies spread over several countries including Australia, Canada, France, Germany, Italy, Japan, Korea, Sweden, and the United States.[3] The final assembling is done here in the United States. The company, therefore, is not only a symbol of America's pioneering spirit but also a symbol of an interconnected corporate world that depends on an intricate network of global supply chains.

Boeing's dependence on manufacturers in other countries is not at all unusual these days. As foreign policy analyst Shannon K. O'Neil points out, "For centuries, countries mostly sent finished goods abroad: olives from Italy; wine from Spain; furs from Canada; and later on, cars from Germany; and sewing machines, printing presses, and cash registers from the United States. Now, countries mostly send abroad pieces or components to be bent, welded, inserted, or sewn together in foreign factories and shops."[4]

Clearly, the nature of international trade has been transformed. Such a transformation has been made possible because of the developments made in transportation, technology, and digital communication. As a result, production, distribution, and consumption of industrial as well as consumer goods have become cheaper. However, if a global supply chain is disrupted, national as well as global economies are disrupted too.

A prime example of disruption is the ongoing war in Ukraine. Along with all the sanctions, the war has disrupted world food supply chains negatively impacting the distribution of wheat and barley, threatening famine in parts of Africa and Asia. Earlier in 2021 when a mega-container ship blocked Suez Canal waterway, it was holding up an estimated $9.6 billion worth of goods each day, severely affecting global supply chains. Similar disruption started to happen in 2020 when the novel coronavirus pandemic struck the Wuhan province in China and quickly spread to other parts of the world. Its ill effects continue even today. More on that below.

It is not just multinational corporations and national economies that depend on global supply chains. We all do. We all need and make use of various goods and services produced, handled, and distributed by global supply chains. Whether we live in a rural area or in a metropolitan city, whether we know it or not, whether we acknowledge it or not, the practice of our everyday life is now entangled in a global web. And with it our sense of Self, our sense of identity. Such an unprecedented entanglement compels us to rethink and reshape who we are, who we want to be. Therefore, in order to understand our identity (re)formation in the world we live in, we must understand the impact of at least two related global realities. One is globalization and the other is digitalization.

GLOBALIZATION AND ITS IMPACT ON IDENTITY

The process of globalization is nothing new in human history. But, in its current phase, it has become a dominant and driving force that is forging novel forms of interconnections among nations, economies, and peoples all over the world. At a broader level, it has been unfolding in three important facets—economic, cultural, and educational.

Educational globalization is marked by an expansion of the physical footprint of Ivy League universities as they rush to compete with each other to open overseas campuses. World-renowned consulting firms such as McKinsey & Company are getting increasingly involved in the education sector, studying and making recommendations about global capital investment in local education. In addition, interested students all over the world can access, and benefit from, free online courses offered by reputed universities like Stanford, Yale, MIT, Harvard, Oxford, and others.

Cultural globalization has created greater awareness about one another than ever before. Cultural images from far off lands flashed across smart phones in our hand, small screens in our living rooms, and big screens in multiplex cinemas have made the world a true global village. Foreign cultures are no longer foreign. Local communities are no longer cultural islands unto themselves. People now have a greater chance of knowing about, and being influenced by, each other's way of life—the good, the bad and, yes, the ugly.

More than educational and cultural globalization, it is economic globalization that has triggered unprecedented transformations in people's lives in many parts of the world, and with it their self-identity.

Global economic activities are likened to a game of Scrabble with millions of pieces (letters) distributed across countries (players) who work in teams to combine the pieces to make products (words).[5] This globalized game touches all of us in simple as well as profound ways.

Take a simple example: A cotton shirt or a dress we buy in a local Macy's or Walmart may simply say "Made in Bangladesh." Hidden behind the label is an intricately woven story that many of us may not be aware of. Bangladesh is "the second-largest garment-producing country in the world." Its "ready-made garment" industry (known by its acronym RMG), employing more than four million people, is worth about $30 billion a year and earns the country's largest foreign exchange.[6] Ironically though, Bangladesh does not grow cotton. It imports 99% of the cotton it needs for its garment industry, mainly from India (nearly 50%) and also from Africa, Australia, and the United States. It does not design the clothes either. The basic designing, one that has to appeal to Western aesthetics of style and color, is originally done by professional designers associated with reputable fashion houses located in cities like Paris, Milan, and New York. Most of their designs are displayed in international fashion shows. Nor is Bangladesh involved in distribution and marketing. What it does, and does well, is stitching the garments. The stitching is done in its crowded sweatshops in hazardous conditions by low wage workers (nearly 85% of whom are women) and sent to seaports in Singapore or Malaysia (because Bangladesh's largest port in Chittagong is ill-equipped to handle the load), and then possibly shipped on a French freighter operated by a Spanish or Italian crew, eventually reaching retail stores in North America and Europe.

What drives this "Scrabble game" are global flows of capital, materials, people, ideas, information, and communication prompted and promoted by large multinational corporations that are aided by governmental policies and agencies. Together, they pose challenges never before encountered in the reconstruction of national as well as individual identities.

In the wake of the collapse of communism-inspired state-controlled economy, many countries in the world are opting for some form of capitalist economy. Some of the countries (such as China) are successfully trying out what is called "state capitalism."[7] According to global analyst Ian Bremmer, in state capitalism, the state plays the role of the principal actor and decision-maker and uses the local and global markets for economic benefit and, more importantly, for political gains. State capitalism is not a new and improved version of the discredited communist central planning, but it is "a form of bureaucratically engineered capitalism" tailor-made to suit governmental policies and practices. It is argued that state capitalism, aided by the processes of economic globalization, will disrupt the foundations of the Western-oriented World Order, and with it the lifestyles of millions of people.

The foundations for the World Order were laid after the World War II when the victorious United States along with its allies met at the Bretton Woods International Monetary Conference in 1944 and decided to establish two major global institutions—International Monetary Fund (IMF), and the International Bank for Reconstruction and Development (also known as the World Bank) with the view to regulating international monetary systems.

Characterized as a reconstructive developmental strategy, which it partly was, the real intention was to steer the global economy in the direction that mostly favored the Western nations and Western-style capitalism. One of the ways in which American supremacy was ensured was to peg most nations' currency to the value of the U.S. dollar. This was aimed at ensuring the world dominance of the dollar as it became a reserve currency used by most nations for international trade. Later, the General Agreement on Tariffs and Trade (GATT) which became the present World Trade Organization (WTO) was vested with the task of supervising international trade and resolving trade disputes between member nations.

Of late, the carefully conceived and constructed foundation of the World Order appears to be shaking, partly because some of the countries pursuing state capitalism have started challenging the dominance of the dollar. The prime mover and shaker is, of course, China. It is reported that about five years ago, China conducted international trade almost entirely in dollars.

Now, more than a quarter of that trade is settled in its own currency Renminbi (RMB), also called Yuan (CNY/CNH).

Internationalizing the use of the RMB has been China's long term national ambition and is attempting to achieve it in three stages: first promote global use of RMB in small-scale international trade, then extend it to commodity trade, and finally transform it into a reserve currency. In a crucial move initiated in 2017, China set up crude oil-futures trading in RMB fully convertible in gold at Shanghai and Hong Kong stock exchanges, thereby side-stepping the use of the U.S. dollar, and consequently weakening it.

There are also other countries which are wary of the continuing dominance of the U.S. dollar and are taking steps to protect their economic interests. The BRICS countries (Brazil, Russia, India, China, and South Africa) have already started carrying out their bilateral and multilateral trade in their respective currencies bypassing the dollar. They have also established a New Development Bank to help member-states to ease pressures from the U.S. dollar-backed IMF and the World Bank in international trade.

In addition, China and Brazil trade in yuan and reals, Beijing and Moscow in yuan and rubles. India trades in local currencies in its trade with Iran, Malaysia, and countries in the Middle East. The ten-member Association of Southeast Asian Nations (ASEAN) trade and invest in local currencies. France has started conducting some transactions in yuan.

All these developments do not necessarily mean that RMB will soon become the main reserve currency dethroning the U.S. dollar. To assuage any uncertainty in the global marketplace, the U.S. Treasury Secretary Janet Yellen informed a Congressional committee in June 2023 that in spite of all the de-dollarization efforts, the dominance of the dollar is not at risk. Maybe. The expanded BRICS countries are now considering a BRICS common currency. Most of those efforts will lead to substantial weakening of the dollar as well as the World Order.

It is fairly clear that the familiar World Order is dying; and a new one is struggling to be born. In fact, Richard Haass, an American expert in international relations, goes a step further and categorically declares that "the old order is never coming back and that efforts to resurrect it will be in vain."[8]

In addition to global economic activities, China has also been investing in science and technology, and there is an American connection to it. In an in-depth investigation conducted in 2018, the online magazine *Politico* reported that China has been investing in high-tech industries like artificial intelligence, robotics, and space travel, and also in the latest 5th generation (5G) wireless technologies.[9] In 2017 alone, China struck deals with 165 start-up companies, mostly American. Quoting a Pentagon official, *Politico* reports that Chinese acquisition of top-notch American technology is enabling a "strategic competitor to access the crown jewels of U.S. innovation." In fairness, the report also points out that there are entrepreneurs in Silicon Valley who treat the Chinese investment not as a threat but as a blessing. They believe that without Chinese money, they will not be able to innovate and maintain American supremacy.

In the context of the rise of China, and its inevitable impact on American global power, a cautionary note struck by Harvard economist Graham Allison in his 2017 book, *Destined for War: Can America and China Escape Thucydides's Trap?* is worth considering:

> In the three and a half decades since Ronald Reagan became president, by the best measurement of economic performance, China has soared from 10 percent the size of the US to 60 percent in 2007, 100 percent in 2014, and 115 percent today. If the trend continues, China's economy will be a full 50 percent larger than that of the US by 2023. By 2040 it could be nearly three times as large. That would mean a China with triple America's resources to use in influencing outcomes in international relations. Such gross economic, political, and military advantages would create a globe beyond American policymakers can now imagine.[10]

Such an outcome, even if it is delayed, will have a detrimental effect on American image abroad and has the potential to reshape its national identity.

While globalization seems to be disrupting the foundations of the Western-oriented World Order, it has not in any way disrupted the fortunes of American multinational corporations. On the contrary, it has helped them thrive in a global economy. Unlike state capitalism where the state is the principal actor, in a free-market economy multinational corporations are principal actors free to act on their own with very few regulations. They focus single-mindedly on increasing corporate profit, decreasing production costs, innovating new designs, targeting new customers, and expanding their global reach. Thanks to globalization, many multinational corporations have become more powerful than they have ever been before. A recent report identified twenty-five companies that are considered to be more powerful than many countries in the world in terms of Gross Domestic Product (GDP), which is the standard monetary measure of the economic performance of nations and companies.[11] These companies span various sectors such as technology (for example, Google), the oil and gas industry (for example, Exxon Mobil), telecommunications (for example, AT&T), and investment banking (for example, Goldman Sachs). The cash that Apple Inc. alone has is considered to exceed the GDPs of two-thirds of the countries in the world.

Globalization has also helped some of the multinational corporations become stateless. They have been dubbed *metanationals*. According to global analyst Parag Khanna, "Clever metanationals often have legal domicile in one country, corporate management in another, financial assets in a third, and administrative staff spread over several more."[12] Khanna goes on to point out that there was a time, not long ago, when a president of GM proudly and patriotically declared: "What was good for our country was good for General Motors, and vice versa." No longer. Now, the metanationals would rather remain stateless in order to put the interests of their company above those of their country.

In putting their company above their country, multinational corporations do not hesitate to compromise certain core values of America and its national identity if that is what is required to tap huge markets such as China. "Anybody who does business with China compromises some of their core values," admits John Hennessy, former President of Stanford University and former chairman of Alphabet Inc., the parent company of Google.[13] In their relentless pursuit of market and profit expansion, American tech giants such as Apple, Google, and Facebook are only eager to do business with a country of 1.3 billion people even if they subject themselves to onerous censorship and curtailment of operational freedom—which they would vehemently oppose if happened in their own country.

With American multinational corporations flourishing in a globalized world, corporate executives have continued to establish an enviable cosmopolitan identity for themselves. As globe-trotting citizens of the world, they benefit from intermingling of cultures and peoples, producing opportunities for them to absorb new forms of cultural beliefs and practices that further their elitist cosmopolitan identities. As political scientist Francis Fukuyama observes in his recent book on identity, global cosmopolitans "argue that the very concepts of national identity and state sovereignty are outmoded and need to be replaced by broader transnational identities and institutions."[14] Noting the enviable lifestyle of corporate executives and other celebrities, British cultural critic Pnina Werbner describes them as "gorgeous butterflies in the greenhouse of global cultures." They have become "gourmet tasters who travel among global cultures, savouring cultural differences as they flit with consummate ease between social worlds."[15]

Sadly, the identity of these "gorgeous butterflies" is very different from that of the worker bees who populate the bottom rungs of the corporate world. The story of General Motors (GM) during and after the 2008 recession offers a good example of how a combination of government policies, corporate greed, and outsourcing has affected the lives of blue-collar workers, sapping their confidence about themselves and their idea of who they are. The economic malaise that caused the 2008 recession resulted in millions of lost jobs, and the auto industry was one of the worst hits. GM alone cut more than 100,000 jobs since the recession began. The Obama administration bailed out GM (along with Chrysler) and forced the company to file for bankruptcy protection and to take certain necessary restructuring. In a couple years, GM's fortunes turned around resulting in significant profit. A report released in January 2019 reveals that GM has now become the top automotive producer—no, not in the United States, but in Mexico, with its outsourced production there accounting for a quarter of the company's output.[16]

According to the same report, despite earning hefty profits, the company announced in 2018 that it was shutting down plants affecting nearly 14,000 employees (about 8,000 salaried workers and about 6,000 hourly workers).[17] The announcement came just a few weeks before the workers were getting ready to celebrate Christmas with their family. The layoff was reported to have saved GM about $ 6 billion by 2020, money it said it wanted to invest in the future. Never mind the hardships some of its employees face in the present.

Reporting the news, a *Washington Post* journalist whose father lost his GM job, articulated the prevailing mood: "He'd call my mom and say in a calm voice, 'Hey, I'm free once again.' I guess when the ax so often hangs over your head, you find relief when it falls—or you become desensitized to it."[18] A year earlier, a blogger captured the big picture equally succinctly: "When people talk about the loss of manufacturing jobs, they are really talking about the loss of old-fashioned cultural norms, gender roles, and the forced confrontation with a lost sense of identity. When we hear about the opioid epidemic in the Midwest, we are talking about escaping from the pain and confusion of identity-loss."[19]

Globalization is seen as one of the causes behind the pain and confusion of identity-loss experienced by working-class Americans, most of whom have only high school education or less. It has also created a wedge between people who work in the older industrial-economy and those who work in the newer ideas-economy, as explained by author and journalist John B. Judis. According to him, the older industrial-economy based mostly on manufacturing jobs has faded away as the newer ideas-economy based on finance, technology, and electronics has flourished. These two economies "have produced very different ways of living—and, crucially, very different personal identities."[20] Many of those who once lived a comfortable life working in the older economy "had important parts of their identity stripped away," while those working in the newer economy see many avenues for shaping new identities and new personas. In short, the way of life and the identity of people working in these two economies have changed and diverged considerably.

Globalization has been a mixed blessing. It has lifted millions of people in developing countries from poverty, propelling them into a new middle class. It has broadened and deepened international trade. It has certainly helped countries become aware of and take coordinated actions to deal with fast spreading epidemics such the Ebola virus and Zika virus, as well as the recent pandemic, COVID-19 virus. It has also fostered interconnections that seem to bring people together in terms of fashion and lifestyle. Young people everywhere seem to wear the same type of blue jeans and Nike shoes, and walk around listening to the same music, with the same brand name headphones unfailingly attached to their ears. They use the same social media to communicate with each other wherever they live. All this and more seems to be promoting a common set of cultural behavior that has the potential to shape and reshape individual identities.

There is also no dispute that globalization has resulted in wide-spread discontent. Given the globalized nature of the economy, many national leaders are struggling to lessen the sufferings of their citizens. The loss of manufacturing jobs largely because of outsourcing has caused untold miseries to hundreds and thousands of blue-collar workers. The unbearable scale of inequality caused by globalization has intensified the social tension between various segments of society. As Bremmer observes, globalization "doesn't just move factory-built products. It also moves *people*, feeding public anxiety by shifting the racial, ethnic, linguistic, and religious make of communities sometimes abruptly."[21]

For most of the ills of globalization, many politicians and pundits blame globalism, "the belief that the interdependence that created globalization is a good thing."[22] A closer look, however, shows that more than the idea of globalism, it is how governments, corporations, and individuals responded to the resultant globalization that seem to have caused the hardships some of which could have been anticipated and alleviated. First of all, certain governments are ideologically wedded to unbridled forms of capitalism and hence shied away from putting in place necessary regulations that will safeguard the interests of the common people. As Harvard economist Dani Rodrik wrote in the *Milken Institute Review,* "The benefits of globalization are distributed unevenly because our current model of globalization is built on a corrosive asymmetry. Trade agreements and global regulations are designed largely with the needs of capital in mind. The interests of labor—good wages, decent work environment, employment security, voice in the workplace, bargaining rights—are scarcely paid lip service."[23]

The ill effects of economic globalization have been aggravated by the introduction of automation and the advent of artificial intelligence (AI), particularly its latest avatar: ChatGPT. Governments and corporations have not adequately come up with actionable strategies to upskill and reskill American workers so that they may remain employable and productive in the workforce. Unlike the United States, Singapore and several countries in Europe have put in place extensive safety nets and implemented retraining programs in collaboration with corporations in order to mitigate adverse effects globalization.

It is with this backdrop, the year 2020 dawned with a deadly Coronavirus spreading all over the world. It has created doubts in the minds of certain politicians and pundits about the sagacity of economic globalization. Some of them believe that the pandemic has actually set in motion the process of deglobalization or decoupling. Prominent among them is Spanish foreign policy analyst Andrés Ortega. His main argument is that because of the breakdown of global supply chains, particularly from China, the world has been experiencing "a human shock, a supply-side shock (involving production) and a demand-side shock (involving consumption), with the added danger of a new financial crisis."[24] As a result, national borders are coming back, he says. There are, however, others such as O'Neil who point out that all we need to do is not dependent on one major supply chain, as we now do on China. "Reshoring" will cause more problems; therefore, we need to diversify our transactions," she says.[25] All that needs to be done to address the risks of high levels of global interconnectivity is to redistribute and reshape supply chains. In fact, several countries, including the United States, are already exploring alternative supply chains. So, the answer for the breakdown of economic globalization seems to be more, not less, globalization—but a new and improved variety.

Good or bad, globalization is here to stay. It is irreversible. It will, whether we like it or not, continue to shape our national and individual identities. And, the engine that drives it all is digitalization.

DIGITALIZATION AND ITS IMPACT ON IDENTITY

Digitalization is described as "the way in which many domains of social life are restructured around digital communication and media infrastructures."[26] It has diffused digital technology into major forms of communication which are increasingly becoming very common. Many people around the world have fast moved away from analog technologies (such as snail mail, land-line telephones) to digital ones (such as email, social media) whether for their formal or informal communication. This transition has certainly increased the speed and improved the efficiency of communication. Aided by the Internet, the digital interface has revolutionized business models, marketing techniques, customer relations, as well as personal, professional, and social life. In other words, digitalization has become an integral part of the practice of everyday life in the twenty-first century.

Digitalization is also revolutionizing the nature of globalization. As James Manyika and Susan Lund of McKinsey & Company observe, "Globalization was once driven almost exclusively by the world's governments, large multinational corporations, and major financial institutions. But now—thanks to digital platforms with global reach—artisans, entrepreneurs, app developers, freelancers, small businesses, and even individuals can participate directly."[27] This has opened up tremendous business opportunities for entrepreneurial individuals everywhere, and with it, opportunities to realize their fullest human potential and become what they want to be. They can now bypass any constraining systems that are stacked against them, and instead can build their own global connections, can join e-commerce marketplaces such as Amazon, eBay, or Alibaba to sell their products directly to their customers who are exposed to these products through social media wherever they may live. Their Small and Medium Enterprises (SMEs) can become, as the McKinsey report points out, micromultinationals in their own right, and start-ups can be "born global." The gig economy too has empowered the individual. Thanks to enterprises like Uber and Airbnb, millions of people around the world are transacting business among themselves.

The opportunities opened up by digitalization are not limited to business-minded individuals. New technologies carry much needed knowledge for those who seek it. The global communication network makes available for millions of people around the world many tools that they can use for personal and professional development. Anybody who has access to the Internet—whether a scholar at Harvard, an investment banker in Hong Kong, a farmer in Hyderabad, a school kid in Harlem—all can access valuable information they want and need.

Digitalization also has the potential to foster meaningful cultural enrichment, particularly among the users of social media since nearly a billion people have at least one international connection on social media platforms, and nearly half of active Facebook users have at least one friend beyond their national borders.[28] Arguing that "Connectivity is destiny," Khanna states that "Global connectivity gradually undermines national roots and augments or replaces them with a range of transnational bonds and identities."[29]

Augmenting one's identity, without at the same time undermining one's cultural roots, is precisely what is needed in this globalized and digitalized society. It is not an easy task to achieve. A prerequisite for that to happen, as I see it, is critical self-reflection that will enable us to question our own taken-for-granted beliefs and practices. In other words, we have to equip ourselves with knowledge, skill, and disposition necessary to develop a capacity for self-interrogation so that we will be able to make informed judgements about who we really are, who we want to be, and what would be the challenges if we, as we must, reassess and reshape our self-identity on a continual basis.

Take for instance, the idea of *individualism* which is considered to be a quintessential part of American identity. American journalist and author Richard Rodriguez has a critical perspective on it:

Americans are so individualistic; they do not realize their individualism is a communally derived value. The American "I" is deconstructed for me by Paolo, an architect who was raised in Bologna: "You Americans are not truly individualistic, you merely are lonely. In order to be individualistic, one must have a strong sense of oneself within a group." (The "we" is a precondition for saying "I.") Americans spend all their lives looking for a community: a chatroom, a church, a support group, a fetish magazine, a book club, a class-action suit.[30]

And yet, Rodriguez says sarcastically, "they swear by individualism."

Whether we agree with that assumption or not, the idea of individualism has always been a contested concept. As early as in 1835, the French aristocrat Alexis de Tocqueville in his oft-quoted book *Democracy in America* defined American individualism as "a calm and considered feeling which disposes each citizen to isolate himself from the mass of his fellows and withdraw into the circle of family and friends."[31] He went on to criticize American individualism which he thought was inadmissibly indifferent to the welfare of the society at large.

Many sociologists have emphasized the role of larger society in shaping individual identity. Our sense of Self is strongly influenced by the community we are part of, and also by the larger society. We tend to forget that the personal is inextricably linked to the social. In fact, British sociologist Richard Jenkins goes to the extent of saying that "*All* human identities are *social* identities"[32] That is partly because in constructing our self-identity, we are mindful of our similarities and differences to other members of the group we identify with. Our community/social connections function as a useful resource for us. Hence the use of the term *social capital*, referring largely to "connections among individuals—social networks and the norms of reciprocity and trustworthiness that arise from them."[33]

The social networks that shape our identity have vastly grown because of globalization and digitalization. "For the first time in human history," as British sociologist Anthony Giddens points out, "self and society are interrelated in a global milieu."[34] The interactions many people have, and the exposures they are subject to on a daily basis, are not limited to the family or to the community but extend beyond even their national borders. The community now is not just local; it is global. The expanding connectivity is making the already intricate relationship between Self and society even more complicated.

In her book on *The Digital Evolution of American Identity*, Communications professor C. Waite characterizes the expanding relationship between Self and society, and the resultant need to recalibrate identity (re)formation as "the most significant consequence of the digital revolution."[35] She argues that the digital revolution has ushered in what she calls "the enlightenment of the twenty-first century."[36] She strikes a contrast between the European Enlightenment of the eighteenth century that generated ideas such as freedom, individualism, etc. (see chapter 1 for details), and the still-evolving enlightenment of the twenty-first century.

The European Enlightenment was limited to certain geographical locations whereas the twenty-first-century Enlightenment is borderless. And as such, the twenty-first-century enlightenment is broad-based. Once, freedom merely meant the right to assemble or to interact locally. But now, it means engaging a global community using modern technologies. What this means is that we need to develop a greater degree of awareness of and acceptance of interdependence between peoples, communities, and societies across the globe. We need to acknowledge that our welfare is linked to the welfare of people who we may not even come into direct contact with. Therefore, "the concept of American individualism," Waite asserts, "no longer adequately explains how we coexist in community with others. Americans struggle to understand what it means to be responsible both for one's Self and for the welfare of others."[37]

The lessons we should derive from all this is clear: the processes of globalization as well as digitalization have unmistakable implications for the national and individual identity (re)formation in the twenty-first century. Amid the centrifugal and centripetal pulls and pressures of living in a globalized and digitalized world, the construction of self-identity becomes daunting, to say the least. As the relative security of tradition and custom slowly recedes, new forms of beliefs and practices have to be learned, and conflicts among them reconciled. We are compelled, ready or not, to take a critical look at our Self and our identity, our community, and our country.

Taking a critical look at our sense of Self and our self-identity as Americans demands an understanding of the process and product of being and becoming American.

Chapter 3

Being and Becoming American

Who and what is American?

A question that strikes at the taproot of American identity, one that has preoccupied the minds of eminent Americans right from the early days of the Republic. They have also wrestled with a related question: what does it mean to say being and becoming American?

Then and now, many historians and sociologists, politicians and pundits have been using the words *being* and *becoming* interchangeably. I believe making a distinction may serve a useful purpose in part because "We were always about becoming, not being; about the prospects for the future, not about the inheritance of the past."[1]

If *being* is seen as a product, *becoming* can be seen as a process. *Being* denotes a state of stagnation; *becoming* denotes a condition of dynamism.

Being American implies a label, a legal status, and a citizenship. Achieving the legal status is fairly routine. If you are born here, the U.S. Constitution declares that you are a natural born citizen. If you are not born here, and successfully apply to be a citizen following all the due process, you are a naturalized citizen,[2] like me. And millions more.

Becoming American, however, signifies an understanding of the idea of America, the meaning of America, the spirit of America. And, faithfully acting on that understanding. There is nothing natural or easy about it. One has to work at it consciously and continually.

BECOMING AMERICAN

First of all, there is no prescribed pathway to become American. No constitutional document, no government website, no mapped-out GPS that tells us how to get there. However, there is no shortage of interpretations, opinions, and arguments about it. From time to time, scholars and political leaders have tried to explain what it takes to become American.

According to historian Philip Gleason, "To be or to become an American, a person did not have to be of any particular national, linguistic, religious, or ethnic background. All he had to do was to commit himself to the political ideology centered on the abstract ideals of liberty, equality, and republicanism. Thus the universalist ideological character of American nationality meant that it was open to anyone who willed to become an American."[3]

The "universalist ideological character" of America is, well, universal. It is by no means confined to the geographical boundaries of a place called the United States of America. However, no nation formulated it, articulated it, espoused it, and disseminated it as productively and proficiently as America did. For me and for many Indian Americans born and brought up in independent India, the abstract ideals of liberty, equality, and republicanism are not alien concepts. Many are the ways in which India shares those abstract ideals with America.

Start with republicanism. It is the ideology that, in part, triggered the American Revolution. It is the ideology admired and advocated by the Founding Fathers. It is the ideology they bequeathed to the American people, challenging them to keep it if they can. It is the fountainhead of other foundational values: people have inalienable rights, not just to life, liberty, and the pursuit of happiness, but also to equality, to individual rights, to the rule of law, to democratic governance. Nobody is above the law. Not kings. Not aristocrats. Not Presidents.

"Never, *never anywhere*," asserts historian David McCullough in an authoritative tone, "had there been a government instituted on the consent of the governed."[4] His assertion highlights the fact that primacy of the people is the hallmark of American republicanism. That is why the American Constitution begins with "We the people." So does the Indian Constitution. It was informed by the American Constitution which considers individual rights as sacred, and was inspired by the Declaration of Independence which considers the consent of the governed as sacrosanct. Even before I came here, I enjoyed the fruits of republicanism: duly elected representational governments at the local, state, and federal levels, the democratic principle of one person one vote, rule of law, independent judiciary, free press, and freedom of expression. Republicanism, therefore, is not a novel idea to me.

There are also other ideals shared by the two countries. Chief among them is the separation of church and state. Both the nations are a kaleidoscope of religions. Both are deeply religious. Faith is fundamental to their way of life. And yet, their Founding Fathers wisely decided and declared that it is not the business of the government to influence or to interfere with peoples' faith. People have the freedom to practice any faith, or no faith.

Pluralism is yet another commonly cherished value. Very few countries are as richly pluralistic as America and India are—religiously, ethnically, culturally, linguistically. As a nation of immigrants, America has become intrinsically pluralistic. As an ancient country, India has been indigenously pluralistic. The diversity of identities is characteristic of both societies. American motto is *E pluribus unum*, "From many, one." Often this motto is misunderstood. As political scientist Michael Walzer explains, the motto "seems to suggest that manyness must be left behind for the sake of oneness." But in reality, as he rightly points out, "there is no movement from many to one, but rather a simultaneity, a coexistence—once again, many-in-one."[5] That is also true of India. Its slogan is *Unity in Diversity*. It too signifies a many-in-one simultaneity. The idea is to ensure unity without demanding uniformity. The purpose is not to denigrate difference but to celebrate it.

Gaining independence from Britain 171 years after America did, India benefited from the American ideals, from the American Experiment. The idea of America has left an indelible impression in the Indian psyche.

What, after all, is the idea of America?

The question is as old as the Republic itself. One that is revisited from time to time. Renewed from time to time.

In 2007, political scientist Anne-Marie Slaughter raised the same question and answered it in her book titled, *The Idea That Is America*. In it, she succinctly stated that the idea of America "is the idea of a nation founded on a set of universal values—self-evident truths—that come not from blood, or soil, or skin color, or wealth but from the fact of our common humanity. It is the idea of a nation bound together not by territory or religion or ethnicity but by a self-conscious commitment to shared values, for ourselves and for all peoples."[6]

The same year, the editors of the *Atlantic Monthly*, celebrating the 150th year of its publication, explained the idea of America even further: "It is the fractious, maddening approach to the conduct of human affairs that values equality despite its elusiveness, that values democracy despite its debasement, that values pluralism despite its messiness, that values the institutions of civic culture despite their flaws, and that values public life as something higher and greater than the sum of all our private lives."[7]

Most Indians and Indian Americans will feel at home with this picture of America, with all its messiness, elusiveness, and flaws. If America continues to be roiled by racial strife, India continues to be roiled by religious strife. If America is troubled by its two-party democracy tainted by partisan squabbling, India is tripped by its multi-party democracy tainted by parochial bickering. Coincidentally, both the countries are at present trying to cope with identity related jingoistic disharmony with its discordant notes emanating from the instruments of political ideology and cultural nationalism.

All this is not to say the United States and India are the same. They clearly are not. No two countries are. But, at the level of "ideological character" and "abstract ideals," there are unmistakable commonalities. The extent to which the two countries have been able or unable to translate and transform the abstract ideals into desired outcomes in the political, social, religious, economic, and cultural arena is what makes the difference between the two countries.

As a proud Indian American, I consider myself a border-crossed speck floating in the vast American landscape. All my dreamy abstract ideals along with decent English language skills, desirable work ethic, and durable family values have propelled me into the orbit of a community that is one of the most educated, most employed, most productive, and most paid immigrant communities in this country. My Indian heritage has certainly rendered my immigrant experiences less challenging and more rewarding. Thanks to the manifold opportunities that America offers, I have been able to do what I came here to do: learn, teach, serve.

Let me hasten to add. I am not claiming anything special about me, or unique about me. I am merely using me as an example. Many thoughtful people born and brought up in any pluralistic country that is wedded to genuine participatory democracy with meaningful secular credentials, deep-rooted sociocultural values, and dedicated work ethic can legitimately claim that they have already been experiencing and enjoying certain abstract universal ideals that characterize the elusive, widely used, term "American Spirit."

If properly understood, it should be clear that the American Spirit is something that is admired, absorbed, nurtured, and refined. It is certainly not something that is transmitted through genes.

We have been told time and time again that becoming American is not about race and religion or about blood and soil but about the spirit and the soul. Like all matters of the spirit and the soul, the idea of becoming American is one of those abstractions that is difficult to define and has been open to varied interpretations in various times, coupled with varied insinuations by various people. That is why some people define it by negation. That may largely explain the reason behind the frequent use of the accusatory word *un-American*. Notice, this epithet is something that is hurled at native-born citizens as well as naturalized ones, historically more at the former.

WHO OR WHAT IS UN-AMERICAN?

Nobody has a definitive answer. But everybody has an opinion. Everybody—from Presidents to politicians to pundits. On every aspect—from the profound to the trivial.

Presidents normally invoke the term when there are consequential happenings that they think conflict with desired American ideals and desired American identity. No President in recent times has referred to un-Americanism more than Barack Obama. Instead of un-American, he has preferred a less accusatory phrase: "that's not who we are" or "that's contrary to who we are." He has used these expressions or their variations several times during his days in the White House. President Trump called Democrats in Congress un-American because they did not clap during his 2018 State of the Union address even when he said positive things. President Biden termed attempts to restrict voting rights as un-American.

Some of the American authors are not far behind in airing their views about being un-American. Recently, Andrew L. Seidal, a constitutional lawyer, wrote a book subtitled, *Why Christian Nationalism Is Un-American.*[8] Conservative columnist Pat Buchanan, referring to investigations conducted by the Democrats about the alleged Russian connection to the Trump campaign, thinks that "the endless airing of unproven allegations" is "inherently un-American."[9]

The use of the term "un-American" is nothing new. According to a research article, the term appeared as early as in the 1810s.[10] It, however, did not gain prominence and official backing until 1938 when the House of Representatives created The House Un-American Activities Committee to investigate citizens and organizations suspected of engaging in subversive activities. The main target of the Committee was Hollywood directors, actors, screenwriters, and others alleged to have Communist ties. The Committee became very unpopular as it was widely criticized for witch-hunting. Echoing the common sentiment, in 1959 President Harry Truman denounced the Un-American Activities Committee (HUAC or HCUA) as the "most un-American thing."[11] Despite the Presidential rebuke, the HCUA continued to function until 1975 when it was abolished.

There were other reasoned voices too, raised from time to time. The *New Yorker* magazine argued in 1948 that "Literally, nothing in this country can be said to be un-American. 'Un' means 'not,' and anything that happens within our borders is American, no matter what its nature, no matter how far off the beam it may be."[12] Commonsense, isn't it? In spite of such sense-making, the narrative about being un-American has continued unabated.

There has been a noticeable surge in the use of the term un-American since President Trump assumed office. Justifiable or not, several commentators have accused him of being un-American for one reason or another. Just to name a couple: Anne Applebaum, a *Washington Post* columnist, lists a few of the ways in which Trump's 2017 state visit to Saudi Arabia "was bizarre, unseemly, unethical and un-American."[13] Republican Senator Bob Corker describes President Trump's comments about the killing of Saudi journalist Jamal Khashoggi, as un-American.[14]

When hundreds of members of fringe groups violently stormed the Capitol on January 6, 2021, looking to grievously harm government officials including U.S. Vice President Mike Pence and House Speaker Nancy Pelosi, several politicians and pundits deplored the incident calling it un-American.

The saga of Un-Americanism continues.

The checkered history of the negative term un-American, and its recurring politicization is to some extent understandable because of its connection to the notion of American identity and the idea of Americanism. The political churning the country has witnessed during and after the Presidential elections in 2016 and 2020 can be seen as a continuing quest for the meaning of who we are, what the country is about.

No doubt, eternal vigilance is the price we have to pay to protect the American republic and the American ideals. But that can hardly be done by engaging in unrelenting and uncritical use of a negative term and by creating a specter of the end of America as we know it.

"THIS IS NOT THE APOCALYPSE."

That is what President Obama was reported to have told his dumbfounded staff members on the morning after Donald Trump was elected President of the United States. Apparently, some of his supporters and some of the media personnel have ignored his words of caution. They were all preparing the country for the apocalypse. They warned us that we are now faced with the danger of Fascism and Nazism. No less. Consider this: Robert Kuttner, the cofounder and coeditor of the *American Prospect*, a reputable magazine, asks hyperbolically: "How, pray tell, do we escape American fascism this time, now that this is no fantasy?"[15]

Well, the thought of Fascism and Nazism assailing and overpowering twenty-first-century America is itself a fantasy. Unquestionably, the country is blessed with many features that mitigate against any Fascist take over: a strong democratic system, a properly elected legislature both at the federal and at state levels, an independent judiciary, a vibrant free press, well-established civic institutions, and citizens who are politically aware and active.

How quickly the constitution was preserved, and democracy was restored in the aftermath of the January 6th storming of the Capitol in 2021 dispels all the unfounded fears about Fascism and Nazism taking over America. It shows that Constitutional checks and balances are working as intended. As political scientist Francis Fukuyama points out, "Unlike a parliamentary system, the U.S. Constitution firmly vests most powers in Congress; the president is powerful only to the extent that he can be a cheerleader and consensus-builder in a system of widely shared powers. . . . And even if Congress approves, the courts and states will have a major say in how and whether projects are executed."[16]

That is precisely what the country witnessed during the Trump presidency. In a June 2020 ruling, the Supreme Court ruled against his administration's attempt to end an Obama-era program called Deferred Action for Childhood Arrivals (DACA). Earlier, the Court found unconstitutional a clause in the federal law that allowed deportation of foreigners charged with any crime or violence, an issue that was central to the President's agenda. Above all, Trump and his aides failed when they approached the courts asking them to overturn the result of the 2020 Presidential election. At the state level, at least eighty-six judges, ranging from state to federal courts, rejected all the post-election lawsuits. At the national level, the U.S. Supreme Court rejected a lawsuit filed by Texas and seventeen other Republican-run states alleging election fraud in four swing states that voted for Biden.

In a sobering assessment, a dozen historians who recently shared their views with a prominent on-line magazine about the current political climate categorically declared that our time is certainly not the craziest time in U.S. political history.[17] They highlight several events which could have easily torn the fabric of American national identity beyond repair: in 1865, the country was plunged into political turmoil when the assassination of the nation's emancipator Abraham Lincoln ushered in an unapologetic racist, Andrew Johnson, as President just about the time Ku Klux Klan was emerging as a force to reckon with. Jumping closer to recent historical memory, the year 1968 marked unprecedented sociopolitical turbulence because of a combination of events: the opposition to the Vietnam War, the assassination of Martin Luther King, Jr. and Robert Kennedy, the ascendance of segregationist George Wallace, the civil rights movement, and the feminist movement.

If the country has seen tougher times and has yet retained the essence of its identity, there is no reason to believe that the apocalyptic forebodings emanating from certain quarters will come true. No amount of fringe groups storming the Capitol, no number of them displaying Swastikas in the streets of Charlottesville, Virginia will drag this nation into an abyss. Recall how on the eve of the first anniversary of Charlottesville, the well-advertised and well-guarded march organized by fringe groups in Washington, DC was dwarfed by counter-protesters hailing American ideals.

In the contentious times we are living in, it is understandable that genuine concerns and uncertainties crop up about potential threats to the nation's core character. American identity, however, is not a fragile glass menagerie that will break at the slightest jolt. It is constructed on steely foundations strong enough to withstand political earthquakes and ideological aftershocks.

AMERICA'S CREEDAL IDENTITY

The unshaken and unshakeable structure of American national identity draws strength from its cornerstone—the American Creed.[18] It constitutes the primary component of American national identity. It is an idea, a noble idea that pervades vital documents such as the Declaration of Independence, the U.S. Constitution, and the Bill of Rights. It captures the quintessential character of America, the Spirit of America: its principles of individual freedom, its model of a government that is "by the people, for the people and of the people," its determination to work to ensure equality and justice for all, its emphasis on the rule of law, and its belief in people's inalienable rights to "life, liberty, and the pursuit of happiness."

Much has been written about how the Founding Fathers went about conceptualizing Creed, and hence the nation—its destiny, its identity. According to the Swedish historian Gunnar Myrdal, the inspiration for the Creed came mainly from three sources: the English Law, the French Enlightenment, and Christianity.[19] The British Magna Carta, signed and sealed on the banks of the River Thames more than 800 years ago, provided the basic principle that nobody is above the law, and everybody has the right for a fair trial. The French Enlightenment spearheaded lofty ideals such as liberty, fraternity, equality, and separation of church and state. The Christian source is traced all the way back to the original settlers who, escaping religious persecution, brought with them unquestionable Protestant piety, and undeniable work ethic. People came and still come to America attracted by the promise of its creedal principles, and the opportunities afforded for them to strive to live a happy life.

Striving to live a happy life is what was in the mind of the Founders when they included the famous phrase, "the pursuit of happiness" in the Declaration of Independence. It was an extraordinary move on their part. Incidentally, it is only now, in the twenty-first century, that top universities such as Harvard, Yale, and Stanford have started offering courses on happiness. Students who take these courses will for sure recognize that happiness is an elusive concept. It means different things to different people in different times. For most of us, it means material possessions and pleasures associated with a home, a well-knit family, a car, a well-earned vacation, and the like. But for the Founders, it meant much more. The very fact that Thomas Jefferson edited out the word "property" in the draft version of the Declaration of Independence and inserted "happiness" in its place demonstrates his intention to philosophize the pursuit of happiness.[20]

THE PHILOSOPHY OF HAPPINESS

Jefferson's use of the term "happiness" has been attributed to Greek and Roman philosophers, particularly Aristotle. For Aristotle, happiness should be the ultimate goal if and only if it is pursued for ultimate good. It sure includes wealth, health, and other markers we usually associate with a good life. But it goes beyond the mundane. It signifies all that is virtuous: justice, generosity, discipline, moderation. It also values civic responsibility. Individuals should strive not only for personal happiness but also for public happiness; not only for personal freedom but also for public freedom. It abhors excesses and seeks balance. Thus, Aristotelian and Jeffersonian happiness "is as much about equanimity as it is about endorphins."[21]

The idea of the pursuit of happiness has a universal character to it. The Aristotelian and Jeffersonian philosophical slant is not confined to Western thought alone. Ancient Eastern traditions have taken a similar approach to happiness. Confucius thoughts connected happiness with self-cultivation, high morals, and virtuous life. Buddhism propagated the concept of *ānanda* (its closest equivalent in English is *bliss*). It is a state of mind that nurtures good thoughts and good deeds in all aspects of human life. It is the result of a tempered attitude that does not succumb to temptations of excessive pleasures. In this respect, it is to some extent akin to the austere Puritanical way of life associated with a particular form of Protestantism practiced by a segment of early American settlers. At a higher level, it is tied to the Buddhist notion of Enlightenment aimed at a heightened state of awakening, self-realization, and renunciation. Similar views can be seen embedded in Hindu scriptures such as the Vedas, Upanishads, and Bhagavad Gita as well.

We may not measure up to the philosophers' or the Founders' exalted idea of happiness. But, are we measuring up to our own, rather weak, version of happiness? Nearly two and a half centuries after the Founders declared the pursuit of happiness as one of the inalienable rights, where do we stand in terms of exercising and enjoying that right? A survey conducted by the National Opinion Research Center at the University of Chicago in May of 2020 found that only 14% of adults say they are very happy, down from 32% recorded in 2018. A *World Happiness Report* released in 2024 ranks America 23rd among 146 countries. The authors measured the state of global happiness using six key variables linked to human well-being: income, healthy life expectancy, social support, freedom, trust, and generosity.[22] No, they would not dare to include elements of Aristotelian happiness or Buddhist bliss.

Amid the humdrum of daily life, amid the cacophony of electoral noise, amid the onslaught of fake news, amid the coldness of info wars, we tend to forget that the Creedal principles are intrinsic to American national identity.

We tend to forget that, unlike Europe and many other countries in the world, the United States enjoys a singular advantage: it had no feudal history, it had no tribal allegiances, it had no rigidly stratified caste system. Socioeconomic mobility, if worked at it, is achievable. With no particular baggage weighing them down, Americans are free to experiment with different ways of social and cultural living. Hence, most except the fringe elements are less judgmental about the gods we worship, the languages we speak, the clothes we wear, the food we eat, or the person we marry. We tend not to see that ordinary Americans are constantly shaping and reshaping American identity, quietly preserving and joyously celebrating the quintessence of American Spirit.

In light of all this, I will explore in the subsequent chapters how Americans construct and reconstruct their individual identity in a way that addresses the challenges and opportunities of a fast-changing world. I will start with two taken-for-granted concepts: assimilation and multiculturalism and explore the extent to which they live up to their expectations in constructing American identity.

PART II

Exploring the Persistence of Myths

Chapter 4

Meltable or Unmeltable Ethnics?

Picture this: A well-known automaker in America hires some of the newly arrived male immigrants to work in their assembly lines. It gives them classes in English language skills and cultural assimilation strategies for about a year. After they complete their apprenticeship, a graduation ceremony is held in an open-air theater. On the stage is a giant pot. Painted on the side in big letters and bright colors are the words: MELTING POT. At one end, the proud students, wearing their ethnic clothes, climb up a small ladder and step into the pot. A couple of instructors carrying long ladles stand around the pot and mime the action of stirring the pot. Inside, the men shed their old ethnic clothes, change to new American blue suits donated by the company, and step out on the other side happily waving American flags. They are supposed to have successfully gone through an intensive course in the process of Americanization. They are all now deemed to have culturally assimilated themselves, and to have become part of their adopted land.

Some of you may think that this is a figment of my imagination. Not at all. It is a fragment of American history. It actually happened, almost annually, during the early part of the twentieth century at the English School run by Ford Motor Company, Detroit, Michigan. It was probably the brainchild of Henry Ford, the Company's patriarch, who was keen on helping his newly arrived European employees quickly absorb American mainstream cultural beliefs and practices.

Unlike the simple and simplistic portrayal by the auto maker, cultural assimilation is a complex, long-term process spanning generations. Many scholars have attempted to define it. Among them are two prominent sociologists of the early twentieth century, Robert E. Park and Ernest W. Burgess. According to them, cultural assimilation is "a process of interpenetration and fusion in which persons and groups acquire the memories, sentiments, and attitudes of other persons and groups and, by sharing their experience and history, are incorporated with them in a common cultural life."[1] The emphasis seems to be on "interpenetration," on "fusion," on caring and sharing

45

experience and history, memories, and sentiments, resulting in mutual learning and mutual enrichment.

It is instructive to see the extent to which the inclusive thought depicted in the above definition was advocated and pursued by thinkers and activists during the late nineteenth and early twentieth centuries, and to what extent it has percolated down to present day America.

The concept of cultural assimilation, along with its popular melting pot metaphor, has two major strands represented by nativists and by idealists.[2] There are, of course, minor variations of the theme, but I believe all of them can be subsumed under one or the other of these two broad categories.

NATIVISTS AND THEIR ANGLO-CONFORMITY

When the settlers—those "intrepid Europeans" as historian Arthur M. Schlesinger called them[3]—came to this country in the seventeenth and early eighteenth century, most of them were escaping religious persecution in Britain. As I have written elsewhere, the original settlers "came with the English language on their tongue, the Protestant faith in their heart, and a noble cause in their mind."[4] Their chief mission was to build a nation of individual liberty and religious freedom. They welcomed immigrants of their own racial and religious stock, that is, White Anglo-Saxon Protestants (WASP). As Harvard sociologists Nathan Glazer and Daniel P. Moynihan observed, they "had a frame in their minds, which became a frame in reality, that placed and ordered those who came after them. It was important to be white, of British origin, and Protestant. If one was all three, then even if one was an immigrant, one was really not an immigrant, or not for long."[5]

The original settlers and their immediate descendants were actually expecting immigrants from England and other northern European regions, who were all the product of religious beliefs and cultural values similar to theirs. They were, therefore, alarmed when immigrants from eastern and southern Europe, mostly Catholics, arrived on the American shores in huge numbers.[6] Consequently, the frame of mind to place and order those who came after them grew into a movement in the late eighteenth and early nineteenth century. A movement that was later labeled nativism. According to sociologist John Higham, nativism is "an intense opposition to an internal minority on the ground of its foreign origins and connections."[7]

Avowing the Anglo-Saxon character of a nation they wanted to build, nativists showed undiluted antipathy toward all other immigrants, Catholics in particular. They thought that immigrants would corrode the basic values of the country, and Catholicism would pose an existential threat to its Protestant character. They were determined to construct and to consolidate a homogeneous America that has no place for racial, religious, or cultural differences. In fact, they looked upon cultural difference as cultural deficiency. Therefore, cultural assimilation for them was a one-way process. The melting pot boiled for others, not for them, even though they were in it. Their role, like that of a catalyst in a chemical reaction, was to facilitate a unilateral transformation, without them undergoing any change in the process.

In order to facilitate such a cultural transformation, the nativists put in place a vigorous, institutionalized program called Americanization. As the term suggests, the goal was to Americanize the immigrants by accelerating the assimilation process through classes and through assistance offered in schools, factories, trade unions, etc. The purpose was to increase the heat so that the melting pot melted well and soon. The immigrants were required to abandon their religion, their culture, and their language in a hurry. The sooner they did it, the better for them and for the country.

Determined to sustain their Americanization project, and also to stem the flow and influence of immigrants, the nativists established political and social organizations, the most prominent of which was a fraternal order called the Order of the Star-Spangled Banner. It came to be known as Know-Nothing Party because members were told to say "I know nothing" if they were asked about the Order. According to historian Tyler G. Anbinder, the party formally entered the American political scene in 1854 and within a short time, it became so popular that it had elected eight governors, more than one hundred Congressmen, the mayors of Boston, Philadelphia, and Chicago, and hundreds of other local officials.

The political agenda of the nativists aimed primarily at restricting immigration and at regulating citizenship. At the national level, they focused on revising the naturalization laws. "It was not the elimination of manyness," notes Anbinder, "but its disenfranchisement that the Know-Nothings championed."[8] They succeeded in passing laws including the *National Origins Act of 1924* that promoted immigration of people of their own racial stock. But they failed in their attempt to extend the naturalization period from five years to twenty-one-years, and to limit public offices to native-born citizens. At the local level, they tried to make sure that the immigrants and their children stopped using their home language and started learning English. They especially worked to curtail German language programs in public schools which were spreading fast at that time.

Capitalizing on their limited success, the nativists converted their fraternal Order into a conventional political party and called it "American Party." They never enjoyed majority support of the American people. They never became a national party, and their influence was confined to certain regions of the country. They could not sustain their momentum. Their popularity quickly declined. Eventually, many members of the party found their way into the Republican Party.

It is not at all difficult to see the connection between this historical precedence and what we witness in parts of today's America: anti-immigrant sentiments, resentment about ethnic diversity, systematic disenfranchisement of certain minorities, opposition to bilingual education, and more. Remnants of nativism are still alive and are part of our contemporary sociopolitical spectrum, fueled from time to time by ideologically-slanted politicians, columnists, and academics.

It is the nineteenth-century nativist sentiment that constitutes the central thesis of a twenty-first-century book on American identity, *Who Are We? The Challenges to America's National Identity* written by Harvard political scientist Samuel Huntington, prompting a prominent reviewer of the book to call him a "native son."[9] The book is a well-known, exalted, and recent representation of the age-old Anglo-conformity argument of the nativists, and so it is worth delving into it a little bit.

Simply stated, Huntington asserts that "America was created as a Protestant society just as Pakistan and Israel were created as Muslim and Jewish societies."[10] And, it should be kept that way.

So, what is his prescription to keep it that way? He dispenses it in just a couple of sentences: "Americans of all races and ethnicities could attempt to reinvigorate their core culture. This would mean a recommitment to America as a deeply religious and primarily Christian country, encompassing several religious minorities, adhering to Anglo-Protestant values, speaking English, maintaining its European cultural heritage, and committed to the principles of the Creed."[11]

Simple. Or, is it?

To me, this statement is a bundle of ambiguities and contradictions. It hides more than it reveals. If we read between the lines, we might be able to get a glimpse of Huntington's nativist mindset. Given his frequent contention in the book that religion and culture are inextricably linked, what does it mean to say Americans of *all races and ethnicities* could attempt to *reinvigorate their core culture*? If Jews, Muslims, Buddhists, Hindus, and other Americans of various religious persuasion reinvigorate their own core culture linked to their own religion, how can they be urged to make a religious recommitment to an America that is *primarily Christian*[12] and also commit to maintain its *European cultural heritage*? Is not their religion primary to them, just as some denomination of Christianity is primary to Christians? And, how are they supposed to *reinvigorate their core culture*, if they have to commit to European cultural heritage?

One aspect of *Anglo-Protestant values* that Huntington highlights is *Protestant ethic* referring mainly to hard work. "The work ethic," he argues, "is a central feature of Protestant culture, and from the beginning America's religion has been the religion of work. In other societies, heredity, class, social status, ethnicity, and family are the principal sources of status and legitimacy. In America, work is."[13]

Huntington's account of hard-working Americans is not disputable. What is disputable though is the glaring hint that markers of heredity, class, social status, ethnicity, family, etc. play a role only in other societies and not in the American society, and that hard work is a prerogative of Protestant culture. Seriously? In the final part of the book, even he concedes that Asian Americans have "brought with them values emphasizing work, discipline, learning, thrift, strong families, and in the case of Filipinos and Indians a knowledge of English. Because their values are similar to those of Americans and because of their generally high educational and occupational levels, they have been relatively easily absorbed into American society."[14] So, where do Filipino and Indian cultures leave the value of the adjective *protestant* that he unfailingly attaches to work ethic?

In his 2018 book on identity, Stanford political scientist Francis Fukuyama, an illustrious student of Huntington, refutes the wide-spread criticism that Huntington was a racist, and defends his views on American identity in general. But even he does not hesitate to take his professor to task on "Protestant" work ethic (the qualifying quote marks are Fukuyama's). "Empirically," he writes based on experimental evidence, "Americans do work much harder than many other peoples around the world—less hard than many Asians, but certainly harder than most Europeans. The historical origins of this work ethic may indeed lie in the Puritanism of the country's early settlers, but who in the United States works hard these days? It is just as likely to be a Korean grocery-store owner or an Ethiopian cab driver or a Mexican gardener, as a person of Anglo-Protestant heritage living off dividends in his or her country club."[15]

Finally, on the matter of the principles of the Creed, Huntington is right about its importance to American identity. But then, he strikes a discordant note when he makes religion the center piece of the Creed. For him, that religion is obviously Protestant religion. If there is one crucial word that has been generously sprinkled all over the book, it is the variation of *Protestant*: Anglo-Protestant religion, Anglo-Protestant culture, Anglo-Protestant values, Anglo-Protestant identity, Anglo-Protestant ethic, etc. He loudly proclaims that American identity *is* Protestant identity. At times, he is gracious enough to expand Protestant to Christian to include Catholics, but only after trying to convince his readers that Catholics have successfully undergone a transformational process of absorbing certain principles of Protestant religion. He offers this qualified extension in order to claim that America is a Christian nation. Historian Jon Meacham, among others, has sharply repudiated such a thought by saying rather curtly, "A nation of Christians is not a Christian nation."[16]

The center piece of American identity is its Creed, not religion. As documented in chapter 3, American Creed was inspired not just by Christianity but also by the English Law (Magna Carta) and the French Enlightenment. Furthermore, to claim that religion is the center piece of American identity is to go against the letter and spirit of what the extraordinary documents Founding Fathers handed down to us. There is no mention of God in the Constitution. The Declaration of Independence does mention God—not a Christian God, but a generic God, represented by the words "Nature's God," "Creator," and "Supreme Judge." A clear testimony to the genius of our Founding Fathers. Even the words "Under God" were added to the Pledge of Allegiance only as recently as in 1954, that too, after considerable controversy.

The conventional version of nativism, where all immigrants were expected to get assimilated continues to persist in certain quarters in America even today. There was, however, another version—an idealistic version—that was also short-lived.

IDEALISTS AND THEIR EURO-CONFORMITY

Nearly 240 years ago, in 1782 to be precise, Hector St. John de Crèvecoeur, a naturalized American citizen of French origin, a farmer, diplomat and writer published in London a volume of essays entitled, *Letters from an American Farmer*. His goal was to provide Europeans with glimpses of American life during the frontier days. He writes, for instance, about an American family "whose grandfather was an Englishman, whose wife was Dutch, whose son married a French woman, and whose present four sons have now four wives of different nations."[17] Different European nations, that is. He marvels at the diversity that prevailed in America of his time—at European cultural diversity, and at intra-Christian denominational diversity.

de Crèvecoeur poses the question who is an American? and answers it himself. In doing so, he is credited with using the metaphor of melting for the first time. "He is an American," he writes (ignore his gendered expression; after all, he was writing in the eighteenth century), "who leaving behind him all his ancient prejudices and manners, receives new ones from the new mode of life he has embraced, the new government he obeys, and the new rank he holds. He becomes an American by being received in the broad lap of our great Alma Mater. Here individuals of all nations are melted into a new race of men, whose labour and posterity will one day cause great changes in the world."[18]

"Individuals of all nations are melted into a new race of men." What a noble, sublime, festive thought from this Frenchman—except that by "all nations," he means only European nations.

The thought was imagined further by the British-Jewish author and playwright, Israel Zangwill. His play, *The Melting Pot*, premiered in 1908. Through the voice of the protagonist of the play, the playwright lays out his vision of a new America:

> America is God's Crucible, the great Melting Pot where all the races of Europe are melting and re-forming! Here you stand, good folk, think I, when I see them at Ellis Island, here you stand in your fifty groups, with your fifty languages and histories, and your fifty blood hatreds and rivalries. But you won't be long like that, brothers, for these are the fires of God you've come to—these are the fires of God. A fig for your feuds and vendettas! Germans and Frenchmen, Irishmen and Englishmen, Jews and Russians—into the Crucible with you all! God is making the American. . . . the real American has not yet arrived. He is only in the Crucible, I tell you—he will be the fusion of all races, perhaps the coming superman.[19]

Like de Crèvecoeur, Zangwill too visualized the American as the fusion of all European races, "perhaps the coming superman."

The coming superman did not come. Perhaps, never will. Zangwill himself realized it. Within a decade his popular play was first staged, he said with a tinge of sadness that it was wrong to "declare that there should be neither Jew nor Greek. Nature will return even if driven out with a pitchfork, still more if driven out with a dogma."[20] In fact, when he died in 1926, a *New York Times* obituary remarked that his dream of a melting pot was as dead as the author.[21]

MELTDOWN OF A DREAM

The dream of a melting pot died young primarily because we humans are tribal by nature. Zangwill was right. Our natural instinct will return even if driven out with a pitchfork. The idealist version of assimilation was too idealistic even for Europeans in spite of the fact that at a broad level, they are thought to share a common Judeo-Christian tradition. Within Protestant or Catholic faith, worshippers flocked to different denominational/ethnic churches then as they do now. It was, for instance, reported that in the 1920s and 1930s when the discourse on European melting pot was loud and clear, "in one square mile of Chicago near the stockyards, there were two Polish, one Lithuanian, one Italian, two German, two Irish, a Croatian, a Bohemian, and a Slovak Catholic church."[22]

The nativist version of assimilation was also destined to die because of yet another basic human instinct—treating strangers as outcasts. As mentioned earlier, the nativists fancied an American identity made up of immigrants of their own religious and cultural beliefs and practices. All others must be cleansed of theirs. They treated cultural assimilation strictly as a one-way process that had nothing to do with "interpenetration and fusion." For them, the melting pot was a convenient, and a deceptive, metaphor.

In an absorbing sociological study, Glazer and Moynihan tracked the role of ethnicity in the lives of the African Americans, the Puerto Ricans, the Jews, the Italians, and the Irish living in New York City. Their report, published in 1963 in their book, *Beyond the Melting Pot*, concluded that "the notion that the intense and unprecedented mixture of ethnic and religious groups in American life was soon to blend into a homogenous end product has outlived its usefulness, and also its credibility."[23] These two Harvard scholars were unambiguous in declaring that the melting did not happen at all.

Their definitive conclusion was strengthened by another sociologist, Michael Novak, who studied the lives of a different generation of European immigrant groups of Polish, Italian, Greek, and Slav origin. The title of his book, published in 1971, says it all: *The Rise of the Unmeltable Ethnics.* Unmeltable indeed. He found that the immigrants were all in close touch with, and continued to cherish, their ethnic heritage. It was for them "a source of values, instincts, ideas, and perceptions that throw original light on the meaning of America."[24]

American sociological literature is full of studies that demonstrate similar findings. In spite of such an undeniable truth, the discourse on classical assimilation, along with its melting pot metaphor, keeps coming back to life, phoenix-like, wearing different masks at different times. Obscuring the reality is an unhelpful proliferation of terms found in American sociological literature: accommodation, acculturation, adaptation, adoption, assimilation, enculturation, incorporation, integration, and more. It is not as if any of these labels define cultural assimilation fundamentally differently. They overlap in meaning and in application. There seems to be a disguised agenda behind such a semantic obfuscation. I wonder whether that is what prompted sociologists Richard Alba and Victor Nee bemoan that some in the field of sociology may have committed "intellectual sins?"[25] Whatever the motive, there is no doubt that terminological ambiguities hide the truth, cloud the issues, and provide a distorted picture of America, thereby causing unnecessary confusion.

Confounding the general confusion is a 2015 book by a Brookings Institute demographer, William Frey,[26] titled *Diversity Explosion: How New Racial Demographics Are Remaking America*. In it, the author divides the country, demographically speaking, into three regions: Melting Pot region (consisting of seven states including California, Texas, New York, Florida), New Sun

Belt Region (fifteen states including Utah, Colorado, Arizona, the Carolinas), and Heartland Region (twenty-seven states including Midwest, interior South, New England).

Setting aside the rationale or the need for such a geographical division, a question begs itself: Why is a whole region consisting of large states called a Melting Pot region? The author is not, as one would expect, christening them based on either the nativist or the idealist or any other version of cultural assimilation. Rather, he uses the term simply to refer to the number of immigrants who have recently moved to and living in that region. He also maintains without any sense of contradiction that this melting pot region, is merely "where new minorities are clustered" and so he calls such an assimilation, "spatial assimilation."[27] I contend that spatial assimilation is not the same as sociocultural assimilation, which is what the term assimilation has historically meant. The use of the classic metaphor of "melting pot" in this context is misleading in the sense that simply because immigrants of different religious, racial and ethnic background share the same zip code with the mainstream community does not mean they are assimilating in the traditional sense of the term. Clearly, the author is blurring the distinction between mixing and melting (see the next chapter for details).

Many are the ways in which the myth of the melting pot is kept alive. Sadly.

THE PERSISTENCE OF A MYTH

Joseph Campbell, that inimitable master narrator who schooled us in the meaning of ancient mythologies from the West and the East, says this about myths: "Throughout the inhabited world, in all times and under every circumstance, the myths of man have flourished; and they have been the living inspiration of whatever else may have appeared out of the activities of the human body and mind."[28]

Yes, myths can be inspirational. Yes, they are a vital source of many human activities. Myth-making is also an integral part of nation building. Every nation creates new myths, modern myths. The nineteenth-century German philosopher Friedrich Hegel stressed the importance of creating new myths. "We need a new mythology," he said, but added a caveat. "However, this mythology must be in the service of the ideas, it must become a mythology of reason. . . . Thus the enlightened and the unenlightened must finally shake hands. Mythology must become philosophical in order to make people reasonable."[29]

A mythology of reason. To make people become reasonable. At some point in our myth making and myth worshipping, reason must prevail. A recent incident I encountered may serve as a pointer. A couple of years ago, I visited a friend's house early evening on a Christmas day. As soon as she opened the door for me, her three-year-old daughter came running to me flaunting her new toy and started dancing and singing: "saann . . . taaa gave meee; saann . . . taaa gave meee." It was a delight to watch the joy in her face. It did not last long. Her mother interjected to say, "no . . . Santa didn't give you. I gave you. There's no Santa." And, she continued, imitating the girl's song and dance, "you thank me and sing: mummee gave meee . . . mummee gave me." The child seemed a little puzzled but ignored her mom and continued to happily play with her toy. I later chided my friend for spoiling the unalloyed joy of a little girl.

There certainly is a place for the Santa myth in the life of little ones every-where. However, if this three-year old believes that Santa is for real when she is thirteen (or worse, thirty), then, society would have failed her, and failed her miserably.

I see a parallel in the persistence of the melting pot myth among many American citizens. It is perfectly understandable if school kids at the elemen-tary level are introduced to this myth. But, should not the difference between myth and reality be acknowledged at some point? If we stop ten adults in the street or on a college campus and ask them if they believe America is a melt-ing pot, chances are seven or eight out of ten would say, yes. That, I believe, is a testimony to how our educational system has done an excellent job of turning a true myth into a false reality. If we quickly peruse textbooks used in middle and high schools, we will notice, with very few exceptions, that textbook writers do acknowledge the myth around the melting pot theory, but they would mention it cursorily in a sentence fragment or in a couple of sentences, and then go on to discuss at considerable length how America is a veritable melting pot.

History, research, and lived experience tell us that assimilation, in the clas-sical sense, did not happen. Neither the nativist version of Anglo-conformity nor the idealist version of Euro-conformity became a reality. If it did not become a reality in the eighteenth, nineteenth, and early twentieth centuries when the nation was racially and religiously less diverse, it is not likely to become a reality in the twenty-first century when the nation has become much more pluralistic. And, much more conscious of it.

Considering the reality of the past and the present, should we not then acknowledge and disseminate a simple truth: America has never been a melt-ing pot; and America will never be a melting pot.

The story of multiculturalism, the conceptual and historical twin of assimi-lation, is no different, as I discuss in the next chapter.

Chapter 5

Multiculturalism or Multiple Monoculturalisms?

My family has the good fortune of living in a quiet, diverse, friendly neighborhood. It is by no means a unique neighborhood, but a special one. It has similar looking houses with well-maintained lawns, and rose plants of gorgeous colors, populated mostly by highly educated and gainfully employed professionals belonging mainly to European American, African American, Chinese American, Indian American, and Japanese American communities.

When I go for my usual evening stroll around a few blocks in the immediate vicinity of my house, I experience the warmth of my neighbors: a middle-aged European American watering his plants smiles and greets me with his usual, "Hey, how you doing?"; a retired Chinese American professor stops me sometimes to talk about his teaching days, now and then asking me when I am planning to retire; a European American woman, meticulously tending to her lawn, tells me good things about the environment-friendly "Eco-lawn" she bought from a Canadian company; an Indian American man prompts his little daughter on a tricycle with training wheels to wave to me; and women walking their dog give me a nod and a smile ever so politely.

In addition to such gestures of neighborly recognition, there are also small acts of cooperation, as happens with a Chinese American family who is our next-door neighbor, and with a Persian American family across the street. When we go out of town for a short period, our Chinese friends keep an eye on our house and collect our mail, and we do the same for them. Our elderly Persian American neighbor who does his own gardening wearing a visible black abdominal brace, borrows our Yard Waste cart whenever his cart overflows, and remembers to share with us the bounty of persimmons that grow in his garden. Another neighbor's daughter comes by seeking the help of my wife (who is a professor of English) to revise her essays and personal statements for college admission. Besides, several residents in the neighborhood use the social network website, *Nextdoor*, to connect with each other for alerts about community events and issues.

On occasions, sitting in my study with windows open, I could hear my next-door Chinese American girl practice her piano lessons, the Jewish American boy in the corner house rehearse his drums in the open garage for his school band, and my daughter practice her Indian classical violin in her room. Sometimes, particularly during weekends, I can hear all three at the same time. No orchestrated symphony, this. Just disconnected music, still enjoyable. And, I see this as a musical metaphor for the sociocultural living in my immediate neighborhood.

I indulge in such a wordy portrayal of my neighborhood just to make a point. And, that is: in spite of the presence of perceptible educated minds, and the prevalence of admirable friendliness and helpful contacts, I see no conscious cultural assimilation taking place, especially of the kind envisioned and propagated by melting pot theorists of various kind. In fact, nobody is eager to know anything about their European American neighbor's or any other neighbor's religious beliefs, cultural practices, way of life, or food habits. But everybody is doing their part to ensure harmonious living in the neighborhood.

In other words, there is certainly mixing, but hardly any melting.

I see a similar scenario being played out in my city as well.

HEART OF THE SILICON VALLEY

I live in Cupertino, a city in Santa Clara County, California. It is the heart of what is well-known nationally and internationally as Silicon Valley. It houses several technology companies, including the first company in the world to reach a market value of three trillion dollars, Apple Inc., with its majestic headquarters dubbed "the spaceship" because of its circularly designed post-postmodern, neo-futuristic architectural model.

The city also boasts of stellar public schools. Monta Vista High has a track record of sky-high test scores, enviable Advanced Placement classes, and graduates who gain admission to prestigious universities. Equally impressive is William Faria Elementary School. Frequently, Faria is placed in the top 1% of all elementary schools in California.

Like my neighborhood, the city is also ethnically diverse. According to 2020 U.S. Census, in this city of about 64,000, a majority of residents are Asian Americans (63.3%), followed by Euro Americans (31.3%), Latino Americans (3.3%), African Americans (0.6%), and a sprinkling of others.[1] Among the people from Asia, Chinese and Indian Americans together constitute a majority, and the rest include people of Japanese, Korean, and Filipino heritage.

The current ethnic diversity is a fairly new development. It is only during the late 1980s and early 1990s that Cupertino started emerging as a minority-majority community. The community was changing rapidly. Too rapidly for some. As a result, tensions among residents in certain areas increased notice-ably. There was, for instance, resentment about Mandarin signs everywhere and about the offering of Mandarin language classes in the school district.

How the community responded to the challenge of change is remarkable. A group of well-meaning activists sensed that most of the tensions were the result of misunderstanding arising from a lack of interethnic communication. They approached the city manager and elected leaders asking them to explore opportunities for discussing their genuine concerns, for identifying explosive issues, and for resolving potential conflicts. The city responded positively and sought the help of the Public Dialogue Consortium (PDC), a California-based non-profit organization consisting of consultants, educators, and practitioners committed to promoting meaningful dialogue in the public sphere. Under the auspices of PDC, a series of activities were conducted over a period of time to promote useful dialogues between residents of various ethnic communities and also between them and city officials. They all had several opportunities to listen and speak to each other with mutual respect, and together they for-mulated actionable plans for fostering intercultural understanding.[2]

A newly formed Citizens of Cupertino Cross Cultural Consortium (5Cs) (on which I had the pleasure of serving for a short time), consisting of citizen volunteers continued the good work. The success of its efforts led to a vast improvement in interethnic relationships and cooperation. As a result, 5Cs soon became redundant, and was disbanded after nearly a decade of service. It was replaced by an ongoing Block Leader Program whose mission is to train interested residents to work towards larger community interests such as safety, education, youth welfare, etc. Some of the 5Cs volunteers became block leaders and started sharing their experiences with other block leaders for the common good.

Every summer, the recreation department of the city organizes a series of free cultural programs staged in various city parks. Recently sponsored programs included musical events featuring Classic Rock (by Johnny Neri Band), Bluegrass (by Busta Groove), Blues (by Big Blu Soul Revue), Fusion music (by Pallejo Seco), and Bollywood-style dance and songs. In addition, on an annual basis and sometimes with the help of the local Rotary Club and Chamber of Commerce, the city facilitates Chinese Moon Festival, Indian Diwali Festival of Lights, Japanese Cherry Blossom Festival, etc.

An easily observable feature of these entertainment programs and cultural events is that they predominantly attract residents from respective ethnic communities. Only a few members of other ethnic communities go to these events. It is rather apparent that the people of Cupertino work together to continue to nurture a socially dynamic, culturally vibrant, educationally excellent, and economically thriving community that fosters harmonious living among its residents. However, each community strives, and succeeds, to maintain and to celebrate its own religious, cultural, and linguistic identity, and takes legitimate pride in doing so.

In other words, there is certainly mixing, but hardly any melting.

From the point of view of cultural assimilation (or the lack of it), what I observe in my neighborhood and in my city is not substantially different from what seems to be happening in several parts of the country.

A quick look at a few representative minority communities in the country shows how they are mindful of the task of preserving and protecting their religious, cultural, and linguistic identities while at the same time working hard to uphold and advance common American ideals and common American identity. Along the way some of them have felt that to be acceptable to the mainstream community, they may have to "become white."[3]

While "becoming white" remains a disputed thesis, there is a general understanding that it is not a reference to the change of official racial classification of non-Anglo-Saxon European immigrant groups but to a change in their acquired socioeconomic and political status. Initially, this change in the status occurred over time among European immigrant groups such as the Jews, the Irish, the Italians, and the Polish mainly owing to their improved education, employability, economic self-sufficiency, and attendant political power. With this change, the groups were deemed to have transitioned from the margin to near the center. No wonder, therefore, minority communities have sought to "become white" in order to advance their aspirations.

One minority group that sincerely tried to "become white" but was repeatedly rebuffed by the mainstream community is the African American community, a community whose history continues to be unique compared to other minority communities in this country.

AFRICAN AMERICANS

Ironically, both the Anglo whites and the Afro blacks arrived at the American shores almost at the same time—four hundred years ago. The difference in the mode of their arrival has made and still makes all the difference. The white settlers voluntarily landed on the Plymouth Rock while the blacks were forcibly brought here, in chains. Theirs is a tortured and tortuous story of people "whose history defying rise from bondage to the highest rungs of society, amassing accolades and power, wealth and land, genius and achievement" is often contrasted with a record of divergence of high rates of illiteracy, unemployment, poverty, and homelessness.[4]

According to the 2020 United States Census, blacks constitute approximately 13.4% of the US population, which equals to about 44 million. They were the largest group of people of color until 2001 when Latinos outnumbered them. Ethnic diversity among the blacks, however, makes it difficult to talk about them as a single group. According to one estimate,[5] after the *Hart-Celler Immigration Act of 1965* eliminated country-specific quotas on immigration, there has been a steady influx of black people who had no experience of slavery or a history of racist segregation in the United States. During 1960 through 1984, more than 600,000 people from Caribbean nations such as Jamaica, and more than 140,000 from Haiti arrived. Between 2000 and 2010, the African foreign-born population nearly doubled in size to 1.6 million people.

In spite of such variations and persistent racial prejudice, the black community as a whole has successfully preserved its distinct identity, particularly with regard to their religion, culture, and education.

In conceiving and in constructing a distinct religious identity for the African American community, perhaps no other institution has played a greater historic role than black churches in America. Going back to the days of slavery, black churches have been a source of not only religious involvement but also of personal enrichment. Most of the Blacks who were brought here as slaves were not Christians. However, they soon embraced Christianity attracted by, as historian Eddie Glaude Jr. observes, "the liberating power of Jesus's example: his sense that all, no matter their station in life, were children of God." He even uses the epithet "African American religion" as it bears "the burden of a difficult history that colors the way religion is practiced and understood in the United States." And it also registers "the horror of slavery and the terror of Jim Crow as well as the richly textured experiences of a captured people, for whom sorrow stands alongside joy."[6]

Even though African Americans became predominantly Protestant,[7] they synthesized their own cultural heritage with what they found acceptable in the religious practices of their white Protestant slaveholders. "In some cases, they reached for traditions outside of the United States altogether. They took the bits and pieces of their complicated lives and created distinctive expressions of the general order of existence that anchored their efforts to live amid the pressing nastiness of life."[8] Even though they mostly opted for Baptist or Methodist denominations, they developed their own version of worship with song and dance reflecting nineteenth-century black life in the United States. Their services routinely figured sermons from black ministers who displayed not only their Biblical knowledge but also literary eloquence. Most of the black preachers played the role of religious and civil rights leaders as well as community activists, Dr. Martin Luther King Jr. being a prime and popular example.

While their religious beliefs and practices are largely limited to the African American community, it is their cultural identity—particularly their music—that found original expressions, and also enjoyed enviable crossover appeal among Americans of various ethnic background as well as the global audience. A recent CNN series "See It Aloud: The History of Black Television" examines the historical impact Black culture has on other cultures. Jazz, with a blend of blues and ragtime, became a popular form of musical tradition in the early part of the twentieth century. A constellation of black stars such as Duke Ellington, Louis Armstrong, and many others enhanced its status and spread its fame. Later in 1970, the celebratory Jackson Five reached No.1 on the *Billboard 100* and became the first group to top the US charts for eleven weeks during that year. That was just a prelude. Fast forward to the twenty-first century. Beyoncé, Jay Z, Drake, Kanye West, Kendrick Lamar, and several others have become legendary singers and song writers. Similar national and global level appeal cutting across color lines can be seen in the achievements of sports figures, particularly in football, basketball, and tennis.

Yet another arena where the African American community strives to preserve its identity is education. Several black-owned, black-sponsored institutions have contributed significantly to that end. Historically Black Colleges and Universities (HBCUs) continue to produce reputable academics, scientists, leaders, and writers. Part of their success is reflected in the fact that during the 1960s and 1970s, many universities and colleges in the country established specialized academic programs in African American studies, enabling African American scholars to present their own perspectives about African American histories, cultures, and lives.

Ever since the successful civil rights movement, African Americans have been making slow but steady progress in terms of their political imprint at the national level. Recently, the country elected and re-elected a black President. Now we have a black Vice President who also happens to be a woman, a first in the history of America. In addition, we learn from a Pew Research Center report that in the newly elected 118th Congress that assumed office in January 2023, African American representation in the House of Representatives has increased to a record 13%, almost equal to the share of African American population in the country.[9]

However, the number of highly educated and reputable professionals in various fields make up only a small fraction of the total black middle class. As in other minority communities, there is widespread educational and income disparity. Between 1988 and 1994, the racial gap in reading grew from 2.5 to 3.9 years; between 1990 and 1994, the racial gap in math increased from 2.5 to 3.4 years.[10] In both science and writing, the racial gap has widened by a full year. Furthermore, only 19% men and 24% of women have bachelor's degree or higher. Partly because of educational disparity, even though the community has produced black one-percenters, as exemplified by media moguls such as Oprah Winfrey, business executives such as Kenneth Chenault, as well as multimillionaire sports and entertainment stars, a large segment of blacks lag behind in wealth with their annual median household income being $48,297.[11]

In spite of the black community's noteworthy achievements, a considerable segment of the mainstream community continued their historical practice of separating blacks from most other new immigrants whom it considered assimilable. During the 1960s, seeing that systemic racism persisted unabated even after their decorated services and sacrifices in World War II, some African American activists, as a mark of protest, tried to revive what was earlier called Afrocentrism. It was during that time, a week-long winter holiday called Kwanzaa was created specifically to celebrate African American history and culture immediately following Christmas holidays. The idea of Afrocentrism was to raise black consciousness and ethnic pride in order to help ordinary African Americans to be aware of their roots in order to regain a sense of self-identity. However, their renewed contact with Africa convinced them that they have more in common with America than with Africa. They discovered that their identity is American.

The steadfast adherence to their distinguished and distinguishing identity has not in any way constrained the African Americans from striving to participate in the construction of a common American identity. But still, a sizable segment of the mainstream community remains indifferent to their growth and development.

The story unfolded very differently for a different minority community.

JEWISH AMERICANS

Perhaps no other minority community worked so hard, for so long, and so well to "become white" as American Jews did. In his award-winning book *The Price of Whiteness: Jews, Race, and American Identity*, Eric L. Goldstein, a historian specializing in Jewish studies, makes a definitive statement about American Jews: "Jews' transition from 'racial' minority to part of the white mainstream was slow and freighted with difficulty, not only because native-born whites had a particularly difficult time seeing Jews as part of a unified homogeneous white population, but also because whiteness sat uneasily with many central aspects of Jewish identity."[12]

The transition of American Jews from minority to mainstream was initially facilitated by two crucial factors. First, the socially demarcated and severely enforced racial color line between free whites and enslaved blacks that prevailed before, during and after the Civil War automatically afforded the fair-skinned Jews a modicum of social acceptance by the whites. Second, American Jews realized early on that in order to survive and to succeed in white America, they have to "become white" in a hurry, and they went about achieving that goal by working hard and by employing their creative talent.

During the early decades of the twentieth century, they initiated, developed, and contributed significantly to, and also benefited from, the popularity of mass media, particularly radio and motion pictures. They are rightfully credited for the invention of Hollywood. Partly to establish their loyalty to the assimilationist Americanization project, Hollywood pioneers such as Louis Mayer, the Warner brothers, and others "projected literally and psychologically," as writer Eric Liu points out, "all their assimilationist dreams of a perfect America onto the screens that in turn framed everyone else's dreams of a perfect America."[13] They realized that celluloid images could have a lasting impact. Some others became opinion leaders shaping American public discourse through their writing and artistic performance.

In spite of "becoming white" and gaining a fair degree of social acceptance that they eagerly sought, American Jews remained uneasy about the likelihood of losing their Jewish identity. Their uneasiness was matched by a segment of the mainstream white Protestant America that remained conflicted about the contours of a stable white American identity that included Jews. In the face of racial adversity and the pressure to assimilate, American Jews were able to protect their identity by practicing their Jewishness in the privacy of their homes and in synagogues for a long time. They also, until recently, scrupulously avoided marrying outside their own community, claiming that it was due to their religious precepts rather than to racial prejudice.

The social and political upheaval the country witnessed during the mid-twentieth century helped the Jews with their identity preservation. As discussed above, African Americans seeing their efforts to integrate with the mainstream community rebuffed, launched the civil rights movement and decided to renew their own cultural traditions and uphold their own ethnic distinctiveness. And, women, through their social activism, fought male domination and decided that the best way to ensure their rightful place in the American society was to underscore their gender identity. American Jews with their active engagement both in the civil rights movement and in the feminist movement saw in them a justification for reclaiming and revealing their own Jewish identity.[14] In addition, as anthropologist Karen Brodkin observes, both Holocaust and the birth of Israel in 1948 "gave Jews a degree of critical distance from mainstream American whiteness, a sense of otherness."[15]

According to Goldstein, it was not until the 1960s that American Jews achieved a high level of success thereby gaining grudging acceptance by the mainstream white community while at the same time feeling safe and secure to display their true Jewish identity proudly and publicly. They eventually became so confident of exhibiting their Jewishness that, when the 2000 U.S. Census included the option of choosing "biracial" or "multiracial" as a category, many of them ignored both, and instead opted to write-in "Jewish" as an alternative category.

The total number of Jews currently living in the United States is uncertain because of various definitions of who a Jew is. A 2013 survey by Pew Research Center estimates that there are 6.7 million Jews in the United States,[16] while a 2016 study by Brandeis University puts that number at 7.2 million.[17] What is, however, certain is that there are well-established and well-funded organizations that seek to preserve and to promote Jewish heritage. It has been reported that, by the dawn of the twenty-first century, there were about 3,800 synagogues in the United States that nourish Jewish religious identity.[18] Also, there were about 400 Jewish Community Centers in North America that provide cultural, social, educational, and recreational programs aimed at Jewish identity-building.[19] Some of them also offer Jewish education for pre-school children, and leadership summer camps for the youth.

Many American Jews now look back at the history of their identity (re)formation, and "seem particularly conscious of the way that being seen as white delegitimized their claim to difference as Jews."[20] The story of American Jews, then, is the success story of a minority community that achieved enviable degree of economic success, political power, social integration, and cultural influence, and one that is legitimately proud of retaining and of enriching its heritage, its identity. Clearly, they adjusted only to the extent of making sure that there is no erasure of their Jewish identity.

A not-so-different story is beginning to unfold with regard to Indian Americans as well.

INDIAN AMERICANS

"How did a population from one of the poorest countries halfway around the world, with distinctive linguistic and religious characteristics and low levels of human capital, emerge as arguably the richest and most economically successful group in one of the richest and arguably the most powerful country in the world—and that too, in little more than a single generation?"[21]

That is a question raised and explored by Sanjay Chakravorty, Devesh Kapur, and Nirvikar Singh in their 2017 book titled *The Other One*

Percent: Indians in America, alluding to about 3.5 million Indian Americans constituting roughly 1% of the current U.S. population. A related question is: how did Indian Americans manage to achieve such a high level of success in America while at the same time maintaining the essence of their religious, cultural, and linguistic identities?

The current status of Indian Americans in the United States can be summed up in two related facts: India-born immigrants are significantly better educated, and therefore have higher household incomes than both foreign-born and native-born Americans. To be more specific, according to a Census report, the median household income in all of America in 2022 is $74,580 while that of foreign-born Indian Americans is $126,705. In terms of higher education, 43% of Indian Americans have postgraduate degrees compared to the national figure of 13%.[22]

How was it made possible?

As with other immigrant communities, the story of Indian Americans is also complicated, with several variables intersecting. But a simplified answer lies in the profile of Indians who came to America. While a small number of low-skilled Indians arrived in late nineteenth and early twentieth centuries, the number mushroomed after 1965 with the passage of the *Immigration and Nationality Act* which abolished nationality-based quota system and instead welcomed high-skilled immigrants, thereby opening up the entry of Indian professionals such as scientists, engineers, doctors, and educators. The number accelerated even more after the year 2000 with the influx of computer specialists who came to work for the rapidly expanding IT industry. Besides, and more importantly, these immigrants come with the benefit of English language education back at home.

We must, however, be wary of overgeneralizations and stereotypes. The rosy picture about education and occupation presented above is somewhat skewed because of the higher educational profile of India-born immigrants who constitute nearly 62% of the current Indian population in the United States. There is substantial inequality in income and in occupation between the first generation (that is, India-born) and other generations of people of Indian origin. Only a few of the earlier generations of Indian Americans are highly educated professionals. There are several who own and run small motels and gas stations all across the country. Many others work in transportation, agriculture, nursing, and retail trade sectors.

Whether they belong to the first or subsequent generations, Indian Americans have by and large safeguarded the basic tenets of their religious, cultural and linguistic identities. They have formed several voluntary organizations to ensure identity preservation, particularly religious identity. Based on an authoritative database, Chakravorty, Kapur and Singh report that there are at present 966 Indian organizations of which 481 are religion-based. Three-fifths of them are Hindu temples or temple-related, and the rest belong to the Sikh, the Jain, the Muslim, and other religious communities.[23] Indian Americans throng to their places of worship, particularly on festival days of which there are many. In addition, many homes, especially the Hindu ones, will have a small *Pooja* room or a corner displaying colorful pictures and bronze statuettes of some of their favorite gods and goddesses selected from the pluralistic Hindu pantheon.

Some of the religion-based organizations also double as Sunday schools teaching Indian regional languages, thereby preserving the linguistic identity of successive generations of speakers of major Indian languages such as Hindi, Punjabi, Telugu, Tamil, Gujarati, or Bengali. For instance, it is reported that there are about 150 Gurdwaras across the country, many of which run Sunday Punjabi Schools where children go to study Sikh history, philosophy, and their heritage language using a well-designed curriculum put together by the Sikh Research Institute.[24] There are also organizations such as the California-based International Tamil Academy that offer regular weekend language classes. In addition, Indian Americans keep their classical artistic and musical talents alive by helping their children learn and perform string instruments like the Indian Violin or Sitar, percussion instruments like Mridangam or Tabla, and traditional dances like Bharatanatyam or Kathak.

It is believed that there are two main factors that largely contribute to the preservation of the identity of Indian Americans: their value system and their marital behavior. Survey after survey reveal that Indians believe in strong family ties that foster acceptance of diversity, group harmony, hard work, frugality, and a fair degree of religiosity. Moreover, like Jewish Americans, Indian Americans too married, until recently, within their own communities, and this practice largely continues beyond the first and second generations. Their family values are also credited for keeping their marriage rate high and divorce rate low.

Augmenting all the religion- and language-based organizations are India Community Centers and Chinmaya Missions across the country that inculcate in the younger generation cultural knowledge, civic responsibilities, and overall Indian value systems. It is in the close-knit family and in sociocultural activities that a sense of belonging, a sense of Indianness is passed on to successive generations. This is not to say that there are no intergroup or intergenerational variations particularly in terms of identity formation and preservation. It is natural that, compared to first-generation Indian Americans, subsequent generations, particularly the second, will exhibit greater integrationist tendencies. But the fact remains that Indian Americans by and large successfully manage to preserve and to protect their religious, cultural, and linguistic identities while at the same time working hard to prosper in and contribute to the American society, and proudly playing a part in strengthening a common American national identity.

LATINO AMERICANS

With about 58 million, constituting nearly 18% of the total U.S. population, Latinos[25] as a racial/ethnic community are second only to the whites in number. Contrary to popular misconception about immigration, more than 90% of Latinos under the age of eighteen are born in the United States to Latino parents.[26] While a significant number of Latinos (64%) are of Mexican origin, there are also many from Puerto Rico, Cuba, Salvador, Guatemala, Dominican-Republic, Honduras, Colombia, and other places, all of them sharing a common religion (Catholicism) and a common language (Spanish). They have settled in large numbers in states such as California, Texas, Florida, and New York, with an increasing number of them now moving to southern states like Georgia and North Carolina.

Wherever they are from, many first-generation Latinos are faced with challenges to fit in with the American society at large. One major reason is their difficulty in finding gainful employment. Nearly three quarters of adult Latino immigrants have only a high school diploma or even less. With limited education and English language skills, many of them end up as low-skilled workers.

The picture changes remarkably, as can be expected, when we look at the second and subsequent generations of Latinos. As demographer Paul Taylor reports, the second-generation Latinos have a higher educational experience and, as a result, have a higher median household income and a higher rate of home ownership. An interesting feature of the Latino communities in the United States is that, as a Pew Research survey reveals, nearly 25% of Latino newlyweds in 2015 have married a non-Latino spouse, and that the rate of Latino intermarriage is higher than that for whites or blacks.[27] "By the third generation," going by the Pew report, "most have assimilated and are English speaking."

The phrase "most have assimilated" should not mislead us to think that by the third generation, most Latinos have socio-culturally assimilated to the mainstream culture, diluting their heritage. That is just not the case. In fact, generational differences as well as economic and educational differences have not in any significant measure changed their identity preservation. Although the second-generation Latinos show greater integrationist tendencies, as in other ethnic communities, Paul Taylor finds that even they "retain strong ties to the land and language of their ancestors. . . . A majority say they most often identify themselves by their family's country of origin . . .

However, with only half of third-plus-generation Hispanics saying they typically describe themselves as Americans, assimilation has come to mean something different."[28]

That difference is the result of what PBS correspondent Ray Suarez calls "the push and pull factors of identity" that vary among various groups of the Latino population. He points out how in parts of cities like Los Angeles and San Antonio, Mexican culture is "alive and thriving" and how "Miami became a bilingual city as Cubans grew in cultural influence and economic clout, but also as Miami became an offshoot of Central and South America."[29] What is therefore clear is that, like other racial/ethnic communities in the United States, a vast percentage of Latinos of second as well as subsequent generations are seriously and successfully engaged in their identity preservation, while at the same time attempting to transcend their ethnic boundaries in certain aspects of their American life.

Similar trajectories of identity preservation can also be seen, with marginal differences, in other immigrant communities from Europe such as the Irish and the Italians, and from Asia such as the Chinese and the Filipinos. Many in the mainstream white community, it is fair to say, have been living in their own cultural cocoons expecting others to "become white." The community, however, is beginning to open up to interracial and interfaith marriages which were, until recently, considered unacceptable and even illegal in some states. More on that in later chapters.

The brief sketch of the neighborhood, the city, and the country presented above points to the same pattern of immigrant experience that author Maria Laurino observed about Italian immigrants: "an isolated first generation dedicates itself to finding work and raising a family; a more secure second-generation, recognizing the chasm between its parents and the culture, seeks to eliminate ethnic traits; and the third and fourth generations set about reclaiming ancestral roots to better define the self."[30]

I see yet another element to this pattern: immigrants of subsequent generations, with very few exceptions, gradually settle down to the daunting task of overcoming racial, political, economic, and social barriers in order to claim their rightful place under the American Sun. Making use of the many opportunities America offers, they strive to build up their economic, educational, social and political capital, with the fervent hope that they will eventually be able to reduce the equality gap so as to enable them play a useful role as American citizens. Some achieve their American dream in a relatively short time; others find their dream deferred.

This predictable regularity of the pattern casts serious doubts about the prevailing academic and political discourses on American multiculturalism and their adequacy to explain what happens on the ground.

AMERICAN MULTICULTURALISM

"We are all multiculturalists now"—declared Harvard University sociologist Nathan Glazer.[31] He was not being frivolous. He was referring to the diffused nature of American-style multiculturalism which means all things to all people, making it rather vacuous. I say "American-style multiculturalism" because many nations in the world describe themselves as multicultural but each one believes in its own version of multiculturalism. Even within Western liberal democracies, multiculturalism is understood and practiced in different ways. American multiculturalism in particular has so many facets that it has been characterized variously as weak multiculturalism, muscular multiculturalism, radical multiculturalism, benign multiculturalism, state multiculturalism, critical multiculturalism, corporate multiculturalism, boutique multiculturalism, and more. At a broader level, the politics of American multiculturalism is such that progressives and conservatives see the concept of multiculturalism differently and hence address its challenges differently. A common feature is that they both ultimately failed to achieve their stated goals.

The progressive aspect of American multiculturalism started during the early part of the twentieth century as a reaction to the strong version of nativism which demanded that immigrants erase their cultural heritage and assimilate into the dominant white Anglo-Saxon Protestant culture. Alarmed by its stridency, many progressive intellectuals raised their voice against it. Horace M. Kallen, a Jewish immigrant and a prominent philosopher of the time, was one of those who spearheaded the opposition to the Americanization project. Questioning the validity of the melting pot theory, he proposed what he called "cultural pluralism" premised upon the rationale that "Democracy involves not the elimination of differences but the perfection and conservation of differences" and that "the hyphen unites very much more than it separates."[32] He firmly believed that human beings cannot divest themselves from their sentimental attachment to their ethnic heritage wherever they may choose to live. "Men," he reasoned, "may change their clothes, their politics, their wives, their religions, their philosophies, to a greater or lesser extent; they cannot change their grandfathers. Jews or Poles or Anglo-Saxons, in order to cease being Jews or Poles or Anglo-Saxons, would have to cease to be."[33]

Kallen's idea of cultural pluralism gradually evolved into present day multiculturalism during the mid-twentieth century. African Americans were the ones who primarily triggered and accelerated this change. The reason was simple: in spite of their high-sounding liberalism, cultural pluralists such as Kallen and other progressive thinkers of the time (such as the celebrated educational philosopher John Dewey) excluded Native Americans and African

Americans from their pluralistic vision. If nativists were Anglocentric, plural-ists were Eurocentric. Privileging only the European whites, cultural plural-ists excluded black, red, brown, and yellow people.

As highlighted earlier, African Americans, rejected by the mainstream community, were left with no option but to reaffirm and to reassert their racial/ethnic identity. They sought to expand the narrow vision of the concept of cultural pluralism into one that will include them and other non-European minorities as well. In the wake of their successful civil rights movement in the 1960s, they decided to work to build a nation that recognized and respected people of all colors and creeds. They achieved concrete but limited success as evidenced in the declaration of February as Black History Month, and in the establishment of African American and African Studies programs in leading universities and colleges. Their role in the development of multiculturalism is so central that Glazer aptly called them "the storm troops in the battles over multiculturalism."[34]

Multiculturalism gained greater importance during the 1980s and early 1990s when it became a major impetus for academic, political, and social activism across the country. Following the positive response to African American Studies, other ethnic studies programs such as Asian American Studies and Latin American Studies emerged in several educational institu-tions. Many schools, particularly in big states like California and New York, introduced new curricula focusing on ethnic histories and ethnic cultures. The impact of the practice of multiculturalism in American school education as well as its popularity among the general public has been so significant that it alarmed an influential segment of American conservatives.

Conservative columnists (for example, Patrick Buchanan), commentators (for example, Lynne Cheney), politicians (for example, Newt Gingrich), edu-cators (for example, Diane Ravitch), writers (for example, Peggy Noonan), and others saw in multiculturalism an undesirable force that is eroding the very foundation of America's sociocultural edifice. They genuinely feared that the edifice would collapse if its Eurocentric foundation were weakened. Although they were opposed to the very idea of multiculturalism, in a grudg-ing recognition of its popularity, some of them appropriated it to claim that they too practiced multiculturalism because they accepted the transition from its narrow Anglocentric emphasis to a larger Eurocentric emphasis. For them, that is multicultural enough.

Given their Eurocentric emphasis, there is no wonder that some of the conservative thinkers and activists were and still are vehemently opposed to ethnic diversity in America. In a recent blog, Buchanan reiterates the familiar conservative stance that there is no scientific, historical, or empirical evidence to prove that racial, ethnic, cultural, and religious diversity makes a nation strong. For him, the reverse is true: "The more diverse a nation, the greater the danger of its disintegration."³⁵ To support his argument, he cites the examples of multi-ethnic countries such as former Soviet Union which split into fifteen separate nations, former Yugoslavia which split into seven separate nations, and other countries which are encountering ethnic conflicts bordering on civil wars. He thus implies that a diverse America may also face a similar fate.

In making such a false parallel, Buchanan seems to have conveniently ignored certain historical facts: in most of the disintegrated and disintegrating countries, various ethnic groups were original inhabitants of the land, living in their own fairly autonomous regions which were forcefully annexed into a larger, fabricated nation-state either by their colonial conquerors or by their autocratic leaders who emerged victorious from bloody civil wars. After a long struggle, many of these ethnic groups succeeded in regaining their original autonomy thereby causing the disintegration that Buchanan is referring to. America, on the contrary, is a nation of immigrants. With the exception of Native Americans who originally belonged here, and African Americans who were brought here in chains, immigrants from all over the world came here voluntarily to build a new life in a new country. Buchanan's analogy is fallacious. When was the last time any of the immigrant ethnic groups in the United States sought or fought for a separate nation in a coordinated, concerted way? And, what's the likelihood of that happening in the near or distant future?

Buchanan and some other conservatives suggest that American diversity will certainly make the nation strong if immigration is limited to people of European origin, and not extended to people from non-European countries. Clearly, they are all driven more by the desire to make the country exclusively Eurocentric rather than by the fear of national disintegration and ethnic conflict. "Where is the evidence," Buchanan asks, "that the more Americans who can trace their roots to the Third World, and not to Europe, the stronger we will be?"³⁶ He would rather keep America a nation of European in color and creed because, according to him, it "is a country that belongs to a separate and identifiable people with its own history, heroes, holidays, symbols, songs, myths, mores—its own culture."³⁷ But the fact is Europe itself is not an ethnically homogenous region. Europeans are not an ethnically homogenous people. The continent consists of several ethnic groups each with "a separate and identifiable" histories and heroes, songs and symbols, myths and mores. Just ask the French, the Germans, the Danes, the British, the Spaniards, the Italians, and others. Evidently, the political agenda to build an America that is in the image of an imagined Europe is an age-old mission of the nativists—a mission that remains unaccomplished.

THE SHORTCOMINGS OF AMERICAN
MULTICULTURALISM

At a theoretical level, the idea of multiculturalism makes eminent sense because in a pluralistic, democratic society such as ours, it is imperative that various racial, ethnic, and religious entities live and work together harmoniously in order to maintain peace and prosperity. This is simply not possible if communities, including the mainstream community, feel that there is a real or perceived threat to their sense of identity. Therefore, an important function of governmental agencies and educational institutions in America's state multiculturalism is to put in place policies and practices that will not only empower all communities to preserve and protect their identities but also enable them to operate within the purview of an overall national identity and pursue a common national agenda.

The most important promise of state multiculturalism is to ensure equality of freedom, equality of treatment, and equality of opportunities for all people so that they recognize that they are all valued stakeholders in the wellbeing of the nation. In America, both the right and the left have failed to create and sustain an environment that is needed for that to happen. Inequality in our country, as we all know, is rampant.

The right, at least a prominent and powerful segment of it, has been fixated on a narrow vision of America that is premised upon race and religion, blood and soil. Is not this view antithetical to the very idea of American identity that the Founding Fathers envisioned and enacted? Intrinsic to the right's narrow vision is an unequal society that valorizes the mainstream community and demonizes the Other. The question of ethnic diversity, then, is anathema to their agenda. However, a vast majority of Americans never historically endorsed the idea of an ethnically and culturally homogenous America. As mentioned earlier, it did not materialize even during the late nineteenth and early twentieth centuries when nativism was a political force to reckon with, and when immigrant population consisted predominantly of people of European origin. All that changed after the mid-twentieth century, particularly after the enactment of the *Immigration and Nationality Act of 1965*, which heralded the steady arrival of skilled immigrants from non-European countries. The country is now unquestionably pluralistic—racially, religiously, ethnically, culturally, linguistically. The chances of nativistic vision materializing now in twenty-first-century America are remote indeed.

The left, in spite of their progressive stance, could not deliver its promise of a truly multicultural nation where members of all the racial/ethnic communities enjoyed a comfortable level of equality. Instead of dismantling the widespread structural inequality in the American society, they frittered away

their energy and enthusiasm by focusing on superficial aspects of multicultur-
alism. They promoted ritualized celebration of difference by designating dif-
ferent months for different ethnic groups. Thus, for instance, we have Black
History Month in February, Irish American Heritage Month in March, Jewish
American Heritage Month in May, Asian Pacific Heritage Month again in
May, Latinx Heritage Month in September-October, and American Indian
Heritage Month in November. And more.

These month-centered festivities have become no more than transient
Kumbaya moments, prompting a scholar in cultural studies derisively remark
that multiculturalism has been "aestheticized and packaged as an exciting
consumable collage: brown hands holding yellow hands holding white hands
holding male hands holding female hands holding black hands in a spirit of
post-historical contemporaneity."[38] Another scholar belittled the cosmetic
aspect of multiculturalism as "boutique multiculturalism."[39] Yet another
scholar disparaged "corporate multiculturalism" that treated ethnic diversity
as a commodity of exotic artifacts to be sold and bought only to be exhibited
in drawing rooms.[40] No doubt, celebrating heritage months, and incorporat-
ing ethnic stories written by ethnic writers in the school curriculum do serve
the cause of creating diversity awareness. However, they are not an end in
themselves; they are a means to an end, the end being creating conditions
necessary for ensuring freedom for all, equality for all, and prosperity for all.
The left has failed to ensure that, miserably squandering away their energy
and effort on superficialities.

Overall, then, both the right and the left interpreted the concept of multiculturalism in their own way to suit their own political agenda. And yet, both
fell short of achieving their primary goal. The right was unable to dislodge
ethnic/racial pride of minority communities, and the left was unable to tackle
economic, social, and political inequality. Both, however, managed to solidify
group-oriented identity politics, mostly for electoral gains, with the right
underscoring white identity, and the left accentuating the identities of all other
minorities and LGBTQ+ community. Consequently, repeated invocation of
the mantra of multiculturalism has become no more than a convenient slogan
that is at variance with reality.

MULTIPLE MONOCULTURALISMS

If we take the ground reality portrayed in this chapter seriously, and if we
recognize the deceptive nature of American multiculturalism, then, a different
way of describing (and hence understanding) contemporary America presents
itself: America is not a nation of multiculturalism; America is a nation of
multiple monoculturalisms.[41]

To put it briefly and briskly, what makes America a nation of multiple monoculturalisms is that it is a vibrant, pluralistic liberal democracy populated by descendants of original settlers, and of successive immigrants from Europe and other parts of the world all of whom bring to this nation the richness of racial, religious, ethnic, cultural, and linguistic diversity. And, each minority community, after initial attempt by its second generation to culturally assimilate by losing some of their ethnic heritage, eventually strive to preserve and to protect their religious, cultural, and linguistic identities while at the same time contributing to the advancement of an overall American identity and American progress.

Such a nation of multiple monoculturalisms is made possible by other attendant beliefs and practices if its citizens: Attracted by the American Dream, immigrants from all over the world come here aspiring to start a new life in a new country, and most of them, with notable exceptions, follow the same trajectory. They try to equip themselves with a higher level of knowledge and skill necessary for gainful employment, for economic self-sufficiency, and for political participation. In the process, they demonstrate their abiding allegiance to, and energetic engagement with, American ideals. They also recognize that preserving and celebrating particular identities is not antithetical to working toward, and appropriating, a common national identity. They demonstrate their patriotism by enlisting in the military and being ready to die for the country. They join the nation in mourning tragic moments such as 9/11 by spontaneously hoisting the Stars and Stripes in their homes. They show their pride by rejoicing at American successes in competitive events like the Olympics. As Pew Research Center researcher Paul Taylor found out, "Today's immigrant—nearly 9 out of 10 of whom are not Europeans—look very different from the previous waves of settlers and immigrants who created America. But when it comes to embracing what we think of as traditional American values, it's hard to find more fervent devotees."[42]

In the subsequent chapters, I will detail the contours of how mainstream as well as minority communities adhere to American values in order to weave a cohesive and colorful tapestry of national identity. I will start with how they shape and reshape the nation's religious, cultural, and linguistic identities.

PART III

Transforming the Sense of Self

Chapter 6

Religious Identity
Faith and the Faithful

"Amen." Nearly a thousand boys, including me, would shout in unison following a cue from our Headmaster. Every working day, at the start of school, all of us would be lined up in the school assembly hall, class by class, led by our home-room teacher. The Headmaster would use the occasion to make house-keeping announcements. And more.

The *more* would come at the end of the announcements. A prayer. The Headmaster would open his well-preserved Bible and read to us a short passage. Often, it would be a Psalm. He would always explain the Psalm, connecting it to a current event or a moralistic story. Sometimes, the same Psalm with a different topical story. He would end the session with "Amen" and out of disciplined practice, we would all enthusiastically repeat after him.

The high school I attended (in the mid-1960s) was a private Christian school located in the city of Coimbatore in the state of Tamilnadu in South India. It was (and still is) run by the Church of South India (CSI). The CSI was formed in 1947 with a union of many Protestant denominations in South India including Anglicans, Methodists, Presbyterians, and later Baptists and Pentecostals. My school was named Union High School in honor of the union of the Churches. Recently, it was rechristened (no pun intended) as CSI Boys' Higher Secondary School. It was one of the many institutions—schools, colleges, hospitals—run by the CSI. The Headmaster and most of the teachers were (and still are) Christians, although the student body consisted mostly of Hindu students along with a sprinkling of Christian and Muslim students, reflecting the population profile of the city. Nobody—not pupils, not parents, not the public—raised any objection to the Christian prayer. Everybody treated it for what it was—a prayer, and a learning experience.

I remember my Headmaster Mr. Michael Ponnuswamy as an affable gentleman. He taught us Math and English. He never talked about Christianity or the Bible inside or outside the classroom, except in the Assembly hall during morning prayers. His dignified persona was a role model for all of us. Every time I passed him by in the school corridor, he made it a point to stop to enquire not only about my studies but also about my father who he knew was an elementary school teacher. On the last day of my final year, he called me to his office. He said I should go on to college, study well, and make myself and my family proud. When I told him that it is doubtful whether I could go to college given the financial condition at home, he simply said, "Believe in yourself." Then, to my surprise, he opened his table drawer, took out a neatly wrapped gift package, gave it to me saying, "this should keep you busy during the summer holidays."

As per our cultural practice, I did not open the package in his presence. I rushed home and opened it with anxious expectation. I found two books: *The Lion, the Witch and the Wardrobe* by C. S. Lewis, and *The Power of Positive Thinking* by Norman Vincent Peale. I sure enjoyed reading them both during the holidays. But then, I read the Narnia volume just as a story, nothing more. I did not fully realize the Christian connotation deeply embedded in the book. It was only much later, when I was doing my degree program in English Literature, I could reread, analyze, and understand the unmistakable parallel between Aslan the Lion and Jesus Christ. Peale's book was simpler and more inspirational. I did not fail to notice that it contained the inspiring words that my Headmaster used: "Believe in yourself."

Clearly, my introduction to and interest in Christianity started in my high school, and my Headmaster played a key, although a subtle, role in it. His favorite Psalms became my favorite ones too. I soon realized that Psalms have universal appeal. Who has not, in moments of despair, cried out to their favorite God the equivalent of: "My God, my God, why have you forsaken me?" I sustained my interest in Christianity by occasionally going to a local church along with my Christian friends, both out of curiosity and out of a desire to learn.

I carried that mindset with me when I joined the University of Michigan, Ann Arbor, in 1984 for my doctoral program. I was staying in the International Student Housing on North campus in what was called an "efficiency," or what is commonly known as a studio. Two unexpected and regular visitors sustained my interest in Christianity, though not with the desired outcome.[1]

Almost every Sunday morning, there would be a gentle knock at the door. Two middle-aged women with a leather-bound Bible in their hands, an unfailing evangelical zeal in their hearts, and a never-fading smile on their face would be waiting there wanting to come in. I always ushered them in.

They would open a page in the Bible, read it to me, and occasionally offer some sketchy explanation. I listened to them with interest, sometimes delighting them with choice quotations from the Bible, particularly from the Psalms, thus showing off my knowledge of the Scripture. They were surprised to learn that I had gone to a Christian school in India where, every working day, I attended a prayer meeting in which the headmaster read a passage from the Bible.

My Sunday sessions with the visiting ladies usually lasted about thirty minutes. I started liking the sessions, especially because they gave me an opportunity to re-acquaint myself with some parts of the Bible, and also because they offered me a welcome diversion from my hectic doctoral work. A couple of months later, tired of their sermonizing and occasional sardonic remarks about Hinduism that revealed how little they knew about my religion, I thought I should do something about it. I came up with an idea.

"You talk about Christianity during the first 15 minutes, and I'll talk about Hinduism the next 15," I said. "That way, we can learn about each other's religion."

Their faces brightened. Their eyes sparkled.

"That's a neat idea," they both said excitedly. I was quite pleased with my suggestion.

"We look forward to next Sunday," they promised as they took leave.

That was the last time they ever came to my place.

Nearly twenty years later and hundreds of miles away, I had another noteworthy experience. A couple of weeks before 2001 Christmas, two evangelical visitors knocked on my door in Cupertino. I invited them in.

Inside the house, close to the front door, there is a wooden statuette of serene looking Buddha in the familiar meditation pose, sitting under a small jade plant, with its top branches and leaves spread out as if to provide a shade for the Buddha.

"Who is this?" one of them asked me.

I said "Buddha."

"Oh, I see."

"And this is his Bodhi tree," I said teasingly pointing to the jade plant.

"What tree?"

"Bodhi tree. You know under which he meditated and attained Enlightenment."

"Oh," said one.

Asked another: "Are you Buddhists?"

I said, "Not by birth."

They looked puzzled.

I ushered them into our drawing room where there was a small, well-decorated plastic Christmas tree in one corner.

I introduced my wife and our two little children to them.

"That's a cute little Christmas tree," one of them complimented.

"Are you Christians?" asked the other.

"Not by birth" I said. "We were born Hindus and will remain Hindus forever."

They looked even more puzzled.

They wanted to know how the children reacted to having the Christmas tree at home. I told them that every year they have fun decorating the tree with lights and miniature dolls of their favorite cartoon characters, and like most other children, they get up early on Christmas day and eagerly run to the fireplace to see what Santa had brought for them.

"They enjoy Christmas very much," said my wife, "as much as they enjoy Diwali, the Hindu festival of lights."

They looked puzzled again but did not pursue my wife's lead.

As the conversation proceeded, I realized that they had trouble reconciling our positive attitude to other religions with our steadfast adherence to Hinduism. They thought it was high time we converted to Christianity. Disagreeing, I started talking about the concepts of polytheism and secularism.

My wife, who had studied in a Jesuit school in India, tried to offer a simpler explanation.

"We come from a country that has almost all the religions of the world, and we belong to a religion that has many gods and goddesses," she said. "For us and for our children, Jesus is just one more addition to our pantheon of gods, and Christmas is just one more addition to our litany of festivals."

They looked at us as if we were crazy.

They left shortly after. Like the Michigan women, they never came back.

I wondered then as I do now, why people who spend a considerable part of their life seeking to spread the Word of God show very little interest in gaining even a rudimentary knowledge of religions other than their own. I wondered even more why the two gentlemen cringed when I talked about secularism. Later I realized that the reason might lie in the history of secularism in the West, which is different from the Indian concept of secularism. I will briefly outline the two as I understand them and then relate them to American religious identity.

WESTERN CONCEPT OF SECULARISM

The Western concept of secularism originated more than 500 years ago, in 1517 to be exact, when Martin Luther, as the legend goes, nailed ninety-five theses on the door of the Castle Church in Wittenberg, Germany. In his theological treatise, he captured and articulated the widespread resentment among the aristocrats as well as the public against the enormous power exercised, and the excesses perpetrated, by the Catholic Church of his times. His thoughts triggered a religious earthquake that eventually resulted in the flowering of Protestant Reformation. It transformed not only the trajectory of Christianity but also the history of the Western world.

The initial stages of Reformation were characterized as secularization rather than secularism. It was mainly aimed at (a) achieving a meaningful separation of Church and State, thereby curbing the role of the Church in non-religious matters that affected public life, (b) halting the intermediary role the clergy played between God and the believers, thereby giving individuals religious rights they had never before enjoyed, and (c) undermining the extraordinary power the clergy had for possessing landed properties, goods, and assets, and also for taxation, thereby arresting their corrupt practices. Protestant followers fought for and, to a large extent, succeeded in these three major aspects of what was called religious secularization.

As can be expected, the fundamental transformation triggered by Protestant Reformation was opposed by a group of Christians who were genuinely concerned that it would weaken the authority of the Church as well as the doctrinal basis of Christianity itself. They vociferously expressed their opposition during the early days of Protestantism. And yet, Protestantism thrived and became a force to reckon with. The overall result was an irreversible break from the Roman Catholic Church and its ecclesiastical hierarchy, including the Pope.

It was this strand of religious reformation that spread fast to the United States and found ardent supporters and equally fervent opponents. The country witnessed discord among the Founding Fathers during the Constitutional debate. This discord is continued by some religious fundamentalists even today, getting its loudest expression during political campaigns. Then and now, fundamentalists treated religious beliefs as unchanging and unchangeable. Hence, they were/are adamant about giving the Bible a literal meaning. They were/are opposed to confining God in the privacy of ones' home, and to banning religion from the public sphere. Some fundamentalists are also wary of science if it goes, in their view, against their understanding of the Bible.

The Founding Fathers were mindful of their gigantic responsibility to create a credible path for an important aspect of American identity, namely religious identity. And for that purpose, they derived useful insights from the Protestant Reformation movement, particularly from its emphasis on the separation of Church and State, and from its accent on individual liberty. A major bone of contention among them related to the separation of Church and State, and, by implication, whether the nation should be declared as a Christian nation or not.

In the ensuing debate, Thomas Jefferson and James Madison employed all their persuasive skills to prevail over the dissenters and to ensure the Constitutional separation of Church and State. They certainly did not want a theocratic nation, nor a nation where the clergy played a key role in the statecraft. Although, as we learn from historians, they and others rarely used terms such as secularization or secularism, they were determined to guarantee religious liberty to people of all faiths, without any interference from the government.

Recall that at that time, the population of the United States was almost fully Protestant. If the Founders wanted, they could have easily declared the new nation a Christian, or even a Protestant, nation. They did not. They were far-sighted enough to know that religious dogma and governmental power were a dangerous and volatile mix. "The founders," as historian Jon Meacham points out, "were not anti-religion. Many of them were faithful in their personal lives, and in their public language they evoked God. They grounded the founding principle of the nation—that all men are created equal—in the divine. But they wanted faith to be one thread in the country's tapestry, not the whole tapestry."[2] That one seminal thread was cut from the cloth of Protestant Reformation, prompting educator Max Lerner to call America, "the Child of Reformation."[3]

The decision about the separation of Church and State was further fortified by the ratification of the First Amendment in 1791, which states: "Congress shall make no law respecting an establishment of religion or prohibiting the free exercise thereof; or abridging the freedom of speech, or of the press; or the right of the people peaceably to assemble, and to petition the government for a redress of grievances." Six years later, a declaration that explicitly stated "The United States is not a Christian nation any more than it is a Jewish or Mohammedan Nation"[4] was passed unanimously by the U.S. Senate and signed by President John Adams.

The religious identity of America envisioned by the Founding Fathers is something that has not been embraced by religious fundamentalists. They unsuccessfully tried to add the name of Jesus to the U.S. Constitution, first in 1947 and again in 1954. Having failed in Congress, they turned, then and now, to the courts hoping that the wail of separation between Church and State can be chipped away little by little. To be fair, some evangelical leaders have from time-to-time paid tribute to the separation of Church and State. That includes a prominent evangelical preacher, Billy Graham, who during a 1985 sermon at Washington National Cathedral, said: "We have a Constitution which guarantees to all of us human freedoms, of which religious freedom is foremost. In America any and all religions have the right to exist and to propagate what they stand for. We enjoy the separation of church and state, and no sectarian religion has ever been—and we pray God, ever will be—imposed upon us."[5]

One of the major consequences of the Protestant Reformation, according to political scientist Francis Fukuyama, "was the way in which it laid the groundwork for the eventual emergence of the concept of identity, and of what we today call identity politics."[6] Protestant identity has been a pluralistic identity—both religious and political. Protestants themselves are by no means a homogenous group. They are splintered into so many denominations and sub-denominations: Anglicans, Baptists, Evangelicals, Lutheran, Methodists, Pentecostals, Presbyterians—just to name a few large ones. Each Protestant group plays its own group politics, identity politics, in religion and in politics.

While the Founding Fathers were understandably preoccupied with secularization initiated by early Protestant Reformation, Christian fundamentalists have been worried about secularization as well as secularism. Unlike secularization, which was largely confined to religious sphere, secularism sought to expand its reach to all aspects of life in the non-religious sociocultural and political spheres as well. That included the state, the economy, science and technology, law and justice, education, culture, entertainment, etc. Secularism is antagonistic to any form of entanglement between government and religion—a tenet seen as essential for preserving and protecting individual rights and equal rights. Secularism's claims were buttressed during Enlightenment and the onset of modernity which emphasized reason over faith, and heralded individual liberty, democratic principles, and scientific temper (see chapter 1 for details). Rationalization and intellectualization became the hallmark of secularism.

Secularism rarely captured the imagination of the American public. The reason is simple: Christian fundamentalists wrongly equated it with atheism owing to its steadfast belief in the separation of Church and State and made their opposition to it a major agenda. This is in spite of the fact that, as political scientist Mark Lilla explains, the separation "did not presume or promote atheism; it simply taught an intellectual art of distinguishing questions regarding the basic structure of society from ultimate questions regarding God, the world, and human spiritual destiny."[7]

The unpopularity of secularism among the American public could also be because of the religious sentiments deeply embedded in the American mind. Or, it could be because thoughtful advocates of American secularism have not disseminated its principles well enough to the public. They seem to have yielded the public discourse to Christian fundamentalists such as Jerry Falwell Jr. and Pat Robertson who have routinely blamed secularists, atheists, pagans, and feminists for natural disasters and also for the 9/11 tragedy. Most recently, the then Attorney General William Barr blamed secularists for such social ills as drug overdose and violence. Addressing the faculty and students at Notre Dame Law School in November 2019, he further declared secularism as a "social pathology" since, according to him, secularists discord "God's instruction manual,"[8] implying that they are being irreligious.

In denigrating secularism, some of the religious and political leaders misrepresent the essence of secularism. As the French philosopher Bernard-Henri Lévy explains:

What, after all, is secularism? It is not, as we know, agnosticism. Nor is it atheism. And it is obviously not a separation of individuals from churches. It is the utterly distinct separation of churches from government institutions. It is the command given to every state not to favor one faith over another. Likewise, and symmetrically, it's the command given to citizens to believe in whatever they are partial to so long as their faith remains a matter of their own conscience and tolerates the conscience of others. But it is in no way a systematic hostility toward religion in general.[9]

Unfortunately, it is the misrepresented discourse on secularism that seems to have become a widespread belief among many members of the American public.

INDIAN CONCEPT OF SECULARISM

Like the United States, India is a deeply religious nation. Unlike the United States which gradually evolved into a pluralistic society, India has been one from ancient times. India's secularism is fully home grown. It is the birthplace of four major religions of the world: Hinduism, Buddhism, Sikhism, and Jainism. Following the Moghul invasion in the sixteenth century, the country became a home for Muslims as well. Now, Islam is the second and Christianity the third largest religion in the country.

Hinduism is different from other major religions such as Christianity and Islam in that it is not an organized religion. No single scripture. No single Prophet. No single authority. There is no Hindu Pope. It is not a proselytizing religion either and so it is not into religious conversions. Hinduism is more about righteous living than about right belief. Therefore, some argue that it cannot even be called a religion in the normal sense of the term. In his popular book, *The Hindu View of Life,* the philosopher-President of India, Sarvepalli Radhakrishnan offers a well-known explanation: "Hinduism is more a way of life than a form of thought. . . . (It) insists not on religious conformity but on spiritual and ethical outlook in life."[10]

Such an outlook has bestowed Hinduism with a built-in secularistic philosophy. It embraces all religions, and all forms of religious doctrines. Hinduism, like other religions, is not monolithic, within it there are seemingly conflicting variations. "Hindu civilization includes," observes British political theorist Bhikhu Parekh, "monist, monotheist, pantheist, polytheist, agnostic, and atheist strands of thought, which have often been at odds with each other."[11] Hinduism stands for what is called *Sarva dharma sambhava.* Roughly translated, it means all religious Truths are equal. Therefore, all religious thoughts are worth pondering, worth respecting.[12]

The nation's psyche has historically been so imbued with the spirit of secularism that, when the Indian Constitution was written after India gained independence in 1947, it was not even deemed necessary to add the word "secularism" to the all-important document, in spite of the fact that national leaders like Gandhi and Nehru were undisputed secularists. The word was inserted into the Preamble only in 1975 by the then Prime Minister Indira Gandhi. Some say, she did it mainly for political reasons, when she ruled the country by decree after declaring Emergency.

Indian secularism has been described as "audible secularism" because India is perhaps the only country in the world where one can hear at the dawn musical sounds of religiosity: Muslim *aazan* blaring from Mosque loudspeakers, the ringing of bells from Hindu temples, recitation of Guru Granth Sahib from Sikh temples, and the pealing of Church bells.[13] In every town, big and small, there are prominently visible places of worship of various religions. On a recent visit to a 450-year-old synagogue in the Hindu dominated southern city of Cochin, Roger Cohen, the *New York Times* columnist and author wrote: "Cochin is dotted with churches and mosques. Nobody cares too much. There's room for multiple truths. It is this that makes the country such a source of hope."[14]

Unlike France which is also a secular country, India does not privatize religion. It does not ban the display of religious signs and symbols from the public sphere. In fact, Mahatma Gandhi, whose name is ubiquitously associated with secularism in modern day India, would start many of his public gatherings with songs drawn from different religions extolling the value of Oneness. Mindful of the Hindu-Muslim tension during the closing part the freedom struggle, one of the chants he favored starts with: *Ishwar Allah tere naam, Sabko sanmati de Bhagwan* (whether people use the name Ishwar or Allah to worship their God, they will all be led to the same path).

The spirit of secularism in India is not confined to religious and political leaders alone. It has seeped down to the practice of everyday life. With the exception of a small vocal group of religious extremists, the general public is comfortable with secular principles and practices in political, social, and cultural arena. From 2004 through 2007, for instance, India had a Sikh as the Prime Minister (Manmohan Singh), a Muslim as the President (Abdul Kalam), and an Italian-born Catholic woman (Sonia Gandhi) as the leader of the ruling Congress party. This, in a country that is nearly 80% Hindu.

Needless to say, when I was growing up in India, I was heavily influenced by the Indian concept of secularism. For me, then, secularism is not a negation of any religion but acceptance of all religions. My respect for my religion does not exclude my respect for other religions. I have all along been interested in the central message of various religions rather than in religious rituals, however ceremonious they are. I consider myself more spiritual than religious. I have come to believe that religiosity without spirituality is blind, and spirituality without religiosity is lame.

It is my spirituality coupled with secularism that drives me to try to acquaint myself with other religions as much as possible. In addition, whenever I go abroad, I seek out a famous place of worship in town, if any. In Leuven, Belgium, I visited UNESCO-recognized St. Peter's Church built in the fifteenth century when Catholicism was flourishing in Europe. In Kent, England, I admired the Anglican Canterbury Church, built in the eleventh century, in Gothic style, recognized as a World Heritage Site. I climbed 268 steep steps to get to the recently completed Tian Tam Buddha temple, with its huge bronze Buddha statue at a hilltop in the Lantau Island of Hong Kong. In Beijing, I revered the image of Confucius and the inscription of the names of more than 50,000 Chinese scholars inside the Confucius temple built in 1302. In Trinidad and Tobago, I worshipped at the Hindu Temple in the Sea built by the descendants of indentured laborers. I had, however, my best learning opportunity at the Blue Mosque (officially the Sultanahmet mosque) in Istanbul, built in the early seventeenth century during the Ottoman Empire. Not only did I marvel at the beautiful blue tiles that are part of the interior design, but I also stepped into the Islamic Information Center located inside the Mosque, which invites guests to come and talk with an ever-present Islamic scholar. I used the opportunity there to try to lessen my ignorance of Islam.[15]

The spirit of religious openness I exhibit is nothing unique to me. It is in tune with the Indian brand of secularism. There are many Indians and diasporic Indians who have similar religious disposition. "Because of this all-encompassing nature," religious scholar Ramdas Lamb correctly notes in his commentary on Hindu polytheism, "it is the One to whom all prayers are offered. This is why it is commonplace for Hindus to be seen in Buddhist or Jain temples, in Sikh gurudwaras, and in mosques and churches. The deity worshipped in each is seen by Hindus to simply be a different manifestation of the deity they already worship."[16]

The secularist tendency is not confined to Hinduism alone. From the Buddhist perspective, the Dalai Lama always talks about "Many Faiths, One Truth." The Reverend Mpho Tutu, the daughter of Bishop Desmond Tutu from South Africa, tells us about herself: "I am a woman of faith, a wife, a daughter and the mother of daughters. I am a world citizen. I have crossed lines of language, religion, race, class, nationality and culture to find my friends and make my family and I have learned that neither I nor my religious faith can contain the whole truth about God."[17]

The reason why I indulged in such a lengthy discourse on my sense of secularism is that, as I try to show below, it is this kind of secularistic religious sentiment that seems to be spreading among young people in many parts of the world including the United States, in spite of the fact that religious fundamentalism—whether Buddhist, Christian, Hindu, Jewish, or Muslim—retains a solid base among a segment of the population everywhere.

THE MANTRA OF THE MILLENNIALS

Even a cursory glance at recent surveys on religious belief of young people from different parts of the world and from different Faiths shows an increasing trend away from established religion and toward secular thoughts.

We learn from a comprehensive 2018 Deloitte Millennial Survey covering 10,455 Millennials from thirty-six countries, and 1,844 Gen Z respondents from six countries including the United States, United Kingdom, and India that young people are getting increasingly disillusioned with religion.[18] A "Europe's Young Adults and Religion" survey conducted in the same year in twelve European countries shows that a majority of young adults do not follow any religion. Stephen Bullivant at St. Mary's University in London, who conducted the survey, says that religion has become "Moribund. . . . With some notable exceptions, young adults increasingly are not identifying with or practising religion."[19] Recent reports from Scotland and Australia tell the same story. The Scottish Attitudes Survey conducted in 2017 found that 58% of respondents said they had no religion at all.[20] An Australian survey conducted in the same year shows that the number of people reporting "no religion" rose from 22.6% to 29.6% in just five years, almost double the figure reported in 2001.[21]

Consistent with reports from abroad, more and more Americans, particularly those belonging to the Millennial and Gen Z generations, are moving toward meaningful secularism. "It may come as no surprise," as 2018 Barna Group report tells us about Gen Z, "that the influence of Christianity in the United States is waning. Rates of church attendance, religious affiliation, belief in God, prayer and Bible-reading have been dropping for decades. Americans' beliefs are becoming more post-Christian and, concurrently, religious identity is changing. Enter Generation Z: Born between 1999 and 2015, they are the first truly 'post-Christian' generation. They are 'drawn to things spiritual.'"[22]

An oft quoted 2014–2015 Religious Landscape Survey conducted by Pew Research Center has quite a few revealing statistics about America's changing religious identity.[23] Some of them are worth reproducing in full: "the number of religiously unaffiliated adults has increased by roughly 19 million since 2007. There are now approximately 56 million religiously unaffiliated adults in the U.S., and this group—sometimes called religious 'nones'—is more numerous than either Catholics or mainline Protestants, according to the new survey. Indeed, the unaffiliated are now second in size only to evangelical Protestants among major religious groups in the U.S." Moreover, "the percentage of adults (ages 18 and older) who describe themselves as Christians has dropped by nearly eight percentage points in just seven years, from 78.4% in 2007 to 70.6% in 2014. Over the same period, the percentage of Americans who are religiously unaffiliated—describing themselves as atheist, agnostic or 'nothing in particular'—has jumped more than six points, from 16.1% to 22.8%." The numbers about Millennials are even more revealing: "Fully 36% of young Millennials (those between the ages of 18 and 24) are religiously unaffiliated, as are 34% of older Millennials (ages 25–33)."

These findings were reinforced in augmented numbers in another survey released by the Pew Research Center in December 2021. It found that 29% of U.S. adults said they had no religious affiliation, an increase of 6 percentage points. About 32% said they seldom or never pray. As expected, Millennials largely prompted the shift. Commenting on the survey, Gregory A. Smith, associate director of research at the Center, said, "the secularizing shifts evident in American society so far in the 21st century show no signs of slowing."[24]

We should interpret the data cautiously. Simply because the "nones" and other Millennials are describing themselves in secular terms, does not necessarily mean that they are becoming non-believers. According to Gregory Smith, ours is still a nation of believers, with nearly 90% of adults saying they do believe in God. The fact is—and that makes all the difference— young people's respect for religion is not confined to their own. Also, they are becoming more knowledgeable about and more sensitive to non-religious problems that beset our globalized world. More specifically, they are paying serious attention to and are demanding actionable plans for promoting religious tolerance, ethnic diversity, social equality, and environmental sustainability. They are highly critical of both religious and political figures who, in their view, are being hypocritical in words and deeds.

Their mistrust of religious figures seems to be well-placed. It is easy to draw a direct correlation, or at least a plausible connection, between the increasing politicization of religion and the increasing alienation from established religion felt by the "nones," including the Millennials. The two developments seem to follow a parallel trajectory during the same period of time, that is, during the 1980s and onward when extreme conservatism became a common cause for the religious right as well as for the political right. According to Robert D. Putnam and David E. Campbell, "during the 1980s, the public face of American religion turned sharply right. . . . Increasingly, young people saw religion as intolerant, hypocritical, judgmental and homophobic. If being religious entailed political conservatism, they concluded, religion was not for them."[25]

The ideologically loaded public role of the Evangelicals became fairly pronounced in the beginning of the twenty-first century, especially during the successful Presidential campaign of George W. Bush in 2000 and in 2004. As President, he took several policy decisions including the establishment of the Office of Faith-Based Initiatives in the White House (see below for more on the Initiatives) that put into action some of the Evangelical agenda. There were critics who thought that President Bush, a self-proclaimed born-again evangelical Christian, became the face of American evangelical Christianity. In his book *American Theocracy*, conservative author Kevin Phillips lamented that "For the first time in our history, ideology and theology hold a monopoly of power in Washington."[26]

It was, however, during and after the 2016 Presidential election that the "hypocritical" stance of the religious right exhibited itself in full measure. Many of the evangelicals supported Donald J. Trump at a level that was far higher than their support for either Ronald Reagan or George W. Bush. Michael Gerson, a nationally syndicated columnist, and a speechwriter for President George W. Bush, wrote in astonishment: "Trump's background and beliefs could hardly be more incompatible with traditional Christian models of life and leadership. Trump's past political stances (he once supported the right to partial-birth abortion), his character (he has bragged about sexually assaulting women), and even his language (he introduced the words *pussy* and *shithole* into presidential discourse) would more naturally lead religious conservatives toward exorcism than alliance."[27] Evidently, some of the evangelicals seem to have made a Faustian bargain with the President: pack the U.S. Supreme Court and Federal Courts with conservative judges, we will turn a blind eye to your religious, moral, and ethical transgressions. Pack the court he joyously did: during his tenure, he appointed three Supreme Court justices titling the Court's balance to six conservatives and three liberals.

As if the compromises made by the evangelicals were not enough to drive the young people away from established religion, they were further treated to a steady stream of news about sinful transgressions from the Catholic Church. The pedophile sex scandal involving some priests, bishops, and even an Archbishop who was part of Vatican inner circle, along with a prolonged, willful cover-up by those in leadership position at various levels were devastating news not only for the Pope but also for trusted believers.

Joining the religious right are politicians who are only too willing to pander to them. Take, for instance, President Bush's Faith-Based Initiatives in the White House. Theoretically, it was aimed at promoting neighborhood partnerships among people of different Faiths. For that purpose, it was supposed to offer aids and grants for both Christian and non-Christian groups on a competitive basis. A noble thought indeed. But, highly hypocritical. The President appointed mostly evangelical political operatives to administer the program.

One of them was David Kuo, who also was a speechwriter to the President. In his book *Tempting Faith: An Inside Story of Political Seduction*, he reveals how the office turned out to be by, for, and of evangelicals. We come to know that "the group that gathered to review the applications was an overwhelmingly Christian group of wonks, ministers, and well-meaning types. They were supposed to review the application in a religiously neutral fashion and assign each applicant a score on a range of 1–100. But their biases were transparent." He gives several inside stories. One female administrator confided in him about what was happening: She said with a giggle "when I saw one of those non-Christian groups in the set I was reviewing, I just stopped looking at them and gave them a zero." When he asked her about others, she said, "Oh sure, a lot of us did. . . . Was there a problem with that?"[28]

Yes, there was a problem with that. A problem that lingers. Thoughtful young people easily see through the hypocritical game and, as a result, continue to distance themselves from established religion altogether. They also see the tendency of candidates for high offices—both Republican and Democrat—to display "an overdose of public piety," as the conservative columnist Charles Krauthammer put it. Referring to a CNN-sponsored debate among the Republican candidates during the 2008 primary, he bemoaned: when "some squirrelly looking guy held up a Bible and asked, 'Do you believe every word of this book?'—and not one candidate dared reply: None of your damn business."[29] The same event drew a disparaging remark from Wendy Doniger, a historian of religions: "I don't care a fig about our next president's personal religious views. The candidate can worship the Great Pumpkin, for all I care, as long as he or she doesn't assume that the rest of us do too, and that the Great Pumpkin told him to do things such as, to take a case at random, invade Iraq."[30]

The conservative columnist and the liberal historian were making the same point, and, that is, neither the question asked at the presidential primary election debate nor the answer was appropriate for a nation that is constitutionally bound by the separation of Church and State. Moreover, we hear Presidents end their official speeches with "God bless America." Obviously, it indicates nothing more than the fact that the nation is imbued with religious spirit. However, when political leaders invoke God in exercising their official duties, many young people are conflicted. They see a misfit between their lived experience in terms of constant invocation of God in official functions and the secular origin of the nation that they studied about in schools and colleges. In cultivating a healthy suspicion about religious and political leaders, without losing their own faith in God, they seem to have developed a tacit understanding of the difference between Faith and the faithful.

FAITH AND THE FAITHFUL

It was Kofi Annan, the former Secretary General of the United Nations, who famously said: "The problem is never the faith; it is the faithful and how they behave towards each other."[31] Many "nones," Millennials, and Gen Zers recognize that what the faithful do in the name of their Faith may be different from, and even antithetical to, their Faith itself. Having Faith is a matter of belief; being faithful is a matter of behavior. There is not a single prophet or prophet-like figure in any established religion who did not teach us about our moral obligation to work for the welfare of all beings, human and animal. They were all social reformers, not just religious seers. A cardinal principle we learn from them is that Faith is more about care and compassion than about rites and rituals.

It is the extremists among the faithful who cling on to untenable beliefs and defend them with passionate intensity. By quietly ignoring them, by refusing to treat people of other religions as children of a lesser God, and by attending to bigger problems such as racial tensions, ethnic conflicts, socio-economic inequality, and environmental degradation that plague the twenty-first-century life, many young Americans are following the scriptures in letter and spirit. They validate that they are becoming secular without necessarily becoming irreligious. In fact, it could be argued that they are the ones who adhere to the true and time-tested "American religious tradition which is at once deeply individualistic, anti-authoritarian, concerned with sin and salvation, yet secular and rationalist in its life goals."[32] They also seem to be listening to Pope Francis, who invited young people all over the world to shake things up. "Make a mess," he urged them, "but then also help to tidy it up. A mess which gives us a free heart, a mess which gives us solidarity, a mess which gives us hope."[33]

What this chapter shows is that, unlike religious fundamentalists, many Americans do not think of their religious identity as immutable and unchanging. American religious identity is fast changing. The churning that is now taking place in the religious sphere may be comparable in scope and impact to the churning that took place in the cultural sphere during the 1960s. Only history can tell. What is clear now is that there are young Americans who seem to be shaking things up about the religious identity of the nation. Their attempt to "make a mess" of religious identity, and to tidy it up also has a serious impact on cultural identity, as I seek to demonstrate in the next chapter.

Chapter 7

Cultural Identity
Mores and Morals

"All I can report is it is a size 10." Quipped President George W. Bush while addressing a press conference at the Prime Minister's palace in Baghdad, Iraq, on December 14, 2008.[1] Earlier, he was warmly received by the Iraqi leaders. They were all grateful to him for ending the dictatorial regime of Saddam Hussein.

Not everybody was grateful, though. There were people in and outside the palace who were resentful of the American occupation. Present among the press corps was a twenty-eight-year-old Iraqi TV journalist working for the Egypt-based TV station *Al-Baghdadia*. He stood up. He did not ask any question; instead, he directed certain choice invectives against the President and hurled his shoes at the visiting dignitary.

The President dodged the shoes. He was not hurt. He took the insult with a dignity that is reflective of his high office, and a humor that is reflective of his jovial personality. He joked about shoe size and continued to take questions from the press.

The journalist was immediately whisked away by Iraqi guards and was promptly sent to prison. He, however, became a cult figure in Iraq and in some other neighboring countries. Not only did he exploit a high-profile event to display the resentment among a section of the Iraqi population, but he also chose a symbolic action that can easily resonate with the Iraqi people.

Shoes. They have a deeper cultural meaning in Iraq.

The shoe is something that is worn on the lowest part of the body and is deemed dirty. That is why people in some parts of the world always remove their footwear before entering a house or a place of worship. Displaying the sole of your shoe to any person or throwing it at a person is considered an insult. Hitting someone with it is even worse. When, at the end of the Iraq War, Saddam Hussein's statue was toppled in Baghdad, jubilant Iraqis danced around it, striking it repeatedly with their footwear.

The American forces won the war so easily; but found it difficult to win the hearts and minds of the Iraqi people. Part of the reason: lack of cultural knowledge and cultural sensitivity. For instance, they did not know about the cultural meaning of the shoe there. Nor did they know that, along with shoes, Iraqis consider dogs also as unclean, and therefore unwelcome inside their house. American soldiers continued to commit double faults when, looking for insurgents, they stormed into people's homes in their dirty boots and with their sniffing dogs that were used to detect explosives. Of course, from their professional and their cultural point of view, they did not see anything wrong with that. But for the Iraqis, it is unbearable. Certainly not the best way to win hearts and minds.

It is not just winning hearts and minds that encountered stumbling blocks. Even some of the military operations were impeded because of a lack of cultural knowledge. "U.S.'s Cultural Ignorance Fuels Iraq Insurgency"—headlined National Public Radio (NPR), citing a military adviser who has written a book about Iraq Insurgency.[2] The American forces knew how to deal with insurgents militarily, but did not know how to deal with them culturally. As a result, the insurgents became more and more belligerent, making it difficult for the army to mop up the military operation.

Cultural tidbits about forms of greetings, etc., are the staple of travel guides, and are easy to understand. However, they generally impart only superficial knowledge good enough for a casual traveler taking a short vacation and can have only a limited value. A real understanding of cultural beliefs and practices of one's own or of others is much more challenging because the concept of culture itself is complex.

THE COMPLEXITY OF CULTURE

"Culture is one of the two or three most complicated words in the English language," observed the British cultural critic, Raymond Williams. That is largely because, as he explains, the word has "come to be used for important concepts in several distinct intellectual disciplines and in several distinct and incompatible systems of thought."[3] As a result, culture as a concept, like identity, continues to defy a clear-cut definition even though it has been widely explored. It has become so diffused as to mean different things to different people at different times.

Writing as early as in 1869, the British literary critic Matthew Arnold asserted that "Culture was the pursuit of our total perfection by means of getting to know, on all matters which most concern us, the best which has been thought and said in the world; and through this knowledge, turning a stream of fresh and free thought upon our stock notions and habits."[4] The British scholar entreated us to keep our windows wide open so that "the best which has been thought and said" will freely flow into our house, not only from our own cultural community but from the outside world as well, enabling us to liberate ourselves from the shackles of cultural misconceptions and stereotypes that we so dearly cling on to.

More than a century later, American anthropologist Clifford Geertz offered a simpler definition. According to him, culture "denotes a historically transmitted pattern of meanings embodied in symbols, a system of inherited conceptions in symbolic forms by means of which people communicate, perpetuate and develop their knowledge about and attitudes towards life."[5] We normally look for such patterns of meanings in art, architecture, theater, dance, music, literature, and in other creative endeavors. We inherit some of the cultural meanings from our parents and close-knit family and learn others through our lived experience. Our inherited as well as learned patterns of meaning solidify our cultural mores and morals—that is, beliefs and practices, customs and habits, norms, and values—which we then use to guide the practice of our everyday life.

Culture, therefore, plays an overarching role in the development of individual identity. That is why it is seen as a form of capital. In coining the term *cultural capital*, on the analogy of its economic counterpart, the French social theorist Pierre Bourdieu argues that cultural capital is generated mainly through socialization and education.[6] Outside one's home, it is the educational system that functions as a vehicle for cultural transmission. It plays a vital role in inculcating wider cultural beliefs and practices in the minds of succeeding generations. Bourdieu also cautions us that schools most often endorse and enforce the cultural values of the dominant segment of a society. They usually do that in the form of curricular design and textbook adoption. And, there are authors who provide necessary textual input for them. A classic example is educator E. D. Hirsch Jr.'s 1987 book *Cultural Literacy: What Every American Needs to Know*. In it, he and his colleagues presented a list of what they called core knowledge necessary to develop culturally literate Americans. The list included bits and pieces of knowledge drawn from historical, literary, and other sources. While some of that knowledge was and still is valid, it turned out to be biased and insufficient.[7] Critics were quick to point out that nearly 80% of that core knowledge was more than a century old and was reflecting a version of America's mainstream culture, ignoring the pluralistic nature of the country.

Regardless of what is exposed to them at home or in school, critically-thinking individuals can and do use their cultural capital to explore alternative cultural practices, thereby contributing to their own cultural growth, and to their community's and the nation's cultural change. But culture change is a slow process. It "moves rather like an octopus," says Geertz, "not all at once in a smoothly coordinated synergy of parts, a massive coaction of the whole, but by disjointed movements of this part, then that, and now the other which somehow cumulate to directional change."[8]

America witnessed such a cumulative directional change during the tumultuous decades of 1950s and 1960s. The period leading up to the 1960s was seen by some as repressive in terms of rigid sociocultural norms—men belong to the cabinet, women to the kitchen, gays/lesbians to the closet, to name a few. In response, a substantial segment of the younger generation rebelled, and generated a countercultural movement which rapidly gathered momentum culminating, some would say, in the Woodstock music festival held in the summer of 1969. This counterculture sought to reshape not only art and music but the American way of life itself. Established norms about family, gender, morality, and sexuality were questioned, and their boundaries redrawn. Undoubtedly, the counterculture yielded lasting legacies, most of which are now irreversible. However, it also generated ideologically-driven, politically-motivated culture wars that are still being waged by certain segments of the American society.

In every society, when suitable social and political climate surfaces, there emerge groups of cultural influencers who seize the moment to try to bring about culture change just as there are those who would vehemently resist such an attempt. For purposes of understanding American cultural identity, I think it is beneficial to categorize such agentive groups as (a) Christian fundamentalists, (b) culture warriors, (c) celebrity activists, and (d) silent deciders. These four groups of people stand out as particularly influential.

CHRISTIAN FUNDAMENTALISTS

The cultural change witnessed during the mid-twentieth century sparked intense opposition among a powerful and well-established segment of the religious community in the United States, particularly, among evangelical Christians. Many among them were, and still are, genuinely troubled by what they think to be the impending demise of traditional cultural values. They are worried about what they see as a deteriorating American family life. They rightly give importance to culture because, along with factors such as history, religion, language, race, class, and gender, culture is a driving force that shapes our lives as well as our identities.

American evangelicalism, however, is not a monolithic entity; it is as diverse as any religious belief system. A sub-section of the evangelicals, dubbed fundamentalists, opposed any cultural change with uncompromising vehemence. Fundamentalists of any religious persuasion—Buddhist, Christian, Hindu, Jewish, or Muslim—are scriptural determinists who believe that there's One Absolute Truth about their religion, and therefore, there is no place for any dissent. They also venerate ancient religious texts, believe in literal meaning of those texts, and claim to speak with the authority of traditional interpreters of those texts. For fundamentalists, religion and culture constitute immutable beliefs and practices and so any change that challenges the traditional belief system is unacceptable.[9]

In our times, well-known among the Christian fundamentalists are Rev. Jerry Falwell Jr. and Rev. Pat Robertson. Both Southern Baptists and trained ministers, they proved to be charismatic and successful televangelists. With Falwell as founder of a megachurch as well as Liberty University in Virginia, and with Robertson as chairman of the *Christian Broadcasting Network*, numerous practicing evangelical Christians were treated to a steady stream of a fundamentalist version of evangelical doctrines. As religious and cultural absolutists determined to play a key role in protecting what they considered to be the purity of American culture, they never hesitated to denigrate those who, in their view, have been a corrupting influence on American culture— whether they are fellow Christians or non-Christians.

Falwell and Robertson often directed their ire towards secularists, atheists, feminists, unionists, and other usual suspects. Either alone or jointly, they condemned all those in favor of abortion at any stage of pregnancy. They characterized AIDS as God's punishment for the American society for tolerating the LGBTQ+ community. They even blamed what they called secular immorality for the 9/11 tragedy. They often combined the religious and the cultural with the political as, for instance, when they tried to persuade their listeners to vote for George W. Bush in the 2004 Presidential election. Robertson revealed how he heard directly from God: "I think George Bush is going to win in a walk. I really believe I'm hearing from the Lord it's going to be like a blowout election in 2004. The Lord has just blessed him."[10] Unlike Robertson, Falwell did not share any voice from the Lord but made a general plea: "It is the responsibility of every political conservative, every evangelical Christian, every pro-life Catholic, every traditional Jew, every Reagan Democrat, and everyone in between to get serious about re-electing President Bush." As Jim Wallis, a moderate evangelical Christian activist said: "These leaders of the Religious Right mistakenly claim that God has taken a side in this election, and that Christians should only vote for George W. Bush."[11]

Moreover, knowing the importance of schooling, both Falwell and Robertson criticized the educational system for not producing religiously pious and culturally conservative citizens. If they had controlling power, they would even abolish all public schools. For his part, Falwell hoped "to live to see the day, when, as in the early days of the country, we won't have any public schools. The churches will have taken them over again, and Christians will be running them."[12] It did not happen during his lifetime; nor is it going to happen ever, unless the American people and the government decide to disregard the constitutional separation of the church and the state. The preachers, however, did the next best thing: they made it a point to encourage their supporters to contest elections for local school boards so that they can redesign the curriculum and rewrite textbooks, as has often happened, for instance, in states like Arizona and Texas, and now in Florida.

In 1979, Falwell founded the Moral Majority, and used it to orchestrate several activities related to cultural issues such as opposition to abortion and to homosexuality, and support for school prayer and right-wing politics. Within ten years, terming his efforts successful, he disbanded the Moral Majority. The changing cultural scenarios of late twentieth- and early twenty-first-century America clearly showed that his expectations were not realized.

Closely aligned with religious fundamentalists in goals and objectives, if not in strategies and tactics, are those who call themselves culture warriors.

CULTURE WARRIORS

"My friends, this election is about much more than who gets what. It is about who we are. It is about what we believe. It is about what we stand for as Americans. There is a religious war going on in our country for the soul of America. It is a cultural war, as critical to the kind of nation we will one day be as was the Cold War itself."[13] That is Patrick J. Buchanan at the 1992 Republican National Convention at Houston, speaking as a contestant in the party's primary elections. As noted by others, his invocation of a war image is significant. The image of war brings to mind antagonistic forces arraigned against each other. An organized fight between a virtuous *us* and a vicious *them*. A fight with a single-minded purpose of defeating the enemy by any means necessary. Of course, Buchanan is talking about an ideological war, a clash of opposing ideas and principles, supposed to be fought not with deadly weapons but with deadly words. Buchanan's words, according to his own estimate, "ignited a firestorm that blazed on through 1992 and has not yet burnt itself out. My words were called divisive and hateful. They were not. They were divisive and truthful."[14]

Divisive, for sure. Although Buchanan was able to garner the support of only about 20% of the Republican primary voters both in 1992 and again in 1996, his bugle call at the Houston Convention did ignite a firestorm the embers of which still remain hot, and given the right political wind, can reignite sporadic flash fires here and there. We witnessed such a flash fire in Charlottesville, Virginia in 2017, and again in a more dramatic fashion during the January 6, 2021, storming of the U.S. Capitol, arguably as a result of fiery political rhetoric heard during and after the 2016 and 2020 Presidential elections. Referring to Donal J. Trump's presidential victory in 2016, Buchanan proudly told a columnist that his ideas made it, but he did not, adding that Trump's election "is the last chance for these ideas."[15]

What are his ideas? They are worth considering in some detail as they represent the views of many other culture warriors as well. Buchanan stands out among others partly because he articulates his thoughts in a clear, coherent, combative manner, and disseminates them regularly through his books, blogs, and broadcasts. He also played a key role in the Republican administration of President Richard Nixon as his Director of Communications. His prominence as a culture warrior may be attributed to how he so effectively synthesizes features of Christian religion, white race, and white American culture. For him, religious war, racial war, and culture war are all inextricably connected. He argues, in apocalyptic terms, that failure of the culture war would result in no less than the *Death of the West*—which is the title of his 2002 book. He also believes that America's cultural decline is suicidal, and wistfully asks *Will America Survive to 2025?*—which is the subtitle of his 2011 book.

The problems he sees in the American cultural arena can be summed up in a few statements taken from his 2002 book.[16] One, America's religious identity is no longer Protestant, Catholic and Jewish but is now "Protestant, Catholic, Jewish, Mormon, Muslim, Hindu, Buddhist, Taoist, Shintoist, Santeria, New Age, voodoo, agnostic, atheist, humanist, Rastafarian, and Wiccan." Two, immigration threatens the very fiber of our nation by bringing in people who have nothing in common with the American mainstream community in terms of religion, culture, and language, and as a result, we just cannot get along with each other. Three, Western civilization and American culture are superior to any other civilization and culture; therefore, it should not be allowed to be corrupted by the infusion of people from non-Judeo/Christian cultural traditions. Four, the golden era that existed in the America of the 1950s and earlier when, for instance, abortion was considered a shameful act, has been unsettled by the counterculture prevailed during the 1960s and after, and that should be redressed. Five, by capturing institutions that transmit ideas and opinions—institutions such as education, TV, the arts, entertainment—the liberal elites are creating a new people, a new culture alien to traditional American norms, and that should be resisted.

As a true thinker, Buchanan does not merely lament, but offers solutions as well. Two of them are central; others derive from them. First, "If Americans wish to preserve their civilization and culture, American women must have more children."[17] Of course, by "American women," he means White American Christian women. Second, stop illegal immigration; and, limit legal immigration preferably to people of European background.

Clearly, there are problems with his solutions. Buchanan is right about the declining white population. In July 2020, the U.S. Census Bureau released estimates of race-ethnic population in advance of 2020 Census.[18] According to the report, the white population share comprised nearly 80% of the population in 1980, but dropped to 69.1% in 2000, and to 60.1% in 2019. All fifty states have registered a decline. The primary reason: white women, with better education and greater career opportunities, are having fewer babies, and much later in their life, which, by the way, is not very different from what happens in other developed countries. They are not likely to have more babies just to please culture warriors. As for immigration, America needs more, not less, skilled immigrants for its workforce to keep its economy going. It also needs highly educated professionals to continue to thrive in scientific and technological spheres. Even countries like Japan, historically opposed to immigration, is planning to open up its borders. Several European countries already do that. Besides, in these days of globalization and digitalization, closing the American borders will not stop the winds of cultural change from flowing into the country.

Realizing that his solutions lead him only to a dead end, Buchanan in a recent blog agonizingly wonders: "Is secession a solution to cultural war?" Not wanting to see the break-up of the country he loves, he suggests a compromise: a new federation of the United States. He suggests "a devolution of power and resources away from Washington and back to states, cities, towns and citizens, to let them resolve their problems their own way and according to their own principles." What he implies is actually identity-based federalism, culture-based federalism. "Let California be California," he proclaims, "let red state America be red state America." That is, let them shape their own cultural identity in their own way according to their own principles.[19]

In reality, such a loose culture-based, identity-based federalism at various governmental and public levels is already in place in the United States. It is this reality that, in part, led me to argue that America may be described as a nation of multiple monoculturalisms rather than as a nation of multiculturalism (see chapter 5).

An interesting fact is that a notable segment of the American population, particularly the younger generation, seems to be receptive to new ideas and opinions about cultural transformation and identity (re)formation emanating from the very liberal elites who Buchanan despised for creating a new people, a new culture, a new America. Chief among the liberal elites are celebrities.

CELEBRITY ACTIVISTS

America, like any other country, has always been fascinated by celebrities but they mostly included extraordinary individuals such as reformers with relentless devotion, explorers with adventurous spirit, leaders with visionary zeal, and Generals with heroic tales. The late twentieth and early twenty first centuries, however, witnessed the emergence of celebrities of a different kind—pop singers, sports personalities, and film actors whose appeal cuts across class and creed, race and religion. They attract hundreds and thousands of ardent fans who, paying exorbitant rates, regularly throng to concert halls, sports arenas, or multiplex complexes to watch their favorite heroes perform.

The irresistible appeal of the new celebrities is not confined to their stage performance alone; it extends to private life as well. The information revolution, accelerated and amplified through Facebook (now part of META), Twitter (now X), YouTube, search engines, and smart phones, keeps the fans continually exposed to the lifestyles of celebrities, including their intimate relationships. In addition, the consumer market provides a steady supply of books by and about celebrities, not to mention gossip columns in popular magazines that are prominently displayed near check-out counters in stores across the country. All this enables fans to develop strong emotional attachments to their favorite celebrities. It was, for instance, reported that when Hollywood stars Angelina Jolie and Brad Pitt announced their separation, some of their fans expressed sincere grief as if this separation happened in their own family. Later, the separation drama of Kanye West and Kim Kardashian became the staple of social media. These and other developments have taken celebrity adulation to new heights.

For some Americans, the purpose behind the fascination for celebrity stories is not just to derive vicarious enjoyment, but to seek role models. An underlying motivation for them seems to be to learn from the inspirational rag to riches stories, hoping to replicate them in their own lives, at least on a small scale. Using social media, fans are constantly connected to their chosen celebrities, and interact with them virtually through their Twitter feeds, if not in person. With a click of a button or a touch of a screen, they not only get the information that interests them but also spread it among their friends. As sociologist Karen Sternheimer points out, "celebrity stories can help us make sense of our identities—not simply by telling us how we should look, feel, think, or act, but through a social process of negotiation. Symbolic interactions view identity construction as just not an individual experience, but one based on our interactions with others."[20]

For their part, some of the celebrities interact with millions of their fans through such social media as Instagram and Twitter and seek to play an active role in helping them make sense of their cultural identity, and if possible, shape and reshape it. Minimally, they are creating an awareness among their fans about larger religious, social, and cultural issues facing the nation, and, to that extent, they are playing the role of agentive leaders who have the potential to influence their fan's attitudes, behaviors, and identities.

Celebrities such as George Harrison and Richard Gere have not hesitated to tread in matters of religious beliefs. To some extent, they facilitated the advent of Indian gurus and Tibetan monks in the United States. During the 1970s, Harrison, the lead guitarist and also singer and song writer for the Beatles, a true devotee of Lord Krishna, familiarized the deity from the Hindu pantheon to their fans in the United Kingdom and the United States. In his 1970 number one hit song "My Sweet Lord," he chanted "Hallelujah" and "Hare Krishna" seamlessly switching between them.[21] Similarly, during the 1980s and 1990s, Gere, a long-time practitioner of Tibetan Buddhism, contributed in no small measure to American people's interest in Buddhist spirituality as well as in its current chief exponent, the 14th Dalai Lama, who himself has become a celebrity.

It was, however, in the sociocultural arena that some of the celebrity influencers seem to have made a huge impact on the general population. Take, for instance, singer-songwriters Beyoncé Giselle Knowles-Carter and Taylor Swift. Better known by her first name, Beyoncé uses stories of love and infidelity in her groundbreaking album, *Lemonade* released in 2016, to focus on larger issues of race, feminism, and identity—all aimed at empowering young women to regain their sense of Self. In her 2019 Netflix documentary *Homecoming*, she includes quotes from sociologist W. E. B. Du Bois, novelist Toni Morrison, poet Maya Angelou, and others, in order to accentuate the importance of personal transformation through education, particularly among the black community. Her album *Black Is King* released in July 2020 celebrates the peoples, the cultures, the riches as well as the spirituality of Africa and African diaspora. Her "Black Parade" bagged Best R & B Performance honors in the 2021 Grammy Awards.

Unlike Beyoncé, Taylor Swift seems to aim largely at younger female fans often writing and singing songs that matter to them in their personal life. In a 2018 interview with an NPR reporter, she explains that she does not write songs about "big ideas and the big world that's outside" because she wants her younger fans to look inward. Referring to them and to her much acclaimed album *1989* released in 2014, she says, "I think the best thing I can do for them is continue to write songs that do make them think about themselves and analyze how they feel about something and then simplify how they feel."[22] Consistent with that view, in an essay titled "30 Things I Learned Before Turning 30," which appeared in a popular magazine on March 6, 2019, Swift shared with her young readers a lesson about sexual assault. Referring to her own sexual assault case in which the jury ruled in her favor, she wrote: "I believe victims because I know firsthand about the shame and stigma that comes with raising your hand and saying, 'This happened to me.' It's something no one would choose for themselves. We speak up because we have to, and out of fear that it could happen to someone else if we don't."[23] The world witnessed her enormous popularity when her thunderous fans sparked a seismic activity equivalent to a 2.3-magnitude earthquake at her "Shake It Off" concert in Seattle in July 2023. As we approach the 2024 Presidential election, she encouraged her 282 million Instagram followers to vote, without saying for whom thereby triggering fierce speculation in the media about her role as an influencer potentially affecting the election outcome.

There are also celebrities who have added certain elegant phrases to our cultural dictionary, triggering serious thinking about changing cultural norms. British actress Emma Watson's phrase "self-partnership"[24] celebrating single-hood generated several tweets and opinion pieces. Similarly, Hollywood actress Gwyneth Paltrow's "conscious uncoupling"[25] presented a way of staying in a family while going through a divorce.

There are other celebrities who have been active in political, social, and cultural matters. Perhaps, no celebrity has done more and with greater commitment than Hollywood actor George Clooney to help Americans become aware of genocides and mass atrocities, particularly in the Darfur region of Sudan. Recall how, when the Sultanate of Brunei passed a law providing death by stoning for gay sex and adultery, Clooney called for a boycott of nine hotels owned by a government arm called Brunei Investment Agency, all of which are located in the United States, Britain, France, and Italy. He was joined by British celebrities like Elton John. Within a month, the Brunei government climbed down. Welcoming the move, Clooney said it "sends a very crucial message to countries like Indonesia and Malaysia that there is a cost for enacting these laws. And the cost isn't folks boycotting their hotels. The cost is that corporations and big banks won't do business with you."[26]

When Angelina Jolie went public about her mastectomy and created a greater awareness about it among women, medical researchers described it as an Angelina effect in medicine. Lady Gaga used her Facebook account to ask millions of her fans to protest against the government's policy on gays in the military. Kim Kardashian's fashion trend is known to be quickly adopted into the mainstream by many among her more than 100 million Instagram followers. San Francisco 49ers football quarterback Colin Kaepernick's refusal to stand for the national anthem triggered a contentious conversation on race relations in this country. The National Football League (NFL) and its officials who spurned him for kneeling have now changed their attitude. In July 2020, four years after Kaepernick kneeled and was severely reprimanded, NFL Commissioner Roger Goodell welcomed the quarterback's "voice on discussions of social issues" and encouraged teams to sign him up again.[27]

Considering the global reach of the celebrities and the shaping of new cultural norms that are fast spreading to many places in the world, it may not be an exaggeration to say that celebrities may have the potential to help people to begin to overcome some of the artificial divisions based on race and religion, class, and creed. Although the list of celebrity activists who seek to influence American public opinion is long and impressive, any direct correlation between their activism and its true impact on American identity is as yet undetermined. To my knowledge, there does not exist a body of scholarly research that has studied the outcome. However, going by all the available anecdotal evidence and instances of sociocultural shifts in the society, it is fair to assume that the American public at large is seriously listening to their favorite celebrities and, in some cases, deciding to act on their advocacy in shaping their cultural identity.

The three groups of cultural agents—Christian fundamentalists, culture warriors, and celebrity activists—are mostly self-appointed facilitators who believe that they have the conceptual knowledge and communicative skill necessary to advocate certain religious, social, cultural, or political viewpoints to millions of the masses who may not be fully aware of the issues involved. They may also believe that they are doing it in the interest of the larger community and the nation. It is, however, the general public who ultimately decide what kind of cultural transformation they are willing to adopt or adapt at the individual and at the national level. They play the role of silent deciders.

SILENT DECIDERS

As I mentioned earlier, the Christian fundamentalists and the culture warriors have similar goals and objectives. They have more or less similar following and reap similar outcomes. The financial and institutional resources at their disposal is staggering. As legal scholar Joseph Margulies and others have noted, "the religious right has created an extensive network to develop and disseminate its views—a network that includes publishing houses and magazines; television and radio programs broadcast over hundreds of Christian stations; a cluster of universities and seminaries; well-funded lobbying groups and think-tanks; professionally maintained websites; and, of course, tens of thousands of churches and ministries."[28] And yet, their impact on the general public has been rather modest both in religious and in cultural arenas.

A comprehensive study conducted jointly by sociologist Robert Putnam and political scientist David E. Campbell reveals that, in spite of what the Christian fundamentalists and the culture warriors have long been advocating, "a vast majority of Americans seem entirely comfortable in a religiously pluralist world, but several indicators point to a small minority (roughly one in ten of all adults) who are 'true believers.'"[29] They further report that nearly "80 percent of Americans say they follow their own conscience in matters of right and wrong," and are not easily swayed by what Faith leaders and Faith dispensers advocate.

The story is not very different on the cultural front either. A prime example is how the Christian fundamentalists and the culture warriors were staunchly opposed to and fervently campaigned against same-sex marriage, and how a substantial number of the general public soundly rejected their views. In fact, the U.S. Supreme Court handed them a major blow when it recognized the widespread public sentiment and decided to declare that same-sex marriage is constitutional (see chapter 9 for more details). More recently, in June 2022 to be exact, the Court handed a great victory to Christian fundamentalists by reversing the 1973 *Roe v. Wade* decision, ending the constitutional right to abortion. A vast segment of Americans, particularly women across political spectrum, have expressed their opposition to the ruling, opposition that might impact on 2024 elections.

Americans do recognize that culture plays a crucial role in constructing individual and national identity. As a 2017 survey conducted by Pew Research Center reveals, "more than four-in-ten (45%) believe that for a person to be considered truly American, it is very important that he or she share American customs and traditions. Another 39% say such identification with U.S. culture is at least somewhat important. Only 15% voice the view that this embrace of cultural Americanism is not very or not at all important."[30] Most Americans, regardless of class or creed, race or religion, enthusiastically participate in certain customs and traditions—whether it be a patriotic celebration like July 4th, or a national festival like Thanksgiving, or a carnival like Mardi Gras, or a sports event like the Super Bowl. This is in addition to ethnicity-specific, family-oriented religious and cultural festivities, as elaborated earlier in chapter 5.

Contrary to the cultural reality of the American society, several right-wing and left-wing politicians and pundits continue to present skewed and competing arguments about culture wars. Ideologically-biased media have gladly obliged to spread their polemics. The constant drumbeat has inevitably drawn a part of the American population into one or the other competing camps, making it clear that some of them have strongly imbibed certain values of culture war.

However, silent deciders, who constitute the silent majority in this country, have not endorsed the passionate intensity of culture warriors. Recognizing this reality, some scholars in the field of Social Sciences have questioned the widespread opinion that culture wars have polarized the American people into two ideological camps. Consolidating these arguments and doing her own research, sociologist Irene Taviss Thomson presents a comprehensive commentary concluding that "American public opinion is considerably more ambivalent and internally inconsistent than the image of a culture war implies. Most Americans are moderate or centrist in both their political and religious beliefs."[31] She agrees with some analysts that what we have been witnessing is "not a culture war but a class war or a series of political conflicts." A more emphatic assessment comes from Andrew Hartman. Culture wars, says the historian, "*are* history. The logic of the culture wars has been exhausted. The metaphor has run its course."[32]

And yet, both Republicans and Democrats continue to see culture wars as political assets never failing to engage in them aggressively during election seasons. Culture wars are linked to identity politics that both the parties have been following for decades. The legislative games currently being played out in the state of Florida offers a prime example. As a failed presidential candidate for Republication nomination in 2024, Governor Ron DeSantis tried to boost his chances, at least among the Republican voters, by taking on the mantle of a culture warrior. He proudly and loudly led the legislative assembly of the Sunshine State to pass the "Don't Say Gay" bill. Officially called the "Parental Rights in Education" bill, it bans teachers from offering lessons on sexual orientation and gender identity to students in kindergarten through third grade.

In yet another political act masquerading as culture war, DeSantis repealed the "special independent district" status enjoyed by Disney for half a century. It is a self-governing status which has given Disney the right to operate as its own municipal government: levying taxes, building roads, controlling utilities, administering town-planning and zoning, etc. Why did DeSantis do this? Simple: Disney has consistently promoted progressive values and has earlier opposed his "Don't Say Gay" bill. As the conservative columnist Rich Lowry wrote, "Taking on big business when it veers to the left is a huge opportunity for Republicans."[33]

One of the reasons why the particular brand of American culture war waged by Christian fundamentalists and cultural warriors has not succeeded as much as they wanted or expected is because it is basically founded on a false premise. While it is true that culture wars are a response to the counterculture of the 1950s, it is not the whole truth. The root of the cultural conflict in America actually goes deeper and broader. It lies in the erroneous notion that there is something called cultural purity—something that is unmixed, unalloyed, unchangeable; something that must be preserved at all times and protected at all costs. This cultural myth was exploded by anthropologists quite a while ago. In his book, *Myth and Meaning*, the pre-eminent French anthropologist Claude Lévi-Strauss whom many consider to be the Father of modern anthropology, demonstrated that every culture is a hybrid culture with borrowings and mixtures that have occurred since the dawn of human history. "Such history," he says, "has never been produced by isolated cultures but by cultures which, voluntarily or involuntarily, have combined their play and, by a wide variety of means (migration, borrowing, trade and warfare), have formed such coalitions as we have visualized in our example. . . . No single culture stands alone; it is always part of a coalition including other cultures."[34]

Silent deciders seem to have an intuitive sense of the dynamic concept of cultural identity. They hardly attach any value to the static, ideologically-loaded views of culture propagated by religious fundamentalists and culture warriors. They recognize and accept that American cultural identity, like its religious identity, is unmistakably pluralistic. They are comfortable with the cultural state of the nation: every ethnic community celebrating its own cultural events while at the same time absorbing elements of common American cultural traditions. In constructing their cultural identity, they also seem to allow themselves to be guided in part by an aspect of their lived experience that is more and more informed by the triple processes of celebrification, digitalization, and commercialization. In a sense, that is what prompted historian Hartman say: "If any one ethos now represents American culture, it is that promulgated by Madison Avenue and Silicon Valley."[35]

The alliance between the publicity machine from Madison Avenue and the social media apparatus from Silicon Valley have made sure that celebrification, digitalization, and commercialization thrive by feeding on each other. As a result, cultural norms are changing at a faster rate than ever before. Take for instance, how yoga-inspired meditation and mindfulness practices become an instant craze and how celebrities play a part in it. Well-known figures from various fields—actor Richard Gere, businesswoman and actress Oprah Winfrey, sports legend Kobe Bryant, just to name a few—have all practiced meditation, and propagated the valuable role it played in their successful life. And, social media is ever ready to commodify cultural tidbits to satisfy its hungry customers. As a leading therapist Jeremy Safran wrote in the London newspaper the *Guardian*, "It's the marketing of mindfulness practice as a commodity that is sold like any other commodity in our brand culture, a brand that promises to deliver. . . . Mindfulness is the marketing of a constructed dream; an idealized lifestyle; an identity makeover."[36]

The silent deciders have demonstrated that no governmental proclamations, no ex-cathedra pronouncements will have any lasting impact on American identity; it has to emerge bottom-up, organically. They demonstrated it in terms of cultural identity, as we saw in this chapter, and in terms of religious identity as we saw in the previous chapter. And, we will see in the next chapter similar trend with regard to America's linguistic identity as well.

Chapter 8

Linguistic Identity

Mother and Other Tongues

Sujatha Bhatt is a poet. Born and raised in India. Studied in Britain and in the United States. Taught creative writing in colleges in Canada, England, and the United States. Her poems often reflect her multicultural and multilingual experiences.

One of her much-acclaimed poems is titled, "Search for my Tongue." It was choreographed by a dance company in the United Kingdom and was performed several times across England and Scotland. It is included in her award-winning collection of poems, Brunizem. Here it is:

"Search for my Tongue"[1]
Sujatha Bhatt

You ask me what I mean
by saying I have lost my tongue.
I ask you, what would you do
if you had two tongues in your mouth,
and lost the first one, the mother tongue,
and could not really know the other,
the foreign tongue.
You could not use them both together
even if you thought that way.
And if you lived in a place you had to
speak a foreign tongue,
your mother tongue would rot,
rot and die in your mouth
until you had to spit it out.
I thought I spit it out
but overnight while I dream,
મને હુતું કે આખી જીભ આખી
મેં થૂંકી નાખી છે.

પરંતુ રાતૂરે સૂવપૂનાંમાં મારી ભાષા પાછી આવે છે.
ફૂલની જેમ મારી ભાષા મારા
મોઢામાં ખીલે છે.
ફૂલની જેમ મારી ભાષા મારા
મોઢામાં પાકે છે.
it grows back, a stump of a shoot
grows longer, grows moist, grows strong veins,
it ties the other tongue in knots,
the bud opens, the bud opens in my mouth,
it pushes the other tongue aside.
Every time I think I've forgotten,
I think I've lost the mother tongue,
it blossoms out of my mouth.

The mother tongue which the poet thought she had lost, suddenly blossoms out of her mouth. In her dreams. To highlight the surprise blossoming, she breaks her poem in English to insert a seven-line stanza in her native language, Gujarati, without translation.

The poem is about the power of one's mother tongue. It is also about the poet's anxiety about losing her mother tongue. It is a lamentation that echoes her feeling of alienation from her roots, from her linguistic identity. It is a longing for renewal, for re-blossoming. It is a sentiment only those who have lost or are losing their mother tongue can truly relate to.

A similar cry from the heart, couched in a dense philosophical contemplation, comes from Jacques Derrida, a French philosopher. He is well known in scholarly circles in many parts of the world for his original contributions to modern Western philosophy. He has published several books and essays in philosophy and in other areas of the Humanities and Social Sciences. He has also studied and taught philosophy at the prestigious University of Paris, well known as the Sorbonne. Later he taught at the University of California, Irvine.

Derrida was born in 1930 to a Sephardic Jewish family in a province in Algeria, a French colony at that time. He automatically became a French citizen because, by an earlier historical agreement, France had granted full French citizenship to the indigenous Arabic-speaking Jews of Algeria. When he was a teenager, his parents sent him to France to study. There, he had no chance to continue to learn or use his mother tongue because France had put restrictions on the teaching of his language in schools and colleges. He learned French and became fluent in it. He quickly became a competent monolingual speaker/writer of the French language.

In his semi-autobiographical book titled *Monolingualism of the Other*, he philosophically reflects on the loss of his mother tongue. With a tinge of sadness, he raises nagging questions about his linguistic identity, his personal identity. He writes wistfully: "I have only one language and it is not mine;

my 'own' language is, for me, a language that cannot be assimilated. My language, the only one I hear myself speak and agree to speak, is the language of the other."[2] He then goes into the complexity of the language one speaks, and its relationship to the Other, deeply philosophizing his condition of how the only language he speaks is not his. The sentence "I have only one language and it is not mine" occurs again and again in the book. It reveals his sense of loss, his sense of longing.

The philosopher and the poet are not alone.

Mother tongue is rapidly reduced to mother's tongue for many a child born and living in a country where their heritage language is not spoken outside their home. That is, the serene, soothing sounds of the mother tongue which infants got so used to while still in the womb, the one that lullabied them into deep slumber during their early years, and the one that served them as a vehicle for carrying sweet memories of childhood, slowly recedes into the inner crevices of their mind.

That is particularly so in a country like the United States where the children of many immigrant families are put in a daycare center where they hear mostly, and in many cases only English, and also after they enter their elementary school. It is a challenge for them to continue to learn their mother tongue and to retain fluency in it. That is the reality with most children, if not all. However, when they grow up to be young adults and realize the cultural as well as the commercial value of the linguistic capital of their mother tongue, many of them regret their lack of proficiency in it and try to resurrect it with the view to constructing a broader linguistic identity.

In their efforts to construct a broader linguistic identity, many Americans have shown remarkable sense and sensibility about the value of their heritage language, the importance of English, and the usefulness of foreign languages.

THE VALUE OF HERITAGE LANGUAGE

American sociolinguist Joshua Fishman defines a heritage language in the American context as "a language of personal relevance other than English."[3] According to a 2015 report from the U.S. Census Bureau, there are about 350 such languages that are being spoken in American homes, in addition to English. Numerous Americans are exposed to at least one of these languages on a daily basis. Just consider the staggering number of languages spoken at homes in the metro areas of large cities: 192 languages in New York, 185 in Los Angeles, 163 in San Francisco, 145 in Houston. Even though many of these languages are not formally taught in public schools, nearly 25% of school-going children in America are from immigrant families where a heritage language is spoken.[4]

Many are the ways in which various ethno-lingual communities in the country are striving to pass on their heritage language to the younger generation. The most effective way it is being done, apart from speaking the language at home, is by offering heritage language classes either as after school programs, or as Sunday school lessons, or as special classes in ethnicity-based community centers (see chapter 5 for more on this). This is particularly true in large states like California, Florida, New York, and Texas. For the political minded, there are heritage language-based magazines, radio, and TV shows. For the entertainment oriented, there are cinema halls showing movies in their native languages. For the religious minded, several places of worship offer services in heritage languages. For instance, within a five-mile radius from my home in Cupertino, California, I see churches offering Sunday services in Chinese, Korean, Russian, Tagalog, and Vietnamese, not to mention Spanish.

What the plurality of language speakers in the country means is that vital governmental and public health establishments have to offer some of their services in major languages that are spoken in a particular region. Just to give an idea of diverse language use: in California, the basic noncommercial Class C driver license written tests are available in thirty-one languages, besides English. A leading HMO, Kaiser Permanente, offers interpreter services in sixteen languages at its facilities in Santa Clara County. At the federal level, the Centers for Medicare & Medicaid Services under the U.S. Department of Health and Human Services offer their services in sixteen languages. There are also other federal and state agencies that provide multilingual services. A Bureau of Census 2020 notification from the U.S. Department of Commerce offered help to complete the U.S. Census Questionnaire in a dozen languages besides English.

Politicians are also fast finding that being fluent in a heritage language can be a prized possession in the electoral arena, and do not hesitate to show off their bi-/multilingual capacity in order to appeal to citizens who speak a language other than English. Former South Bend Mayor Pete Buttigieg is now the U.S. Cabinet Secretary of Transportation in the Biden administration. As an aspirant for the Democratic Party nomination in the 2020 Presidential election, he surprised the public as a multilingual speaker in half a dozen foreign languages including French, Spanish, Italian, and Arabic. During the first TV debate held in June 2019 among Democratic presidential hopefuls, we heard Spanish interspersed with English. During the 2016 Presidential election, Democratic vice-presidential candidate and Virginia Senator Tim Kaine tried to impress his Spanish speaking supporters by delivering a speech entirely in Spanish during a Spanish-language church service. Former Florida Governor Jeb Bush, married to a Latina from Mexico, speaks fluent Spanish at home and never hesitates to use it in pubic politically strategically.

The availability of multilingual services from state and federal governmental agencies, and the sustained attempts by various generations of immigrants to revive their heritage language does not in any way diminish their realization and acknowledgement that the English language is an integral part of their individual as well as national identity.

ENGLISH IS A MUST

A 2017 study by Pew Research Center found that a vast number of Americans consider proficiency in English "far and away most critical to American identity." A significant majority of the public (70%) says that it is important to be able to speak English fluently to be "truly American." Another 22% think that proficiency is somewhat important, while only 8% say it is not at all important. Even more significantly, there is a remarkable consensus among the people of major racial or ethnic background about English being a central attribute of American identity, with seven-in-ten whites (71%), blacks (71%), and Hispanics (70%) in strong agreement.[5]

Clearly, English is the de facto language of the United States, in the sense that it is used for all governmental, educational, and other civil purposes. And yet, it is not the official language at the national level. There have been repeated attempts both in and outside the Congress to make English the official language. If a law is passed to that effect, it would mean, according to a popular organization in support of making English the official language—USEnglish.org—that "All official documents, records, legislation and regulations, as well as hearings, ceremonies and public meetings are conducted solely in English, with some commonsense exceptions."[6] The commonsense exceptions would allow languages other than English being used for purposes such as public health and safety, and multilingual ballots.

The U.S. Senate has repeatedly failed to pass a federal legislation to make English the *official* language of the United States. In 2006, it struck a compromise and voted 63 to 34 to declare English as a *national* language, directing the federal government to "preserve and enhance" the role of English, without curtailing the current law that requires certain documents and services be provided in other languages.[7]

Declaring English as the official language is to give it a special status over and above all the other languages spoken in the country. There are advocacy groups that have been actively supporting or opposing such a move. The supporters mainly argue that a unifying language is a must for promoting a distinct national identity.[8] Some of them, however, make it clear that they are not in favor of legislation that would ban the use of languages other than English. There seems to be widespread support among the public for making English the official language, cutting across political as well as ethnic divide. This might explain the fact that a majority of the states—thirty-one of them—have passed laws declaring English as their official language.

Among the strong supporters of the attempt to make English as the official language are conservative columnists and pundits who are also generally in favor of cultural assimilation and are against what they see as the divisive forces of diversity. Nearly a decade ago, columnist Charles Krauthammer wrote: "In Plain English: Making it Official. Having a unifying language is a secret of America's success. Why mess with it?"[9] Emphasizing the importance of English in general, yet another commentator George F. Will tells immigrants: "if you are to be welcomed to the enjoyment of American liberty, then America has a few expectations of you. One is that you can read the nation's founding documents and laws and can comprehend the political discourse that precedes the casting of ballots."[10]

Those who are opposed to the idea of making English the official language of the United States point out that it is a non-issue because immigrants do learn English within a couple of generations anyway. This happened in the case of nineteenth- and twentieth-century immigrants such as Germans and Italians, as well as among the twentieth- and twenty- first-century immigrants of Asian and Hispanic origin. More than a common language, they say, what binds the citizens are America's creedal identity and its abstract ideals (see chapter 3 for details). Besides, they are concerned that in a multilingual immigrant society such as the United States, designating and promoting one language as the official language might lead to unnecessary conflicts among various linguistic communities.

Regardless of the discordant note surrounding the status of English, American immigrants are fully aware that English has value in the job market. They are also aware that a person's possession of linguistic capital in a high-value language like English establishes that person's status with individual, national, and other identities. Such an awareness is complemented by the positive attitude shown by the mainstream community that speaks English natively. They are open to the idea of using tax dollars to teach English to immigrant adults and children. They do so because they "view English language," sociologists Carlos Garcia and Loretta E. Bass observe, "as a cohesive force solidifying the United States citizenry, and that a strong willingness exists to meet immigrants half-way in their assimilation process by providing English language education."[11]

Immigrant parents and children of all ethnic communities are increasingly making use of the opportunities available to learn English. According to a 2012 study by the Center for American Progress, "in the decade between the 1997–1998 and 2008–2009 school years, the number of English language learners in public schools increased by 51 percent while the general population of students grew by just 7 percent."[12] The widespread misconception that immigrants from the Latino community lag behind others in English language learning does not accurately reflect the ground reality. We learn from a 2007 study by Pew Hispanic Center in Washington, DC that while only 23% of first-generation immigrants from Latino immigrants spoke English very well, the number jumped to 88% among the second generation, and to 94% among the third.[13]

In spite of the importance of English at the national level and its status as a global language, mobility-conscious Americans are sensible enough not to limit their language ability to English. There seems to be a perceptible recognition among many of them that their linguistic identity needs to be broadened.

"ENGLISH ALONE IS NOT ENOUGH"

That was a definitive conclusion reached by a high-powered committee consisting of business leaders, academics, and educational planners who explored the language needs of twenty- first-century Britain. The committee set up in the year 2000 by a British charitable trust called the Nuffield Foundation declared in no uncertain terms: "English alone is not enough. In the face of such widespread acceptance and use of English, the UK's complacent view of its limited capability in other languages is understandable. It is also dangerous. In a world where bilingualism and plurilingualism are commonplace, monolingualism implies inflexibility, insensitivity and arrogance."[14]

The committee warned the British government that exclusive reliance of English creates a culture of dependence on the linguistic competence and the goodwill of others, leaving the country vulnerable in several areas of national interest. It recommended sweeping reform in language education so that

> the ability to operate in other languages and cultures should be part of the portfolio of skills possessed by all graduates. To meet their own and the country's needs, they will need to be effective communicators and citizens in a multilingual, multicultural world, regardless of their area of specialist study. For many, using languages will be a regular supporting feature of their work, in areas as varied as global finance, defence, diplomacy, public administration or voluntary associations.[15]

Undoubtedly, the warning and the recommendations are relevant to the United States as well. It took only sixteen years after the Nuffield report was published for American lawmakers to wake up. And they are still barely half-awake. In 2016, a bipartisan group from the U.S. Senate and the

U.S. House of Representatives requested the American Academy of Arts & Sciences to examine the following questions: "How does language learning influence economic growth, cultural diplomacy, the productivity of future generations, and the fulfillment of all Americans? What actions should the nation take to ensure excellence in all languages as well as international education and research, including how we may more effectively use current resources to advance language learning?"[16]

A year later, the Academy submitted its report titled, *America's Languages: Investing in Language Education for the 21st Century*. In its introduction, it echoed the British warning: "It is critical that we work together at this moment in history, when there is so much to gain by participating in a multilingual world, and so much to lose if we remain stubbornly monolingual." Its recommendations include: "a primary goal" for every school in the nation should be to offer "meaningful instruction in world languages as part of their standard curricula." In addition, the Academy emphasized that the nation should support heritage language learning opportunities both in classrooms and outside so as to help these languages persist from one generation to the next. To that end, college and university curricula should be revised to offer instruction and course credit for proficiency in a heritage language.[17]

The ongoing processes of economic and cultural globalization have only heightened the need to develop multilingual capacity in our students. As a researcher points out, "Foreign language skills are the ultimate twenty-first-century social skill, and those who do not possess these skills risk being left behind, in the global marketplace of ideas, in the workplace, and even in social and personal life. Americans are among the least likely in the world to learn a foreign language and have the most to lose in the developing global linguistic scenario."[18] A 2012 McKinsey Global Institute report showed that nearly 40% of new jobs in developed countries around the world go to foreign workers because of the multilingual and multicultural skills they bring with them.[19]

In America too, several employers are now seeking bilingual speakers to work for them. A cluster of surveys cited by the National Immigration Forum based in Washington, DC reveals the trend: in California, 66% of small business owners would hire a bilingual job applicant over an equally qualified monolingual one. In Massachusetts, between 2010 and 2015, the number of online job postings for bilingual workers increased by more than 150% in some of the state's large establishments. In Georgia, between 2010 and 2014, the number of job postings seeking bilingual candidates increased 84%. Mindful of these developments, the Forum concludes: "We should ensure that Americans learn other languages and that new Americans do not lose their native language. Rather than losing their home language completely, first- or second-generation immigrant students should be encouraged to be proficient in English and their home language. Multilingualism will be only more important as our economy is increasingly tied to the global economy. The federal government and states should increase their support for foreign language learning."[20]

NATIONAL SECURITY

Apart from the imperatives of economic and cultural globalization, it is a genuine concern about national security that prompted both the British and the American expert committees to issue a fervent appeal for bolstering foreign language education. Various U.S. administrations have shown interest in foreign language education whenever they sense a national security threat. However, when the threat dissipates, the interest also dissipates. During the Soviet era, particularly in the wake of the successful launch of Sputnik, America focused on promoting Russian language, and federal funds were made available for colleges and universities to start Russian language programs. When the Soviet Union collapsed in the early 1990s and the threat receded, the funds dried up, and many programs folded up. It took a devastating national tragedy for the interest in foreign languages to be revived again.

"Tomorrow is zero hour." These ominous words were part of a message that was getting transmitted among al-Qaeda operatives on September 10, 2001.[21] The message, written in Arabic, was successfully intercepted by the U.S. intelligence on the same day, but was not translated until September 12, the day after the 9/11 attack. A reported reason: not enough interpreters and translators, particularly in Arabic. Soon after, the CIA intensified its efforts to recruit Arab-Americans, and went to places like Dearborn, Michigan, where nearly one-third of its residents are of Middle-Eastern origin. There are also reports that during 2006 through 2008, the CIA gathered 46 million files of intelligence, one-third of which were untouched owing to the lack of translation resources.[22] In the context of domestic threat, the FBI is reported to have had thousands of hours of backlogged audiotapes that remain to be translated because of a lack of qualified translators.

In 2006, sensing that our inability to communicate in other languages negatively affects our national security efforts such as counter-terrorism, diplomacy, law enforcement, intelligence gathering, and intercultural understanding, President George W. Bush launched the National Security Language Initiative (NSLI) and allotted substantial federal funds for teaching foreign languages from kindergarten to university. The Initiative focused on languages such as Arabic, Chinese, Farsi, and others. Later, the U.S. Department of State identified fourteen "critical languages," promoted intensive summer immersion courses in them and offered scholarships for students.[23]

Any expert in language leaning would readily attest that two-to-eight-week summer classes are hopelessly inadequate to develop meaningful competence in any language. Translation, in particular, requires high-level linguistic skills. Even the professional translators from the State Department were sometimes found wanting in their translation skills, occasionally resulting in diplomatic *faux pas*. A classic example is what happened in 2009 in Geneva. With the view to improving America's tense relationship with Russia, the Obama administration opted for what it called a reset. When the then U.S. Secretary of State Hillary Clinton met her Russian counterpart Sergei Lavrov, she presented him with a gag gift, with a red button with the word "reset" written in Russian. Lavrov opened it, looked inside, and smiled. He told Clinton that the Russian word on the button, *peregruzka*, actually means "overcharge," not "reset"—not exactly the message America wanted to convey.[24]

What is really lamentable is the fact that policy makers and government officials have all along been turning a blind eye to something that is hidden in plain sight. With nearly 350 heritage languages spoken at home by immigrants and children of immigrants, the United States is blessed with rich linguistic resources that remain under-utilized. Unfortunately, our language policy is such that it not only fails to promote heritage languages in schools and colleges but also does everything possible to let Americans forget the home language they already know. Recall how we are treated from time to time to short-sighted educational policies such as Proposition 227 in California and Proposition 203 in Arizona that deprive schools of opportunities for bilingual and heritage language education programs.

We even punish heritage language speakers for using their language in public. There have been recurrent reports that judges in some southern states ruled against bilingual workers speaking their home language in their workplace even during lunch break. Recently, a Duke University professor and director of graduate studies asked her Chinese students not to speak their native language even in the student lounge. She was actually responding to other professors who complained to her about them hearing Chinese being spoken in the lounge. Her email to students read in part: "To international students, PLEASE PLEASE PLEASE keep these unintended consequences in mind when you choose to speak in Chinese in the building."[25] Unintended consequences. For speaking in native language. In the lounge. During private time. Think about it.

The nation continues to ignore a large pool of American citizens who are exposed to a heritage language at home and end up speaking it with varying degrees of competence. With additional institutional support, they can easily meet the security needs of the country. That is why the American Academy of Arts & Sciences recommended that the American government should

Support heritage languages already spoken in the United States, and help these languages persist from one generation to the next. Encourage heritage language speakers to pursue further instruction in their heritage languages. . . . Provide more language learning opportunities for heritage speakers in classroom or school settings. . . . Expand efforts to create college and university curricula designed specifically for heritage speakers and to offer course credit for proficiency in a heritage language.[26]

The recommendations do not seem to have had the desired effect. Consider this: a 2018 report from Pew Research Center, citing a study by American Councils for International Education, states that in Europe, a median of 92% of students learn a foreign language in school. Among the twenty-nine nations that are part of the European Union, twenty-four have a foreign language learning rate of at least 80%, with fifteen of those reaching 90% or more of students enrolled in language courses, whereas in the United States, in all fifty states and the District of Columbia, only 20% of K-12 students are enrolled in foreign language classes.[27] We also learn from a 2018 preliminary report by Modern Language Association that foreign language enrollments in colleges and universities fell 9.2% between Fall 2013 and Fall 2016. "Most striking," the report says, "is that the total number of enrollments in modern language courses in relation to the total number of students at postsecondary institutions in the United States fell to 7.5, almost matching the low point in 1980."[28]

There is, however, a silver lining. The popularity of Amazon's Alexa, which has the capacity to switch between languages for multilingual homes, testifies to the importance people attach to multilingual skills. Moreover, many parents around the country are also seeking out specific language-focused daycare centers or nannies to give their children a head start in foreign language skills. Perhaps they are aware that, as repeated studies by Toronto University neurolinguist Ellen Bialystok revealed, normal bilingual children develop better cognitive skills than normal monolingual children.[29] In a related move, California has proposed an initiative called Global California 2030 which would triple the number of bilingual high school graduates in the next dozen years. If successful, all the students in the state would be encouraged to be proficient in at least two languages.

There are also those who, undeterred by the lack of adequate governmental and institutional support, have been pursuing foreign language learning beyond what is minimally required for school graduation. More specifically, thanks to their awareness of the economic globalization and the growing importance of China's growing power, many American youth are increasingly enrolling in Chinese language classes. Keeping up with the trend, more and more high schools are also offering classes in the Chinese language. To compensate inadequate governmental financial support, some of them are making use of the help that is coming from China.

As part of its soft power outreach to spread Chinese language and culture, the Beijing-based Office of Chinese Language Council International (also known as Hanban) has, as of 2019, opened ninety-eight Confucius Institutes in schools and colleges across forty-eight states and Washington, DC, with 1,360 teachers and volunteer instructors helping over 419,000 American students learn the Chinese language. Incidentally, Hanban has opened Confucius Institutes in colleges and universities in as many as 154 countries, sending more than 10,000 Chinese language teachers, along with free teaching materials and financial assistance.[30]

Of the ninety-eight or so Confucius Institutes in the United States, only about one-third remains now. The reason: The Trump administration determined that the Chinese were using the Confucius Institutes not merely to spread Chinese language and culture, but also as a propaganda tool. In 2018, the U.S. Congress passed a law barring colleges and universities that host Confucius Institutes from receiving U.S. Department of Defense funding for language programs it sponsors.[31] Consequently, many colleges and universities which depend on such funding closed down the Confucius Institutes partly because of the law and partly because of the objections raised by several academics who were appalled at the Chinese state censorship of certain topics in course materials.

What has been outlined in this chapter confirms a pattern that Americans follow in establishing their linguistic identity, a pattern that has been summed up neatly by political scientist Samuel P. Huntington:

> The large majority of first-generation immigrants do not, unless they come from English-speaking countries, achieve fluency in English. The second generation, who either arrive as very young children with their parents or are born in the United States, have relatively high degrees of fluency in both English and their parents' language. The third generation is completely fluent in English and has little or no knowledge of their family's ancestral language, which creates a problem for communication with their grandparents, but is also often accompanied by a nostalgic interest in and expressed desire to learn the language of their ancestors.[32]

The nostalgic interest does blossom into effective heritage language learning among Americans of subsequent generations, even if sporadically.

"We have room for one language in this country," declared President Theodore Roosevelt in a 1919 address to the American Defense Society, "and that is the English language, for we intend to see that the crucible turns our people out as Americans, of American nationality, and not as dwellers in a polyglot boarding house."[33] These words are music to the ears of certain conservative pundits who are even today fond of quoting them in defense of their opposition to bilingual education. They do not realize that Roosevelt governed a different America, at a different time. What Roosevelt said a century ago is irrelevant to the conditions prevailing in our contemporary American society with its plurality of languages and cultures, and inadequate to meet our national security needs in this era of globalization and digitalization. If Roosevelt were alive today, as a leader committed to and interested in the welfare of the country and its citizens, he would certainly urge Americans to be polyglots.

All available data show that many young Americans do realize the importance of the English language, their heritage language, and foreign language, and are striving to construct their linguistic identity keeping in mind their personal and professional growth, as well as their nation's security interest.

The chapters in Part III on religious, cultural, and linguistic identity indicate that many American citizens do not hesitate to defy political and ideological elites when it comes to shaping and reshaping their individual as well as national identity. More details on that in the next chapter.

PART IV

Realizing the Spirit of America

Chapter 9

How the Ruling Elites Distort American Identity and the Common People Reshape It

World Economic Forum. It has become a prestigious symbol of, and a go-to place for, ruling elites everywhere. For its annual gathering, its founders selected a place far from the madding crowd: Davos, a picturesque little town in the Swiss Alps. It is not only an exclusive club but an expensive one as well. Going by various reports, fees range from $60,000 for ordinary membership to $600,000 for a special membership called "Strategic Partner."[1] Attendees of the annual meeting get different colored badges which determine the level of their access to conference proceedings and social events. It is all free, though, for invited guests who are invariably prominent political leaders, corporate executives, and Hollywood celebrities.

The Forum has evoked strong diametrically opposed views. Those who hold a positive view echo the Forum's own mission statement: it is "committed to improving the state of the world by engaging business, political, academic, and other leaders of society to shape global, regional, and industry agendas."[2] It strives to "demonstrate entrepreneurship in the global public interest" keeping "moral and intellectual integrity" at the heart of everything it does. It is impartial having "no ideological or commercial interests;" it is global attending "to challenges that affect the future of global society"; it is holistic covering "perspectives from all interested parties;" and it is forward-looking focusing "on the long term, not the emergencies of the day." It also believes that "progress happens by bringing together people from all walks of life who have the drive and the influence to make positive change."

Those who hold a negative view such as Anand Giridharadas and Seth Kaplan characterize the Forum as "the high priest of plutocracy, i.e., rule by the ultra-wealthy." They argue that such an exclusive and expensive Forum can no way bring together "people from all walks of life," nor can it cover "perspectives from all interested parties." They see it as a den of capitalist elites who swear by the neoliberal ideology that a free and unregulated market is the only answer for all the ills of humanity. They assert that the Forum is no more than "a family reunion for the people who broke the modern world."[3]

Regardless of which view one subscribes to, there is no doubt that the Forum offers a venue where ruling elites from all over the world come to rub shoulders with people of their own ilk, and to strategize how to run the world in a way that benefits them. What happens at this global level happens at the national level also. Although the term *elites* generally refers to a motley group of people that include political leaders, corporate executives, media personalities, academics, opinion makers, writers, artists, and other celebrities, ruling elites everywhere are not ordinary elites. They are power elites.

POWER ELITES

Power elites are a group of self-chosen people who are either revered or reviled but never ignored. American sociologist Charles Wright Mills who authored *The Power Elite*, an informative book published more than sixty years ago, defines power elites as "men whose positions enable them to transcend the ordinary environments of ordinary men and women; they are in positions to make decisions having major consequences."[4] This elite group is not confined to political leadership alone but includes decision makers in government, industries, military, media, and entertainment. They constitute "a privileged ruling stratum" whose decisions, taken mostly in self-interest, have a huge impact on ordinary people, many of whom may not even be aware that the power elites are among the driving forces that shape the practice of their everyday life.

American power elites, like their counterparts elsewhere, build close-knit networks, mingle with each other in exclusive country clubs, forge personal and professional relationships, and work relentlessly to reinforce their collective interest. Their primary goal is to maintain their grip on power. As self-appointed gatekeepers, they decide who will or will not have access to the levers of power, especially in political, economic, judicial, cultural, and religious institutions. In many cases, their educational preparation for such an exalted life starts early on with attending expensive preparatory schools, and Ivy League universities such as Harvard, Princeton, and Yale. Elitist alumni of these and other prestigious universities make sure that their children and their children's children are easily admitted to these institutions regardless of their academic record. Such a practice is explained and justified in the name of legacy admission; a practice that is being increasingly questioned.

According to researchers, elite educational institutions admit more students form the top 1% of the economic bracket than from the bottom 60%.[5]

Coming from a privileged background, many of the ruling elites are so disconnected with those they want to lead that they know very little about their living conditions, their lifestyle, and their everyday struggle. There is very little that is common between them and the people they swear they serve. Recall how President George H. W. Bush, a Yale graduate and an exemplar of the American ruling class, could not recognize an electronic scanning device at a supermarket checkout counter, because he had never seen one, never been to a supermarket in his lifetime.

In a concerted and coordinated manner, American elites manipulate public opinion with the view to making sure that the entrenched political establishment, regardless of party affiliation, continues to control the levers of power. More often than not, they succeed in using mass media resources at their disposal for "manufacturing consent" among the public who often trust them rather innocently and go along with their plans and programs.[6] Such a seemingly implicit trust convinces the ruling elites that common people desire and deserve to be shown the correct path and that they are the chosen ones to do that. Directly or indirectly, they try to constrain the agency common people have in constructing their own self-identity. Given their unchallenged self-importance and unlimited self-confidence, they tend to overreach their power-play and fail to notice the flaws in their aims and activities.

There are times, however, when common people do not fail to recognize the excesses committed by the ruling elites and decide to defy them. Their collective defiance can happen on matters of political economy that affect their livelihood and also on matters of sociocultural autonomy that affect their identity formation and (re)formation. When that happens, the country experiences political tremors and cultural earthquakes with long-lasting aftershocks.

POLITICAL TREMORS

No developments in recent times demonstrate ordinary people's deep resentment against the ruling elites more than what happened during the initial decades of the twenty-first century culminating in the 2016 Presidential election.[7] A closer look at the political economy of the country during these decades reveals that the American ruling elites, with their outsized power and outsized ego, have continued to turn a blind eye to the real concerns of a large segment of the population. They have relentlessly pursued neoliberal economic policies that benefited them although some of the policies were immensely harming the people they claim to serve, particularly people from the lower-middle class and the working class. The elites have largely been unmindful of weakening the very workforce sorely needed for the successful operation of their industries and corporations which contributed to their enormous wealth and power. As the corporate elites focused single-mindedly on making global companies even more global by shifting plants out of the country and by outsourcing projects to maximize their profits, and as the political elites made that more and more possible by passing corporate-friendly economic policies and by weakening labor unions, the poor and lower-middle-class workers were left to experience untold hardship and fend for themselves.

It is now well known that the rust belt was hard hit. However, that is not the only region to suffer. In southern states, for instance, people have become poorer, as American sociologist Arlie Hochschild observes, with instances of "more teenage mothers, more divorce, worse health, more obesity, more trauma-related deaths, more low-birth-weight babies, and lower school enrolment."[8] In addition, their basic health deteriorated because of industrial pollution made worse by government deregulations. Because of all this, people were losing their livelihood and, in some cases, their lives. With their standard of living plummeting, an unmistakable realization dawned on the lower-middle class and working-class people across the country that they were going to be worse off than their parents and grandparents.

The ruling elites never paid any serious attention to the ever-widening income inequality partly because they continued to reap most of the rewards, no matter what happened to the labor force. And they were never punished for the misery they caused. In fact, none of the leading white-collar offenders went to jail. Over-confident as they had always been, they failed to grasp the groundswell of resentment that was building up against them. They never questioned their own fallibility and frailty. Instead, they disparaged the downtrodden for their failures and dismissed them with contempt. As historian Andrew Bacevich stated: "Anyone counting on members of the policy elite to acknowledge the scope of their collective failure is in for a long wait."[9]

By the turn of the century, the aggrieved people could not afford a long wait. They expressed their resentment through the only means available for them in a democratic society: the ballot box. In the 2016 presidential election, they decided to teach a lesson to the political establishment—both Republican and Democratic. Motivated by a blend of fear and hope, fear of losing their livelihood and hope for better days for them and their children, they rebelled against establishment politicians and opted for an unlikely candidate outside the recognized political spectrum.

They turned to Donald J. Trump. As a billionaire businessman, and as one who hails from an elitist background himself, he is certainly not one of them. And yet, he astutely figured out that one way he could endear himself to a vast segment of the disgruntled electorate is to present himself as one of them, that is, as a non-elite, anti-elite candidate. Sensing people's mindset and echoing their resentment, he ridiculed and mocked America's elites in almost all his campaign stops. He also disparaged globalist urban elites who benefited from economic globalization which created wealth and opportunities for them and not for the lower-middle class and the working class. His catchy slogans such as "America First," and "Make America Great Again" convinced a segment of the electorate, particularly in the crucial rust belt, that he would keep his promise to "drain the swamp." He knew who he should be thankful for. In a victory speech in February 2017, he declared rather candidly: "I love the poorly educated."[10]

It is not just in the field of political economy that the masses occasionally succeed in defying the elites and make history in spite of the powerful forces arraigned against them. The same can be seen in the sociocultural arena as well. Two major sociocultural developments in our times—culture change in the 1960s and same-sex marriage—offer illustrative examples.

CULTURAL EARTHQUAKES

Perhaps no other single decade in recent times transformed American identity—either of the individual or of the nation—more than the 1960s. The transformation was as breathtaking as the transgression that triggered it. What is even more historic about it is that it was all a non-violent, bottom-up endeavor initiated by common people in total defiance of the ruling elites of the time. It was a veritable cultural earthquake and its aftershocks are felt across the country even today. Tom Brokaw, the American television journalist and a longtime anchor of *NBC Nightly News*, was not exaggerating when he wrote, "many of the debates about the political, cultural, and socioeconomic meaning of the Sixties are still as lively and passionate and unresolved as they ever were. Moreover, those debates and the issues involved are a critical and defining part of our contemporary dialogue about where this nation is headed now and how it gets there."[11]

The America of 1950s and earlier was seen as repressive with rigid conservative sociocultural norms imposed on the society by political, religious, and cultural elites. The 1960s was a rebellious but peaceful response to the collective resentment that was building up among the common people. The rebellion left no aspect of American life untouched. A coming together of a bunch of movements—sexual revolution, feminist movement, Gay Rights movement, civil rights struggle, antipathy to Vietnam War—may appear to be separate and coincidental but each one cemented the aims and activities of the other. As the decade unfolded, a counterculture emerged that drastically changed American lives and lifestyles.

The sexual revolution, also termed sexual liberation, defied the moral codes of behavior strictly enforced on interpersonal relationships between men and women. Premarital sex was not a taboo anymore. Free-love rescripted family values. In a hugely consequential development, women were liberated from unintended pregnancies thanks to the invention of birth-control pills. Sexuality redefined heterosexual and homosexual relationships. A direct result was the coming out of the closet of gays and lesbians. The 1969 police raid at the Stonewall Inn, a gay bar in the Greenwich Village, New York, and the riots that followed accelerated the Gay Rights movement.

The feminist movement of the 1960s brought several women's issues to the forefront raising the consciousness of the nation. Betty Friedan's book *The Feminine Mystique* published in 1963 focused sharply on what she called "the problem that has no name"—the widespread unhappiness experienced by housewives in spite of the material comfort they enjoyed at home.[12] Refuting the images created and propagated by mainstream media as well as women's magazines, and collecting irrefutable sociological data, she invoked a disquieting imagery from the Holocaust and labelled suburban homes as a "comfortable concentration camp" for women. The doors that were forced open to women during this decade eventually led their entry into Ivy League universities, professional schools such as medicine and law, state and federal legislatures, and all the way into the Supreme Court. Only the White House remains closed. Perhaps not for long now that we have a female Vice-President just a heart-beat away from the Presidency.

The entertainment industry was not lagging behind in capturing the mood of the changing times. Music found its rebellious voice particularly in rock 'n roll. Among the American players, Bob Dylan expressed the mood of the decade with his lyrics that could "shake your windows / and rattle the walls." Many believe that his 1964 song and album titled *The Times They Are A-Changin'* became the anthem of the times.[13] Motown (short for Motor Town, referring to Detroit), pioneered by African Americans, released music records that combined elements of Rhythm and Blue. The 1969 Woodstock Music and Art Fair attracted nearly half a million young men and women, black and white. Two British groups—The Rolling Stones with its lead singer Mick Jagger, and the Beatles with the quartet of John Lennon, Paul McCartney, George Harrison, and Ringo Starr—rocked the Anglo-American music world.

In general, many historians believe that the 1960s opened up a relatively more tolerant America that respected a variety of perspectives and personal lifestyles. The events unfolded in such a quick succession that it undermined the credibility of the ruing elites. During the 1950s, after the horrors of World War II, American people were enjoying a relative period of peace and prosperity and, as a result, the country hardly anticipated the tumultuous events that marked the Sixties. As the young people were revolting and exploring their sense of Self, a segment of the ruling elites was unprepared to face the sociocultural transformation—one they did not initiate, one they did not lead, one they did not desire.

Conservative elites in particular were appalled at a relatively more liberal, more secular, more diverse America that was fast emerging. They abhorred the feminist movement and the Gay Rights movement both of which they thought would rip apart the carefully stitched social fabric of the conservative America of the Fifties and earlier. With regard to the Gay Rights movement, the 1960s turned out to be just a precursor. What was planted at that time and nurtured for more than half a century blossomed into a constitutionally-guaranteed law of the land, marking a huge victory for common people's defiance over religious and cultural elites.

SAME-SEX MARRIAGE

It was "like a boulder thrown into a pond, it will have public consequences for decades," so wrote columnists Michael Gerson and Peter Wehner. They were referring to the 2015 ruling by the U.S. Supreme Court that a right to same-sex marriage is guaranteed in the U.S. Constitution. The Justices cited the 14th Amendment to rule that all states must issue marriage licenses to same-sex couples, and also recognize same-sex unions legally performed in other states. The ruling, according to these two columnists who have both served Republican presidents as advisers, "placed gay rights firmly within the moral tradition of the civil rights movement."[14]

The momentous nature of the ruling can be understood if we recall the long-lasting antipathy directed towards Gay Rights movement. It came not only from individuals but also from four elitist institutions—religious, social, legal, and scientific. These four formidable sources were dubbed the "Four Horsemen of the Gay Apocalypse." These institutions considered homosexuality a sickness that must be remedied, a behavior that must be reformed, a menace that must be removed.

In recent times, most of the strident voices came from right-wing religious elites who saw themselves as custodians of religious and moral values that, according to them, should be the hallmark of the American identity, and therefore should never be compromised. Prominent among them were popular preachers Rev. Pat Robertson and Rev. Jerry Falwell Jr. They both used their well-oiled religious pulpits to spread anti-gay sentiments among their pious viewers and listeners by telling them that same-sex marriage violates the scripture. Any transgression must be resisted at all costs. Robertson argued that same-sex couples were bent upon destroying the very institution of marriage. He, however, predicted that gays will "die out because they won't reproduce."[15] Falwell reasoned that "the ultimate conclusion" to legalizing same-sex marriage would be legalizing polygamy, bestiality, and pedophilia. In an interview to the PBS program *Frontline*, he further argued that "We will see a breakdown of the family and family values if we decide to approve same-sex marriage, and if we decide to establish homosexuality as an acceptable alternative lifestyle with all the benefits that go with equating it with the heterosexual lifestyle. Everything that America is built on—basically the Judeo-Christian ethic—will be down the tubes."[16]

It is not just the evangelical elites who were opposed to same-sex marriage. Political elites too joined them. For a long time, the Republican Party has made it a point to include its opposition to same-sex marriage in its official Party Platform. The Party has for long been able to galvanize its supporters, or at least its evangelical base, on this issue. Three Gs—God, Gays, and Guns—were its staple campaign slogans, proudly proclaimed particularly in the South. In its 2016 Presidential election Party Platform, GOP included the following language: "Traditional marriage and family, based on marriage between one man and one woman, is the foundation for a free society and has for millennia been entrusted with rearing children and instilling cultural values. We condemn the Supreme Court's ruling in *United States v. Windsor*, which wrongly removed the ability of Congress to define marriage policy in federal law."[17] A dozen years earlier, running for his re-election in 2004, the then President George W. Bush went to the extent of endorsing a constitutional amendment explicitly banning gay marriage. Constitutional amendment, no less.

Even though the Democratic Party has been from time to time making politically correct statements supporting the LGBTQ+ community, its explicit support for same-sex marriage is nevertheless a recent development. Even as recent as in 1996, Democratic President Bill Clinton signed into law the *Defense of Marriage Act* (DOMA) that banned federal recognition of same-sex union. He went along with an overwhelming bipartisan support in the U.S. House of Representatives and also in the U.S. Senate. In 2008, as a Presidential candidate, Barack Obama opposed gay sex marriage stating rather categorically: "I believe that marriage is the union between a man and woman. Now, for me as a Christian—for me—for me as a Christian, it is also a sacred union. God's in the mix."[18]

Leaders from both the political parties, however, could not ignore the ground reality for long. They noticed that the attitudinal tides regarding same-sex marriage have been shifting and shifting fast. Surveys conducted by Pew Research Center confirmed the magnitude of that shift. A 2004 survey revealed that Americans opposed same-sex marriage by a margin of 60% to 31%. The percentage was dramatically reversed in just fifteen years. A

2019 survey showed that a majority of Americans (61%) supported same-sex marriage, while 31% opposed it. Among the Millennials, a massive 74% favored same-sex marriage while only 23% opposed it.[19]

Clearly, ordinary people defied the elites and the elites took notice. As the popular band played on, political elites started marching to the popular tune. In took only three years for President Obama to allow his oppositional thoughts to be "evolved." In 2011, he supported gay marriage saying, "Every single American—gay, straight, lesbian, bisexual, transgender—every single American deserves to be treated equally in the eyes of the law and in the eyes of our society. It's a pretty simple proposition."[20] In 2012, the Democratic Party Platform explicitly stated for the first time: "we support the right of all families to have equal respect, responsibilities, and protections under the law. We support marriage equality and support the movement to secure equal treatment under law for same-sex couples."[21] In 2013, the U.S. Supreme Court struck down the *Defense of Marriage Act*. In 2015, with the blessings of the Supreme Court, the right to marry a person of the same sex became the law of the land.

The cascading developments have compelled the Republican Party to show visible signs of softening. For the first time, the Party invited Silicon Valley entrepreneur Peter Thiel, a prominent gay, to be a speaker in its 2016 Presidential Convention. He condemned the culture war waged by conservative elites against gay marriage as fake culture. "I don't agree with every plank in our party's platform," he said, "but fake culture wars only distract us from our economic decline."[22] Bowing to the trend, a segment of the Republican legislators have been planning to introduce a bill in Congress that would ensure some LGBTQ+ protections at the federal level. By doing so, they hope, they will be able to ensure protection for religious liberty championed by their evangelical base. The bill envisions a compromise where, for instance, a secular company cannot fire a worker for being gay, but a religious agency could. Similarly, religious-minded small business owners can refuse services to gay customers, as reflected in the Supreme Court ruling about the so-called wedding cake case. The idea, they say, is to ensure fairness to all.

Following the evangelical community, the Mormon Church also softened its stand on the gay community. In 2019, the church abandoned its long-standing policy of labelling same-sex couples as "apostates," and started allowing their children to be baptized into the church. A church official announced: "These policy changes come after an extended period of counseling with our brethren in the Quorum of the Twelve Apostles and after fervent, united prayer to understand the will of the Lord on these matters."[23]

A similar softening tendency can be noticed in the entertainment sector as well, as seen in the Christian music industry, for instance. The case of Christian singer Jennifer Knapp illustrates what has been happening. In 1998, she stormed into the Christian music scene with *Kansas*, an album that sold more than half a million copies. She was well-liked by fans and critics alike. In the year 2000, she confirmed a long-standing rumor that she was gay. Even though a segment of evangelical community did despise her, she found acceptance in general, leading her to observe: "nearly every denomination you can think of has an active LGBT inclusive group in their midst, even if not everyone in that church agrees."[24] In spite of the noticeable softening, the shrill voice against gays has not fully subsided as demonstrated by the vocal opposition to the 2020 Democratic presidential candidate, Pete Buttigieg who is gay. According to the popular conservative radio host Rush Limbaugh, America will never elect as President "a gay guy kissing his husband."[25] Well, to start with, Buttigieg is now a cabinet secretary in the Biden administration.

In spite of sporadic dissenting voices, there is widespread support for same-sex marriage across age, gender, religious, and ethnic divisions, as Pew surveys clearly show. It did not come easy. As the author and civil rights campaigner Nathaniel Frank observed, "It took sustained, relentless work to change millions of minds about who gay people were, what marriage meant and ought to mean, and how and whether gay people fit into it. It required battling entrenched religious hierarchies and social and cultural contingents that devoted every last ounce of their energy to defeating the inclusion of gay people and families in the fabric of American society."[26]

In sum, the illustrative examples spread half a century apart demonstrate how, unlike the ruling elites, many pragmatic-minded citizens are not hopelessly blinded by ideological blinkers, nor do they hesitate to express their distrust of the elites whether they are from the Right or from the Left of the political spectrum. Technological changes and the easily accessible social media have empowered common people in terms of their interactive ability. They have effectively used them to reduce the hitherto unchallenged power and prestige of self-serving elites who can no longer manufacture and exploit public opinion to their full advantage. It is becoming increasingly clear that power elites are not the only history-makers. A significant segment of ordinary Americans do make history by collectively defying the entrenched political, religious, and cultural elites whenever they realize that the elites have gone beyond a basic sense of humanity.

In the final chapter, I shall delineate how the ability and willingness of ordinary citizens to defy ruling elites and to make use of their collective history-making capacity have enhanced their potential to shape and reshape American identity and to nudge the nation toward a "more perfect union."

Chapter 10

Has the Real America Arrived Yet?

Two eminent American personalities—one is a former President and another is a scholar—see around them and within them and share with us a fragment of their life.

Two voices. Two profiles. One theme.

The life of Barack Obama is familiar and is presented here in his own voice:

"I am the son of a black man from Kenya and a white woman from Kansas. I was raised with the help of a white grandfather who survived a Depression to serve in Patton's Army during World War II and a white grandmother who worked on a bomber assembly line at Fort Leavenworth while he was overseas. I've gone to some of the best schools in America and lived in one of the world's poorest nations. I am married to a black American who carries within her the blood of slaves and slave owners—an inheritance we pass on to our two precious daughters. I have brothers, sisters, nieces, nephews, uncles and cousins, of every race and every hue, scattered across three continents, and for as long as I live, I will never forget that in no other country on Earth is my story even possible."[1]

The life of Harvard scholar Robert D. Putnam is not so familiar and he presents it in the third person in his book co-authored with David E. Campbell, *American Grace: How Religion Divides and Unites Us*:

He and his sister were raised as observant Methodists in the 1950s. He converted to Judaism at marriage; he and his wife raised their two children as Jews. One child married a practicing Catholic, who has since left the church and is secular. The other child married someone with no clear religious affiliation but who subsequently converted to Judaism. Meanwhile, Putnam's sister married a Catholic and converted to Catholicism. Her three children became devout, active evangelicals of several different varieties. So this homogeneous Methodist household in mid-century America has given rise to an array of religious affiliations (and nonaffiliations) that reflects the full gamut of American religious diversity.

It would be hard to rouse anti-Jewish or anti-evangelical or anti-Catholic or anti-Methodist or even anti-secular fervor in this group.[2]

In their own way, each one marvels at America's diversity. For them and for many others, diversity is not an abstract concept. It is personal. It is familial. For them and for many others, diversity *is* the meaning of America; diversity *is* the spirit of America.

According to a Diversity Index released by the U.S. Census Bureau in 2020, "the chance that two people chosen at random will be from different racial or ethnic groups has increased to 61.1% in 2020 from 54.9% in 2010."[3] And, diversity keeps increasing.

One of the recent manifestations of such diversity can be seen in the ever-increasing rate of interfaith and interracial marriages. Consider the following numbers: interracial marriages in 1960 constituted only 0.4% of all U.S. marriages. It increased to 3.2% in 1980 and jumped to 8.4% in 2010.[4] In the year 2010 alone, 9% of whites, 17% of blacks, 26% of Hispanics, and 28% of Asians married someone from another race.[5] Consequently, the number of children growing up in interracial families has also soared. Clearly, the country has come a long way since the 1920s when, for instance, Virginia's *Racial Integrity Act* prohibited interracial marriage. Nearly half a century later, in 1967, the *Act* was overturned by the U.S. Supreme Court declaring that laws against interracial marriage were unconstitutional.

Interfaith marriages are also on the rise. A 2019 study by Pew Research Center shows that nearly 40% of Americans who got married since 2010 have a spouse who belongs to a different religion.[6] For many of them, a spouse with similar values is more important than a spouse with similar Faith. A growing proportion of them are keeping their separate faiths instead of converting to their spouse's religion. What about their children? Interestingly, "fully 48% of those whose parents had different religious identities now identify with their mother's religion, while 28% identify with their father's religion and 24% identify with neither."[7]

Given these numbers, it is no surprise that a majority of Americans say racial, religious, and ethnic diversity has made the country a better place to live. A Pew Research Center study found that "white, black and Hispanic adults are about equally likely to say it's good that the U.S. population is racially and ethnically mixed, and majorities across these groups say this has had a positive impact on U.S. culture." The study also found that "most Americans have at least some daily interaction with people who do not share their race or ethnicity, but relatively small shares say they have a lot of interaction."[8]

Although diversity is one of the undeniable aspects of American identity, there are people who are perturbed by it. As detailed in previous chapters, there is a segment of political, religious, and cultural elites and their ardent followers who have difficulty in coming to terms with the nation's pluralistic identity. When nation-builders aspire to be wall-builders, they may end up replacing a "shining city upon on a hill" with a walled fortress upon a hillock. By doing so, they downgrade America. They degrade Americans. Sadly, they are nostalgic about a monochromatic America that does not exist anymore and seem to be willing to restore it at any cost. Such an alarming sociopolitical development has prompted a concern that the country may even be at the brink of a civil war. Thomas L. Friedman, a well-known *New York Times* columnist recently lamented: "I began my journalism career covering a civil war in Lebanon. I never thought I'd end my career covering a civil war in America."[9]

Hyperbolic representations of America frequently presented by some of our politicians, pundits, pollsters, and other power elites are at complete variance with what ordinary Americans seem to believe and to behold. Those who look at the nation through ideologically tinted glasses see America as a country hopelessly divided along party lines, color lines, gender lines, and all other imaginable lines. Clinging to the false notion of identity politics they themselves created for their own vested interest, they portray each racial and ethnic group as a monolithic entity believing in the same thing and behaving in the same way. They persist with such stereotypes even though people have repeatedly proved them wrong.

Clearly, common Americans are not as naïve nor are they as polarized as they are portrayed. In the 2016 Presidential election, for instance, contrary to stereotypical expectations associated with identity politics, a surprising number of white women voted against Hillary Clinton. And, a notable number of Latinos and African Americans voted to elect Donald Trump. We are also led to believe that politics and religion are so mixed that devout people let their faith shape their political beliefs and civic duties. A 2019 survey conducted by Pew Research Center disputes that claim.[10] It found that nearly two-thirds (63%) of Americans categorically say that "churches and other houses of worship should keep out of political matters." It also found that three-quarters of the public (76%) believe that "churches should *not* come out in favor of one candidate over another during elections." Most Americans (66%) hold the view that religious and nonreligious people are equally trustworthy and reveal that they do interact with people of different faiths in their daily life.

Concerned by all the troubling reports in the media about how badly the country is polarized, the prestigious American Academy of Arts & Sciences recently appointed a commission consisting of educational administrators, scholars, journalists, and public intellectuals of differing ideological persuasions to assess the current practice of American democratic citizenship. The commission released its final report in July 2020 and the Academy published it with the title: *Our Common Purpose: Reinventing American Democracy for the 21st Century*. Taking the pulse of the country, the commissioners present a different, less troublesome, story.[11] They tell us that the depressing discourse on nationwide divisiveness we hear and read about almost on a daily basis "is not the whole story." While acknowledging the "nihilistic cynicism" thriving in the media, they share a reassuring story. "As we have traveled the United States in recent months and listened to Americans from many walks of life, we have heard disappointment and frustration, but even more, we heard a yearning to believe again in the American story, to feel connected to one another. We heard stories of surging participation and innovation, of communities working to build new connections across long-standing divides, and of individual citizens suddenly awakening to the potential of their democratic responsibilities."

The "nihilistic cynicism" that the report points out is indeed widespread. It thrives in the social media and propagated ad nauseam by ideologically-slanted TV as well as print media, giving us a distorted tale of two nations: red and blue. The ground reality is quite different.

In this regard, social psychologist Jonathan Haidt has made two astute remarks that are worth paying attention to. First, the two-party political system entrenched in our country results in a tribalistic tendency among certain segments of the population. "The worst number of political parties to have in a country is one," he says. "But the second worst number is two."[12] In a two-party system, people are forced to make a choice. Each group takes a moral high ground and subjugates the other group through confrontations focusing mainly on differences rather than similarities. If there are three or more political parties, there will be a motivation to compromise, form alliances, and work toward commonly agreed goals. In fact, a recent survey by Pew Research Center has found that there is no hardcore Right or hardcore Left. There are fifty shades of red and fifty shades of blue. "The gulf that separates Republicans and Democrats," say Pew researchers, "sometimes obscures the divisions and diversity of views that exist within both partisan coalitions—and the fact that many Americans do not fit easily into either one."[13]

Second, social media created by tech companies purely with profit motive amplifies and feeds on extremism. Extremists of the Right and the Left constitute only a fraction of the total population and people in the middle make up about a vast majority. But they are a silent majority. Haidt emphasizes the need to reform social media saying "right now 95 is not larger than 5, but once we get social media reform, I think 95 really can be larger than 5."

If we go beyond the ideologized general and social media, we will find that, as the Common Purpose report highlights, people can and do work together in order to achieve common goals despite their racial and religious, political, and personal differences. They do so by developing mutual trust and by engaging in meaningful interaction which have the capacity to create and maximize intergroup learning opportunities for mutual benefit.

LEARNING *ABOUT* AND *FROM* OTHERS

In the current social media environment which attracts groups of individuals who "like" each other, our prejudices and stereotypes can be easily reinforced. However, when we witness and participate in social interaction or when we engage in serious relationships, we are presented with close encounters that have the potential to help us culturally grow. Such intercultural encounters compel us to rethink critically about ourselves and about others. Critical cultural encounters can be unsettling in the beginning but they can eventually help us with our meaningful cultural growth.

A prerequisite for any meaningful cultural growth is developing an open mind that acknowledges that there is something everybody can learn from others. By gaining greater knowledge of how others think and act, we can become less certain of the knowledge and skills we think we have, which is always the first step toward greater humility and better understanding. As I wrote in a newspaper op-ed more than two decades ago, "we may never know the true measure of our strengths unless we also know the true measure of our weaknesses. And we can know this only if we have an open mind and are willing to learn *about* and *from* others."[14]

The heart of the matter here is a readiness to learn *from* others, not merely *about* them. We learn *about* others when we get to know what they do. We learn *from* others when we delve deeper into why they do what they do. By learning *about* others, we may gain valuable cultural information but it is only learning *from* others that can lead us to valued cultural transformation. Without understanding the Other, our understanding of our Self will be limited and limiting.

In a pluralistic society, we can all enrich our lives if we are conscious of "the gift of one another's presence."[15] Both majority and minority communities stand to gain if they, as the Jewish theologian Jonathan Sacks advices, "learn the art of conversation, from which truth emerges not, as in Socratic dialogues, by the refutation of falsehood but from the presence of others who think, act, and interpret reality in ways radically different from our own."[16] Such a human-centered conversation involving people who are radically different from us will enable us not fall easy prey to sickening stereotypes. To make that happen, we do not actually need any formal, institutionalized education. All we need to do is to keep our eyes, ears, and mind open allowing natural sociocultural osmosis to do its job.

SOCIOCULTURAL OSMOSIS

"I was once at a Muslim wedding in a Christian church on Staten Island in New York, and everybody was dancing to salsa music," says journalist Anand Giridharadas in an interview.[17] Muslim wedding. Christian church. Salsa music. What is happening is not a mystery. In a pluralistic society, no community can live for long in its own cocoon and be completely insulated and isolated from others. As a result, what is bound to happen, especially in a land of immigrants, is sociocultural osmosis in which people, sooner or later, absorb some of the sociocultural practices of others they come into contact with—in schools, in workplaces, or in other contact zones that offer opportunities for sustained social interaction. The permeability of such an osmotic flow is made possible because it comes largely from within, and not enforced from without. This kind of a natural cultural flow, as opposed to forced cultural assimilation, results in desirable and durable solidarity among people of various religions, cultures, and languages. Little do cultural warriors realize that Americans have all along been cultural straddlers happily crossing borders to make sociocultural accommodations in their personal life. Nothing testifies to that more than the rapidly increasing rate of interfaith and intercultural marriages highlighted above.

Another noticeable feature of American cultural osmosis relates to everyday habits—food habits. What we eat is very much influenced by our sociocultural and religious upbringing right from the early stages of our life. Our likes and dislikes for specific food items develop over time and become an integral part of our fairly well-established individual and social identity. And yet, presented with a bewildering array of ethnic food items, many Americans do not hesitate to transcend the boundaries of ethnic culinary practices. Tortilla chips are challenging the dominance of potato chips. Salsa ketchup tests the endurance of Heinz ketchup. Stout is no longer the favorite beer of the Irish alone. Americans are no less patriotic because they gobble French Fries and guzzle French wines. In fact, an ill-conceived attempt by a jingoistic Congressman to rename French Fries as Freedom Fries became a veritable laughingstock.

Americans are also willing to transform ethnic food with the flavors drawn from their homelands. A recent report from *Washington Post* illustrates how, on Thanksgiving days, certain immigrant families convert the American Thanksgiving turkey into Italian Citrus turkey, Chinese Peking-style turkey, West-African tamarind and honey-glazed turkey, Lebanese-style Roast turkey with spicy rice stuffing, Indian tandoori turkey with garam masala, and more.[18] In addition, Americans throng to Chinese, Japanese, Indian, Italian, Mexican, and other ethnic restaurants almost on a regular basis.

The spontaneous sociocultural osmosis that has been quietly taking place is a repudiation of a two century-old attempt by nativists and their contemporary sympathizers to confine and to squeeze American identity inside a melting pot that they fabricated. It is a repudiation of their attempt to compel all the immigrants to adopt the behaviors, values, beliefs, and lifestyles of their community, and get assimilated into it. It is a repudiation of their attempt to mold all Americans in their own image. It is a repudiation of their attempt to urge all Americans to follow their version of American Dream.

There are, however, millions of Americans who wonder why they cannot have their own American Dream without abandoning their religious, cultural, and linguistic heritage. They believe that as law-abiding, tax-paying, and hard-working citizens carrying out their civic and other duties to the best of their abilities, they too should have the opportunity to realize their own dreams following their own path. They believe, as a TV commercial declares, there is no one American Dream; there are 330 million American Dreams.

Many of them, however, have come to the sad realization that all is not well with all that is American. They realize that they still face deep-rooted, systemic discriminations that keep their American Dream a distant destination. They realize that America's imperfection is still holding them back—imperfections that can be traced all the way back to the founding days of the republic.

IMPERFECTION WOVEN INTO
THE AMERICAN FABRIC

The Founding Fathers, for all their visionary zeal, turned a blind eye to, and therefore perpetuated, racial, gender, and other types of discriminations which plague us even today. Chiefly, they did not think it fit to give voting rights to a sizable segment of the population including women, slaves, and those blacks who were free at that time. As relentless advocates of the democratic ethos of "we the people" and of the humanistic tenet of "all men are created equal," they failed to live up to their own core beliefs, thereby exposing themselves to justifiable reproach that they were at best noble hypocrites. As a historical archive shows,[19] the vast majority—forty out of sixty-five—of signers of the Declaration of Independence owned slaves. Ten of the first twelve presidents owned slaves. Four of the widely admired presidents—Washington, Jefferson, Madison, and Monroe—continued to own slaves even *during* their presidencies. The much-praised Emancipation Declaration issued in 1863 by

Abraham Lincoln, contrary to common belief, did not really emancipate all the slaves; it was restricted to slaves in certain rebellious states, and it was also limited in scope.

The Founders were not, however, blind to the fact that they had created an imperfect nation. That is why they left it to subsequent generations of Americans to strive toward a "more perfect union." To be fair, subsequent generations of Americans have indeed taken many historical steps to meet the challenging task. Their continual attempts can only be described as three steps forward and two steps back.

It is obvious that the country has made steady but incremental progress. The march forward is typified in remarkable achievements including but not limited to the advancement of women's suffrage, the adoption of Civil Rights, the ending of school segregation, the decriminalization of interracial marriage, and the declaration of same-sex marriage as constitutional. We can certainly take solace in the fact that the country elected a black man—that too, someone named Barack Hussein Obama—as President, twice. It offers the hope that when the right leader arrives at the right time with the right message, the country can transcend some of its historical racial and religious imperfections.

And yet, the country still has a long way to go. Sadly, "justice for all" remains a mission yet to be accomplished, particularly in terms of gender and of racial equality. The Equal Rights Amendment that aims at banning all forms of discrimination based on gender is yet to be ratified. Recent despicable incidents the country witnessed in places such as Ferguson, Charlottesville, and Minneapolis are a stark reminder that deep-rooted race-based animosity remains an intractable problem. As political scientist Ashley Jardina recently remarked, "the nation today remains marked by an enduring racial hierarchy, one in which whites are at the top, blacks are at the bottom, and other racial and ethnic groups fall somewhere in between."[20] Clearly, the union is far from perfect.

The Founders may have surmised that perfecting the union entails a long journey. A strenuous journey. A never-ending journey. Nevertheless, it is a journey every generation is destined to undertake. A major challenge facing each generation is how to keep the eyes on the prized destination of equality and justice visualized by the Founders but, unlike them, carry all the travelers together regardless of their race, class, and gender, and harmoniously pave a new credible path to get there.

Having laid out a vision for the future, the Founders seem to have taken their own as well as America's earthly imperfections stoically. They perhaps saw what the Victorian poet Robert Browning saw in a different context and at a different time: "On the earth the broken arcs; in the heaven a perfect round."[21]

BROKEN ARCS

Many are the broken arcs that are scattered all over the American historical and sociopolitical landscape. The very birth of the nation was marked by what has been called "a birth defect"[22] or "original sin"[23]—slavery, with its attendant racial discord continuing to afflict the nation even today. From the early days of the republic, Native Americans and African Americans were seen as stains on American identity. The same attitude was extended to certain other immigrant communities from time to time. In the 1790s, Alien and Sedition Acts were passed to curtail the process of naturalization, making it difficult for immigrants to become citizens. In the 1850s, the Know-Nothing Party campaigned against Irish Catholics. In the 1880s, the Chinese faced the exclusion act. In the 1920s, legislative measures regulated immigration based on nationalities. In the 1940s, Japanese Americans were sent to internment camps. In the twenty-first century, the same bigoted sentiment continues in some quarters against certain segments of the society, this time blessed by certain leaders in high places. All these were and are done and explained largely in the name of preserving and protecting America's core identity.

We should never forget these and other broken arcs because they offer valuable lessons for every generation of Americans. However, a heap of broken arcs can present only a heap of distorted images. If we manage to see beyond them, as we must, we see a country that is a beacon, radiating the lights of freedom for all those "yearning to breathe free." We see a country that is a magnet, attracting academic, artistic, and scientific talents from all over the world. We see a country that is a powerhouse, sheltering technological prowess, economic vigor, and political clout. We see a country that is a laboratory, experimenting with disruptive innovations aimed at relentless renewal.

This glorious picture of the country gets tarnished now and then by those who wear ideological blinkers and never fail to see an illusory threat to America emanating from minority communities including immigrants. They can hardly notice that their myopic vision impedes the country's march toward a more perfect union. Some of them who actually admire President Ronald Reagan forget what he said in the last speech he gave as President: "Other countries may seek to compete with us, but in one vital area, as a beacon of freedom and opportunity that draws the people of the world, no country on earth comes close. This, I believe, is one of the most important sources of America's greatness. We lead the world because, unique among nations, we draw our people, our strength, from every country and every corner of the world, and by doing so, we continuously renew and enrich our nation."[24] Without a proper understanding of what this country is all about, they try to define and divide America in terms of racial and religious identity proclaiming that they are actually upholding the much-cherished American Spirit. In reality, they are only diminishing it.

Most Americans all over the country are living the American Spirit on a daily basis, and do not get distracted by a handful of power-hungry politicians and ideology-driven pundits. They allow themselves to be entertained by them but refuse to be entrapped by them. They quietly go about their daily life. They get up early in the morning. Get ready for the day's labor. If they have kids, they ready their kids for the day. Drive or walk them to school. Come back, do their daily chores or go to work. Pick up their kids in the evening. Help them with their homework if they can. Have dinner. Watch their favorite shows. Go to bed. During week-ends, they do their grocery, mow their lawns, water their plants, take a long walk, play golf, or go to a ballpark to watch their local team play. Occasionally, they take a well-deserved family vacation to get away from it all. On national commemorative days and during times of war, they wave their Stars and Stripes with unflinching patriotic fervor. This is how American life unfolds in most cities and towns. This is the routine, although there are exceptions. The practice of everyday life of ordinary citizens leaves them with no time or inclination for divisive politicking, something they leave to their ideologically-skewed politicians and pundits.

The divisive politics have not prevented the country's slow walk toward a more perfect union. Nothing bears greater witness to it than the realm of religion. Minority communities no longer experience the kind of religious discrimination witnessed in eighteenth- or nineteenth-century America. Consider, for instance, the religious composition of the appointed U.S. Supreme Court and the elected U.S. Congress. At present, of the nine judges, six are Catholics, two are Protestants and one is Jew. Chief Justice John Roberts is the very first Catholic to occupy that high office in the history of this country. In a country where a majority of the population is Protestant, in a country that was labelled a Protestant nation by some, there are only two Protestants on the highest court right now.[25] Nobody demurs. Not even the right-wing ideologues. Such a scenario would have been unthinkable just a few decades ago.

The demographics of the current 118th Congress also reflects the expanding diversity of the nation. According to Pew Research Center (dated January 3, 2023), the total number of lawmakers that identify as something other than white is the highest in the nation's history. More specifically, of one hundred members of the Senate, eighty-eight identify as white, six as Hispanic, three as black, two as Asian American, one as American Indian and Alaska Native. Of 434 members of the House of Representatives (as of January 3, 2023), 313 identify as white, fifty-three as black, forty-six as Hispanic, fourteen as Asian American, four as American Indian, and four as multiracial. There are also a record number of 153 women in both the House of Representatives and the Senate.[26]

Recently, the country elected and re-elected an African American as President, and we now have a biracial woman as our Vice-President.

Clearly, in all the three branches of government—the Executive, the Legislature, and the Judiciary—members of racial/ethnic minorities are slowly making their presence felt, and their voices heard.

SEEING AROUND AND WITHIN US

That a majority of the American people feel comfortable with, and appreciate the value of, the country's sociocultural diversity was highlighted in a 2016 international survey conducted by Pew Research Center.[27] Fifty eight percent of the U.S. respondents said increasing diversity makes the country a better place to live; only 7% said it makes the United States a worse place. By contrast, Europeans had a negative view of diversity: only 10% in Greece, 18% in Italy, 33% in Britain, and 36% in Sweden thought diversity improved their country.

It is clear that for a minority of Americans difference disturbs; for many others, difference delights. It is the multiracial, multiethnic crowd that joined together to stage prolonged nationwide protests in the wake of the 2020 Minneapolis police action, showing admirable solidarity and raising the nation's conscience. "In our finest hours," historian Jon Meacham writes, "the soul of the country manifests itself in an inclination to open our arms rather than to clench our fists; to look out rather than to turn inward; to accept rather than to reject. In so doing, America has grown even stronger, confident that the choice of light over dark is the means by which we pursue progress."[28]

If some of us do not seem to notice the streak of light piercing through the clouds of darkness, would it be possible, as the former Czech President and playwright Václav Havel said in a different context, that the bright future "has been here for a long time already, and only our own blindness and weakness has prevented us from seeing it around us and within us, and kept us from developing it?"[29]

Nearly two hundred and fifty independent years may appear to be a long time in the life of an individual, but not that of a nation, particularly when we realize that there are countries in the world that have been around for millennia. America is still young. Still experimenting. Still evolving. Therefore, I may be pardoned for twisting more than a century-old statement of Israel Zangwill's protagonist in his historic play, *The Melting Pot* ("the real

American has not yet arrived. He is only in the Crucible"[30]) to suggest that every successive generation of Americans should raise and ponder over the question:

Has the real America arrived yet?

Notes

PREFACE

1. W. E. B. Du Bois, *The Souls of Black Folk: Essays and Sketches* (Chicago: A. C. McClurg, 1903), vii.
2. Francis Fukuyama, *Identity: The Demand for Dignity and the Politics of Resentment* (New York: Farrar, Straus, & Giroux, 2018), xv.
3. In this book, following the common usage in the United States and in most parts of the world, I use the term "America" to refer to the United States of America, and the term "Americans" to refer to the citizens of the United States of America. We must, however, remember that geographically speaking, the term "Americas" includes references to the vast landmass covering North America, Central America, and South America as well.
4. Clifford Geertz, *The Interpretation of Cultures* (New York: Basis Books, 2000), 5.

CHAPTER 1

1. U.S. Federal Trade Commission, "IdentityTheft.gov," n.d., OMB CONTROL#: 3084–016, https://www.identitytheft.gov/#/ (accessed January 1, 2024).
2. Philip Gleason, "Identifying Identity: A Semantic History." *Journal of American History* 69, no. 4 (1983): 918, https://doi.org/10.2307/1901196.
3. Anthony Elliott, "Introduction." In *Self-Identity and Everyday Life*, by Harvie Ferguson (London: Routledge, 2009), viii. More recently, philosopher Kwame Anthony Appiah, *The Lies That Bind Us: Rethinking Identity* (New York: Liveright Publishing, 2018); and political scientist Francis Fukuyama, *Identity: The Demand for Dignity and the Politics of Resentment* (New York: Farrar, Straus, & Giroux, 2018), have tried to tackle the concept of identity.
4. In discussing *Self* in the context of identity, some scholars use upper case, some use lower case, and some others use both interchangeably. Throughout this book, I will consistently use *Self* with a capital "S" to differentiate it from the common use of *self* in expressions such as myself, yourself, self-conscious, etc.

5. Sarvepalli Radhakrishnan, *The Hindu View of Life* (New York: Macmillan, 1927), 25.

6. Eric Erikson, *Identity: Youth and Crisis* (New York: W.W. Norton, 1968), 314.

7. Charles Taylor, *Sources of the Self: The Making of the Modern Identity* (Cambridge, MA: Harvard University Press, 1989), 27.

8. Étienne Balibar, *Identity and Difference: John Locke & the Invention of Consciousness* (London: Verso, 1998; 2013), xxviii.

9. Amin Maalouf, *On Identity* (London: Harvill Press, 2000), 10.

10. In academic literature, one comes across a bewildering array of terminologies to refer to different periods: ancient, premodern, medieval, early modern, modern, late modern, postmodern, post-postmodern, to name a few. Scholars across and within disciplines also differ on the exact dates of these periods, with overlapping variations. For the purpose of this book, I rely mostly (but not entirely) on authors such as Charles Taylor, *Sources of the Self*; Anthony Giddens, *Modernity and Self-identity: Self and Society in the Late Modern Age* (London: Polity, 1991); and Harvie Ferguson, *Self-Identity and Everyday Life* (New York: Routledge, 2009). I will consistently use the terms *premodern* (to refer to the period prior to mid-seventeenth century), *modern* (from mid-seventeenth to late twentieth century), and *postmodern* (from late twentieth onward, a period that is now being impacted by the on-going processes of globalization, digitalization, etc.). Part of the description in this chapter is drawn from the above authors and also drawn and updated from my book, B. Kumaravadivelu, *Cultural Globalization and Language Education* (New Haven, CT: Yale University Press, 2008), chap. 8.

11. Ferguson, *Self-Identity*, 163.

12. Aleksandra Sandstrom, "Half of All Church Fires in the Past 20 Years Were Arsons," *Pew Research Center*, October 26, 2015, http://www.pewresearch.org/fact -tank/2015/10/26/half-of-all-church-fires-in-past-20-years-were-arsons/ (accessed July 19, 2017).

13. See a summary by non-profit organization, Fraidy Reiss, "Unchained Holds Historic Chain-In to End Forced Marriage," *Unchained At Last*, April 15, 2015, https: //www.unchainedatlast.org/3142015-%E2%80%A2-unchained-holds-historic-chain -in-to-end-forced-marriage/ (accessed January 1, 2024); and also an essay by Anjali Tsui, Dan Nolan, and Chris Amico, "Child Marriage in America: By the Numbers," *PBS: Frontline*, July 6, 2017, https://www.pbs.org/wgbh/frontline/article/married -young-the-fight-over-child-marriage-in-america/ (accessed January 1, 2024).

14. Two popular documentaries: Josh Alexander, *Southern Rites*, directed by Gilliam Laub (Montgomery County, GA: HBO Documentary, 2015); and Paul Saltzman, *Prom Night in Mississippi*, directed by Paul Saltzman (Charleston, MS: HBO: Return to Mississippi Productions, 2000); vividly portray the causes and consequences of some of these racially segregated proms.

15. A well-known example is Augusta National Golf Club in Georgia.

16. Ferguson provides a lucid description of "Selfless" premodern identity in his book (*Self-Identity*, 48–55).

17. Ferguson, *Self-Identity*, 55.

18. C. Taylor, *Sources of the Self*, 27.

19. Maalouf, *Identity*, 22.

20. David A. Hollinger, "Identity in the United States," in *Keywords: Identity*, ed. Mahmood Mamdani (New York: Other Press, 2004), 44.

21. The U.S. Census 2020 questionnaire provides sub-categories within these five major ones, see OBM NO. 0607–1006, https://www2.census.gov/programs -surveys/decennial/2020/technical-documentation/questionnaires-and-instructions/ questionnaires/2020-informational-questionnaire-english_DI-Q1.pdf (accessed January 1, 2024). Bonnie Tsui notes "It wasn't until 2000 that the Census Bureau started letting people choose more than one race category to describe themselves, and it still recognizes only five standard racial categories" in "Choose Your Own Identity," *New York Times*, December 14, 2015, https://www.nytimes.com/2015/12/14/magazine/ choose-your-own-identity.html (accessed January 1, 2024).

22. Amartya Sen, *Identity and Violence: The Illusion of Destiny* (New York: Penguin Books, 2006), 26. Terms such as Asian Americans, Hispanic Americans are all uniquely American inventions fabricated purely for bureaucratic purposes of clustering various ethnic groups. The term Asian American is reported to have been invented during the 1960s to replace a derogatory term "oriental" widely used by American scholars. This umbrella term makes no sense because it is meant to cover a bewildering diversity of people who come from a vast stretch of real estate, differing religiously, culturally, linguistically, and politically. There is an interesting discussion on this issue in Eric Liu's book, *The Accidental Asian: Notes of a Native Speaker* (New York: Vintage Books, 1998).

23. Kareem Abdul-Jabbar, "Let Rachel Dolezal Be as Black as She Wants to Be," *Time*, June 16, 2015, https://time.com/3921404/rachel-dolezal-naacp-race-kareem -abdul-jabbar/ (accessed January 16, 2024).

24. Bobby Jindal quoted in a speech at the Henry Jackson Society (*HJS*), January 16, 2015, http://henryjacksonsociety.org/2015/01/19/a-lecture-by-governor-bobby -jindal-3/ (accessed July 14, 2017).

25. Casey Egan, "Congressman Joe Crowley Defends Irish-American and Other Hyphenated Americans," *Irish Central*, January 30, 2015, http://www.irishcentral .com/news/politics/congressman-joe-crowley-defends-irish-americans-and-other -hyphenated-americans (accessed December 5, 2028).

26. Ashok Malik, "Why India Hates Bobby McJindal," *Deccan Chronicle*, June 28, 2015, http://www.deccanchronicle.com/150628/commentary-columnists/article/why -india-hates-bobby-mcjindal (accessed July 14, 2017).

27. Shashi Tharoor, "Should We Be Proud of Bobby Jindal?" *Times of India*, October 28, 2007, http://timesofindia.indiatimes.com/shashi-tharoor/shashi-on-sunday/ Should-we-be-proud-of-Bobby-Jindal/articleshow/2495846.cms (accessed June 28, 2017).

28. Garance Franke-Ruta, "Is Elizabeth Warren Native American or What?" *Atlantic*, May 12, 2012, https://www.theatlantic.com/politics/archive/2012/05/is-elizabeth -warren-native-american-or-what/257415/ (accessed November 14, 2017).

29. Fred Vogelstein, "The Wired Interview: Facebook's Mark Zuckerberg," *Wired*, June 29, 2009, https://www.wired.com/2009/06/mark-zuckerberg-speaks/ (accessed January 1, 2017).

30. Brooke Hauser, *The New Kids: Big Dreams and Brave Journeys at a High School for Immigrant Teens* (New York: Free Press, 2011), 242.

CHAPTER 2

1. Parag Khanna, *Connectography: Mapping the Future of Global Civilization* (New York: Random House, 2016), 19–20.

2. Jacob Pramuk, "At Boeing, Trump Touts American Manufacturing, Says He's Looking at 'Big' F-18 Fighter Order," *CNBC*, February 17, 2017, https://www.cnbc .com/2017/02/17/trump-heads-to-boeing-facility-to-talk-jobs.html (accessed on June 5, 2022).

3. Soo Kim, "Is the Dreamliner Worth the Hype? Here's 10 Reasons Why It Might Just Be," *Telegraph*, March 28, 2018, https://www.telegraph.co.uk/travel/news/ boeing-787-10-dreamliner-features/ (accessed June 5, 2022).

4. Shannon K. O'Neil, "How to Pandemic-Proof Globalization: Redundancy, Not Reshoring, Is the Key to Supply Chain Security," *Foreign Affairs*, April 1, 2020, https: //www.foreignaffairs.com/articles/2020-04-01/how-pandemic-proof-globalization (accessed May 28, 2021).

5. Khanna, *Connectography*, 148–49.

6. Achim Berg, Harsh Chhaparia, Sadkia Hedrich, and Karl-Hendrik Magus, "What's Next for Bangladesh's Garment Industry, After a Decade of Growth?" *McKinsey & Company*, March 25, 2021, https://www.mckinsey.com/industries/retail /our-insights/whats-next-for-bangladeshs-garment-industry-after-a-decade-of-growth (accessed March 26, 2021).

7. Ian Bremmer, The End of the Free Market: Who Wins the War Between States and Corporations? (New York: Portfolio, 2010).

8. Richard Haass, "How a World Order Ends: And What comes in Its Wake," *Foreign Affairs*, December 11, 2018, updated January/February 2019, https://www .foreignaffairs.com/articles/2018-12-11/how-world-order-ends? (accessed February 13, 2019).

9. Cory Bennett and Bryan Bender, "How China Acquires 'the Crown Jewels' of U.S. Technology," *Politico*, May 22, 2018, https://www.politico.com/story/2018/05 /22/china-us-tech-companies-cfius-572413 (accessed January 10, 2019).

10. Graham Allison, *Destined for War: Can America and China Escape Thucydides's Trap?* (New York: Houghton Mifflin Harcourt, 2017), 216.

11. Parag Khanna, "These 25 Companies Are More Powerful Than Many Countries," *Foreign Policy*, March 15, 2016, http://foreignpolicy.com/2016/03/15/these-25 -companies-are-more-powerful-than-many-countries-multinational-corporate-wealth -power/ (accessed March 10, 2017).

12. Khanna, "These 25 Companies."

13. Isobel Asher Hamilton, "Interview with Alphabet Chairman John Hennessy," *Business Insider*, November 21, 2018, https://www.businessinsider.com/alphabet -john-hennessy-google-returning-to-china-2018-11 (accessed January 10, 2020).

14. Francis Fukuyama, *Identity: The Demand for Dignity and the Politics of Resentment* (New York: Farrar, Straus, & Giroux, 2018), 137.

15. Pnina Werbner, "Introduction: The Dialectics of Cultural Diversity," in *Debating Cultural Hybridity: Multicultural Identities and the Politics of Anti-Racism*, ed. Pnina Werbner and Tariq Modood (London: Zed Books, 1997), 11–12.

16. Martin Placek, "Motor Vehicle Production of the United States and Worldwide from 1999 to 2021," *Statista*, 2022, last updated December 8, 2023, https://www.statista.com/statistics/198488/us-and-global-motor-vehicle-production-since-1999/ (accessed May 14, 2022).

17. Placek, "Motor Vehicle Production."

18. B. J. Bethel, "I Sent My Dad's Manufacturing Job Overseas. My Own Ended Not Long After," *Washington Post*, November 28, 2018, https://www.washingtonpost.com/outlook/2018/11/28/i-sent-my-dads-manufacturing-job-overseas-my-own-followed-not-long-after/? (accessed October 14, 2019).

19. Jonah Hall, "Manufacturing Jobs, Identity and Public Sympathy," *Medium*, March 8, 2017, https://medium.com/@darkoindex/manufacturing-jobs-identity-and-public-sympathy-15b737d22f5 (accessed June 23, 2018).

20. John B. Judis, "It's the Economy, Stupid," *Washington Post*, November 29, 2018, https://www.washingtonpost.com/news/magazine/wp/2018/11/29/feature/the-key-to-understanding-americas-red-blue-split-isnt-ideology-or-culture-its-economics/? (accessed December 19, 2019).

21. Bremmer, End of the Free Market, 20.

22. Bremmer, End of the Free Market, 20.

23. Dani Rodrik, "The Trouble with Globalization," *Milken Institute Review*, October 20, 2017, https://www.milkenreview.org/articles/the-trouble-with-globalization (accessed January 20, 2024).

24. See Andrés Ortega, "The Deglobalization Virus?" *Globalist*, March 18, 2020, https://www.theglobalist.com/coronavirus-covid19-pandemic-globalization-deglobalization-globalism/ (accessed January 20, 2024).

25. O'Neil, "How to Pandemic-Proof Globalization."

26. There are many overlapping definitions of *digitization*, and *digitalization*, and sometimes these terms are used interchangeably. The simple definition I have used here is attributed to J. Scott Brennen and Daniel Kreiss of the University of North Carolina School of Media and Journalism. See J. Scott Brennen and Daniel Kreiss, "Digitalization," *Whiley Online Library*, October 23, 2016, https://onlinelibrary.wiley.com/doi/10.1002/9781118766804.wbiect111 (accessed February 22, 2024).

27. James Manyika and Susan Lund, "Globalization for the Little Guy," *McKinsey & Company*, January 1, 2016, https://www.mckinsey.com/business-functions/globalization-for-the-little-guy (accessed January 23, 2017).

28. Manyika and Lund, "Globalization for the Little Guy."

29. Khanna, *Connectography*, 56.

30. Richard Rodríguez, *Brown: The Last Discovery of America* (New York and London: Penguin, 2002), 200.

31. Alexis de Tocqueville, *Democracy in America* (1835) (New York: Generic, 2003), 506.

32. Richard Jenkins, *Social Identity* (New York: Routledge, 2004), 5; emphasis in the original.

33. Robert [R. D.] Putnam, *Bowling Alone: The Collapse and Revival of American Community* (New York: Simon and Schuster, 2000), 19.

34. Anthony Giddens, *Modernity and Self-Identity: Self and Society in the Late Modern Age* (London: Polity, 1991), 32.

35. C. Waite, *The Digital Evolution of an American Identity* (New York: Routledge, 2013), 3.

36. Waite, *Digital Evolution*, 13.

37. Waite, *Digital Evolution*, 5.

CHAPTER 3

1. Lewis H. Lapham, *Age of Folly: America Abandons Its Democracy* (New York: Verso, 2016), 30.

2. The U.S. Citizenship and Immigration Services' website (https://www.uscis .gov/), reiterates that "We are a nation bound not by race or religion, but by the shared values of freedom, liberty, and equality." The user-friendly website explains the process of naturalization, step by step. If you are eligible, you submit a form. You take the English language test that expects you to know nothing more than basic functional English. You attend an interview in which you are asked about you, including whether you have ever been a communist in your previous avatar. You are then invited to a naturalization ceremony held normally in a federal court presided over by a federal judge. You raise your right hand in front of the judge and take the Oath of Allegiance to "the flag of the United States and the republic for which it stands." You are now an American citizen.

3. Philip Gleason, "American Identity and Americanization," in *Harvard Encyclopedia of American Ethnic Groups*, ed. Stephan Thernstrom, 31–32, 56–57 (Cambridge, Mass.: Belknap Press, 1980), 32.

4. David McCullough, *The American Spirit: Who We Are and What We Stand For* (New York: Simon & Schuster, 2017), 28; emphasis in the original.

5. Michael Walzer, *What It Means to Be an American* (New York: Marsilio, 1992), 26.

6. Anne-Marie Slaughter, *The Idea That Is America: Keeping Faith With our Values in a Dangerous World* (New York: Basic Books, 2007), 1–2.

7. Atlantic Monthly Editors, "What is 'the American Idea'?" *Atlantic Monthly*, January/February 2006, https://www.penguinrandomhouse.ca/books/182828/the -american-idea-by-robert-vare/9780307481405 (accessed October 16, 2007).

8. Andrew L. Seidel, *The Founding Myth: Why Christian Nationalism Is Un-American* (New York: Sterling, 2019).

9. Patrick J. Buchanan, "Is not the endless airing of unproven allegations inherently un-American?" (blog, dated February 17, 2018), http://www.wnd.com/2017/05 /comey-the-saturday-night-massacre/ (accessed March 19, 2018).

10. George Lewis, "An Un-American Introduction," *Journal of American Studies* 47, no. 4 (2013): 871–79, https://www.jstor.org/stable/i24482947 (accessed January 31, 2024).

11. New World Encyclopedia Contributors, "House Un-American Activities Committee," *New World Encyclopedia*, last updated January 14, 2018, ID: 1008788, https://www.newworldencyclopedia.org/entry/House_Un-American_Activities_Committee (accessed July 18, 2021).

12. Written in the *New Yorker* magazine in 1948, cited in William Safire, *Safire's Political Dictionary* (Oxford: Oxford University Press, 2008), 764.

13. Anne Applebaum, "Trump's Bizarre and Un-American Visit to Saudi Arabia," *Washington Post*, May 21, 2017, https://www.washingtonpost.com/news/global-opinions/wp/2017/05/21/trumps-bizarre-and-un-american-visit-to-saudi-arabia/ (accessed September 9, 2021).

14. Senator Bob Corker quoted in, Nicole Gaouette, Manu Raju, and Veronica Stracqualursi, "Khashoggi Was Murdered, Saudis Did It, Leading Republican Says," *CNN*, October 11, 2018, https://www.cnn.com/2018/10/11/politics/trump-saudi-arabia-journalist-corker/index.html (accessed February 12, 2019).

15. Robert Kuttner, "Phillip Roth's 'The Plot Against America' Is Fast Becoming Reality," *Huffpost*, January 15, 2017, updated January 16, 2018, https://www.huffpost.com/entry/phillip-roths-the-plot-ag_b_14190564 (accessed February 24, 2018).

16. Francis Fukuyama, "Trump's a Dictator? He Can't Even Repeal Obamacare," *Politico*, March 27, 2017, http://www.politico.com/magazine/story/2017/03/trumps-a-dictator-he-cant-even-repeal-obamacare-214958 (accessed March 27, 2017).

17. Politico Magazine, Elizabeth F. Ralph, and Contributors, "Was 2017 the Craziest Year in U.S. Political History?" *Politico*, December 29, 2017, https://www.politico.com/magazine/story/2017/12/29/was-2017-the-craziest-year-in-us-political-history-216119 (accessed March 14, 2018).

18. The term "creed" is generally used to refer to religious beliefs and precepts. It is primarily in that sense that, for instance, Kwame Anthony Appiah uses in his book on identity, *The Lies That Bind Us: Rethinking Identity* (New York: Liveright Publishing, 2018). Here, I use the term in a broader sense, as formulated by our Founding Fathers, especially Thomas Jefferson. American Creed, in particular, has been a fascinating subject of thoughtful discussion by many authorities over the centuries. They include eighteenth-century writer Hector St. John de Crèvecœur, nineteenth-century diplomat Alexis de Tocqueville, twentieth-century historian Arthur Schlesinger Jr., and twenty-first-century political scientist Samuel Huntington. For a more recent and comprehensive work on the subject, see Jospeh Margulies, *What Changed When Everything Changed: 9/11 and the Making of National Identity* (New Haven, CT: Yale University Press, 2013), a book in which he talks about the bright side as well as the dark side of American Creed.

19. Shari Cohen, "The Lasting Legacy of an American Dilemma," *Carnegie Results*, Fall 2004, https://www.carnegie.org/publications/lasting-legacy-american-dilemma/ (accessed March 3, 2020).

20. Carol V. Hamilton, "Why Did Jefferson Change 'Property' to the 'Pursuit of Happiness'?" *History New Network*, 2008, https://historynewsnetwork.org/article

/46460 (accessed August 7, 2018). Originally published as "The Surprising Origins and Meaning of the 'Pursuit of Happiness.'"

21. Jon Meacham, "A Nation of Christians Is Not a Christian Nation," *New York Times*, October 7, 2007, http://www.nytimes.com/2007/10/07/opinion/07meacham .html (accessed May 28, 2018).

22. John F. Helliwell, Haifang Huang, Max Norton, Leonard Goff, and Shun Wang, (Eds.). (2024). *World Happiness Report 2024*. University of Oxford: Wellbeing Research Centre.

CHAPTER 4

1. Robert E. Park and Ernest W. Burgess, *Introduction to the Science of Sociology* (Chicago: University of Chicago Press, 1921; 3rd ed., 1969), 735.

2. Part of the introductory section of this chapter is based on my book, B. Kumaravadivelu, *Cultural Globalization and Language Education* (New Haven, CT: Yale University Press, 2008).

3. Arthur M. Schlesinger Jr., *The Disuniting of America* (New York: W. W. Norton, 1992), 13.

4. Kumaravadivelu, *Cultural Globalization*, 75.

5. Nathan Glazer and Daniel Moynihan, *Beyond the Melting Pot: The Negroes, Puerto Ricans, Jews, Italians, and Irish of New York City* (Cambridge, MA: MIT Press, 1963), 15.

6. Early nativists sincerely believed that "the peoples of the Mediterranean region were biologically different from those of northern and Western Europe and that the difference sprang from an inferiority of blood." See Oscar Handlin, *Race and Nationality in American Life* (Boston: Atlantic-Little, Brown, 1957), 96.

7. John Higham, *Strangers in the Land: Patterns of American Nativism, 1860–1925* (New York: Rutgers University Press, 1955; new epilogue, 2002), 4.

8. Tyler G. Anbinder, *Nativism and Slavery: The Northern Know Nothings and the Politics of the 1850s* (New York: Oxford University Press, 1992), 32.

9. Alan Wolfe, "Review Essay: Native Son: Samuel Huntington Defends the Homeland." *Foreign Affairs* 83, no. 3 (May–June 2004): 120, https://doi.org/10.2307 /20033980.

10. Samuel, P. Huntington, *Who Are We? The Challenges to America's National Identity* (New York: Simon & Schuster, 2004), 63. Although Huntington is referring to the time America was "created" (itself disputable?), the analogy is misleading because the Constitution of Pakistan recognizes Islam as the state religion just as the Basic Laws of Israel (which guide the nation in the place of a constitution) recognizes Israel as a Jewish state. On the contrary, the U.S. Constitution does not recognize America as a Protestant or a Christian state.

11. Huntington, *Who Are We?*, 20.

12. In using the phrase "primarily Christian," Huntington is treating Christianity as a monolithic religion ignoring various denominations and various religious and cultural practices.

13. Huntington, *Who Are We?*, 71.
14. Huntington, *Who Are We?*, 298.
15. Francis Fukuyama, *Identity: The Demand for Dignity and the Politics of Resentment* (New York: Farrar, Straus, & Giroux, 2018), 161.
16. Jon Meacham, "A Nation of Christians Is Not a Christian Nation," *New York Times*, October 7, 2007, http://www.nytimes.com/2007/10/07/opinion/07meacham.html (accessed October 23, 2018).
17. Hector St. John de Crèvecoeur, *Letters from an American Farmer* (London: Thomas Davis, 1782), 51.
18. de Crèvecoeur, *Letters*, 53.
19. Israel Zangwill, *The Melting Pot* (play), Columbia Theatre, Washington, DC, October 5, 1908. https://www.gutenberg.org/files/23893/23893-h/23893-h.htm (accessed January 24, 2024).
20. Israel Zangwill, quoted in Glazer and Moynihan, *Beyond the Melting Pot*, 290.
21. David R. Roediger, *Working Toward Whiteness: How America's Immigrants Became White* (New York: Basic Books, 2005), 145.
22. Roediger, *Working Toward Whiteness*, 167.
23. Glazer and Moynihan, *Beyond the Melting Pot*, v.
24. Michael Novak, *The Rise of the Unmeltable Ethnics: Politics and Culture in the Seventies* (New York: McMillan, 1971), 290.
25. Richard Alba and Victor Nee, "Rethinking Assimilation Theory for a New Era of Immigration," in *The Handbook of International Migration: The American Experience*, ed. Charles Hirshman, Philip Kasinitz, and Josh DeWind (New York: Russell Sage Foundation, 1999), 137.
26. William Frey, *Diversity Explosion: How New Racial Demographics Are Remaking America* (Washington DC: Brookings Institute Press, 2015).
27. Frey, *Diversity Explosion*, 178.
28. Joseph Campbell, *The Hero with a Thousand Faces* (Princeton, NJ: Princeton University Press, 1949; 2nd ed., 1968), 3. He is, of course, talking mostly about religious mythologies from different parts of the world.
29. Georg Wilhelm Friedrich Hegel, quoted in Mark Lilla, *The Stillborn God: Religion, Politics, and the Modern West* (New York: Alfred A. Knopf, 2007), 171.

CHAPTER 5

1. U.S. Census Bureau, "2020 Census Results," last revised September 21, 2023, https://www.census.gov/programs-surveys/decennial-census/decade/2020/2020-census-results.html (accessed November 21, 2022).
2. For details, see Shawn J. Spano, *Public Dialogue and Participatory Democracy: The Cupertino Community Project* (New York: Hampton Press, 2001).
3. There is considerable scholarship on how non-Anglo-Saxon European immigrants such as the Irish, Italians, and Jews "became white." Well-known works include Noel Ignatiev, *How the Irish Became White* (New York: Routledge, 1995); Karen Brodkin, *How Jews Became White Folks & What That Says About Race in*

America (New Brunswick, NJ: Rutgers University Press, 1998; 2004); and David R. Roediger, *Working Toward Whiteness: How America's Immigrants Became White* (New York: Basic Books, 2005).

4. Henry Louis Gates Jr. and Kevin M. Burke, *And Still I Rise: Black America Since MLK* (New York: HarperCollins, 2015), ix. In narrating African American history, I draw mainly from Henry Louis Gates Jr. and Kevin M. Burke, and from Eddie S. Glaude Jr., *Democracy in Black: How Race Still Enslaves the American Soul* (New York: Broadway Books, 2016).

5. Glaude, *Democracy in Black.*

6. Eddie S. Glaude Jr., "What is African American Religion?" Oxford University Press (blog), October 17, 2014, https://blog.oup.com/2014/10/african-american -religion/ (assessed May 15, 2017). All the three quotes in the paragraph are from this source.

7. A small percentage of African Americans became Muslims following the leadership of Elijah Mohammed and later Louis Farrakhan.

8. Glaude, "What is African American Religion?"

9. Katherine Schaeffer, "U.S. Congress Continues to Grow in Racial, Ethnic Diversity," *Pew Research Center*, January 9, 2023, https://www.pewresearch.org/short-reads /2023/01/09/u-s-congress-continues-to-grow-in-racial-ethnic-diversity/ (accessed February 2, 2024).

10. Abigail Thernstrom and Stephan Thernstrom, "Black Progress: How Far We've Come, and How Far We Have to Go," *Brookings*, March 1, 1998, https://www .brookings.edu/articles/black-progress-how-far-weve-come-and-how-far-we-have-to -go/ (accessed January 24, 2024).

11. U.S. Census Bureau, "Income, Poverty and Health Insurance Coverage in the United States, 2021," Press Release Number CB22–153, September 13, 2022, https: //www.census.gov/newsroom/press-releases/2022/income-poverty-health-insurance -coverage.html (accessed October 19, 2023).

12. Eric L. Goldstein, *The Price of Whiteness: Jews, Race, and American Identity* (Princeton, NJ: Princeton University Press, 2006), 1. My rendering of the history of American Jews owes much to him.

13. Eric Liu, *A Chinaman's Choice: One Family's Journey and the Chinese American Dream* (New York: Public Affairs, 2014), 159.

14. Particular mention must be made here to the young Jewish activists who loosely organized themselves as the Jewish Renewal movement to work toward the preservation of Jewish identity.

15. Brodkin, *How Jews Became White Folks*, 141.

16. Pew Research Center, "A Portrait of Jewish Americans, Chapter 1: Population Estimates," October 1, 2013, https://www.pewresearch.org/religion/2013/10/01/ chapter-1-population-estimates/ (accessed December 7, 2015).

17. Steinhardt Social Research Institute (SSRI), "American Jewish Population Project," *Brandeis University*, 2016, https://www.brandeis.edu/cmjs/constructs/2016/ population-estimates.html (accessed February 2017).

18. Alon Pinkas, "American Rabbis, Tell your Congregants: The Israel You Knew Is a Relic of the Past," *Haaretz*, September 11, 2023, https://www.haaretz.com

/us-news/2023-09-11/ty-article/premium/american-rabbis-tell-your-congregants-the
-israel-you-knew-is-a-relic-of-the-past/0000018a-848c-d37d-a19a-e5ac49030000
(accessed October 10, 2023).

19. Jewish Federations of North America (JFNA), "Meeting the Needs of North American Jewish Community," 2023, https://www.jewishfederations.org/about-jfna (accessed October 10, 2023).

20. Goldstein, *Price of Whiteness*, 236.

21. Sanjoy Chakravorty, Devesh Kapur, and Nirvikar Singh, *The Other One Percent: Indians in America* (New York: Oxford University Press, 2017), x.

22. U.S. Census Bureau, "Quick Facts: United States," 2023, https://www.census .gov/quickfacts/fact/table/US/RHI225222 (accessed February 1, 2024).

23. Chakravorty et al., *Other One Percent*.

24. Raja Abdulrahim, "Punjabi Schools: Language Is the Key," *Sikhchic* (*Los Angeles Times*), May 7, 2011, https://www.sikhchic.com/people/punjabi_schools _language_is_the_key (accessed July 25, 2021).

25. Although "Latino" generally refers to people from Central and South America, and Caribbean countries, and "Hispanic" refers to people from Spanish-speaking countries (including Spain), the two terms are often used interchangeably in the United States.

26. Suzanne Gamboa, Sandra Lilley, and Sarah Cahlan, "Young Latinos: Born in the U.S.A., Craving Their Own Identity," *NBC News*, September 14, 2018, https: //www.nbcnews.com/news/latino/young-latinos-born-u-s-carving-their-own-identity -n908086 (accessed May 4, 2021).

27. Survey report by Mark Hugo Lopez, Ana Gonzalez-Berrera, and Gustavo López, "Hispanic Identity Fades Across Generations as Immigrant Connections Fall Away," *Pew Research Center*, December 20, 2017, http://www.pewhispanic.org /2017/12/20/hispanic-identity-fades-across-generations-as-immigrant-connections -fall-away/ (accessed July 25, 2018).

28. Paul Taylor, *The Next America: Boomers, Millennials, and the Looming Generational Showdown* (New York: Public Affairs, 2014), 74.

29. Ray Suarez, *Latino Americans: The 500-Year Legacy that Shaped a Nation* (New York: Celebra, 2013), 210.

30. Maria Laurino, *The Italian Americans: A History* (New York: W. W. Norton, 2015), 192.

31. Nathan Glazer, *We Are All Multiculturalists Now* (Cambridge, MA: Harvard University Press, 1997), 160.

32. Horace M. Kallen, *Culture and Democracy in the United States* (New York: Boni and Liveright, 1924), 102.

33. Kallen, *Culture*, 116.

34. Glazer, *We Are All Multiculturalists Now*, 94.

35. Dispatch Editorial Board, "Patrick J. Buchanan: The Unpardonable Heresy of Tucker Carlson," *Dispatch*, September 17, 2018, https://cdispatch.com/opinions/ patrick-j-buchanan-the-unpardonable-heresy-of-tucker-carlson/ (accessed, September 28, 2018).

36. Dispatch Editorial Board, "Patrick J. Buchanan."

37. Dispatch Editorial Board, "Patrick J. Buchanan."

38. R. Radhakrishnan, "Postcoloniality and the Boundaries of Identity," *Callaloo* 16, no. 4 (1993): 750.

39. Stanley Fish, *The Trouble with Principle* (Cambridge, MA: Harvard University Press, 1999), 57.

40. Kwame Anthony Appiah, "Is the Post- in Postmodernism the Post- in Postcolonial?" *Critical Inquiry* 17, no. 2 (Winter 1991): 336–57. http://www.jstor.org/stable /1343840?origin=JSTOR-pdf.

41. In using the term "multiple monoculturalisms," I am inspired by a reading of Nobel Laureate Amartya Sen's book, *Identity and Violence: The Illusion of Destiny* (New York: Penguin Books, 2006). Commenting on the current form of multiculturalism (American, British and others), Sen rightly asks: "Does the existence of a diversity of cultures, which might pass each other like ships in the night, count as a successful case of multiculturalism?" (156). He therefore prefers the term "plural monoculturalism." Note the singular. And, he uses the term rather narrowly to refer to contexts in which cultures are "sequestered" (157) based on religion as, for instance, done some time ago in the case of faith-based schools. He emphasizes that we should avoid "the confusion between multiculturalism with cultural liberty, on the one side, and plural monoculturalism with faith-based separatism on the other" (165). I decided not to opt for the term plural monoculturalism for two reasons: first, I believe that, from a linguistic point of view, the term "plural monoculturalism" could be misunderstood to mean a type of monoculturalism that is in itself pluralistic in nature (a meaning, I think, Sen may not have intended). Second, I do not believe that different religious, racial or ethnic communities in America are "sequestered," either inside schools or outside as it happened in the case of, for instance, South African apartheid. By using the term "multiple monoculturalisms." I am highlighting the historical fact that cultural assimilation as proposed by nativists and pluralists did not materialize as intended, and that every racial/ethnic community is striving and largely succeeding to preserve its religious, cultural, and linguistic identities. This does not mean each community is "sequestered" because, as I discuss in chapter 10, there's a lot of cultural osmosis taking place between racial/ethnic communities in America.

42. P. Taylor, *Next America*, 4.

CHAPTER 6

1. This Michigan episode and the Silicon Valley episode below are an expanded version of a 2003 opinion piece I wrote with the title [Kumaravadivelu], "Evangelical Zeal Not Matched by Humility, Curiosity," *San Jose Mercury News*, September 13, 2003, http://www.bayarea.com/mld/mercurynews/entertainment/6762441.htm (accessed April 28, 2017); now available at *Hindu Vivek Kendra*, https://www.hvk.org /2003/0903/154.html (accessed January 25, 2024).

2. Jon Meacham, "A Nation of Christians Is Not a Christian Nation," *New York Times*, October 7, 2007, http://www.nytimes.com/2007/10/07/opinion/07meacham .html (accessed October 23, 2018).

3. Max Lerner, *America as a Civilization: Life and Thought in the United States Today* (New York: Simon & Schuster, 1957), 704.

4. Byron Williams, "The U.S. Is Not a Theocracy, Nor Should It Be," *Winston-Salem Journal*, September 3, 2022, https://journalnow.com/opinion/column/byron-williams-the-u-s-is-not-a-theocracy-nor-should-it-be/article_b234298c-294b-11ed-a7b8-f3edfed215c0.html (accessed February 5, 2023).

5. Billy Graham, 1985, quoted in Jon Meacham, *American Gospel: God, the Founding Fathers, and the Making of a Nation* (New York: Random House, 2007), 214.

6. Francis Fukuyama, "Political Consequences of the Protestant Reformation, Part II," *American Interest*, November 2, 2017, https://www.the-american-interest.com/2017/11/02/political-consequences-protestant-reformation-part-ii/ (accessed August 5, 2018).

7. Mark Lilla, *The Stillborn God: Religion, Politics, and the Modern West* (Toronto: Random House, 2007), 278.

8. William Barr, quoted in Jerry Johnson and HBU Editors, "Celebrating Diversity & Distinction," *Pillars: Houston Baptist University (HBU)* 56, no. 1 (Spring 2020): 1–72, https://hc.edu/publications/pillars/PillarsSpring2020web.pdf (accessed January 6, 2020).

9. Bernard-Henri Lévy, *American Vertigo: Traveling America in the Footsteps of Tocqueville* (New York: Random House, 2006), 278.

10. Sarvepalli Radhakrishnan, *The Hindu View of Life* (New York: Macmillan, 1927), 55.

11. Bhikhu Parekh, *A New Politics of Identity.* (London: Palgrave Macmillan, 2008), 159.

12. This statement about religious equality in India may sound odd for those who have been following the religious strife in modern day India, particularly the Hindu-Muslim conflicts dating back to the time of India's struggle for independence, which resulted in partition and in the creation of Pakistan. Considering the hoary past of India's history, these religious conflicts are rather recent developments. Any objective historian would testify that deep down, these conflicts are more political than religious. Politicians give a religious mask to social conflicts and economic grievances in order to instigate their base aiming at electoral gains. Besides, as I discuss in the later part of the chapter, we need to separate Faith from the faithful, as Kofi Annan advised us to do (see n31). What we learn from him is: there are Christian extremists but we should not blame Christianity for their actions. There are muscular Buddhists but we should not blame Buddhism for their actions. There are Hindu extremists but we should not blame Hinduism for their actions.

13. M. J. Akbar, "Hear It? Indian Secularism Is Both Enduring & Audible." *Times of India* (blog), December 8, 2014, http://blogs.timesofindia.indiatimes.com/TheSiegeWithin/hear-it-indian-secularism-is-both-enduring-audible/ (accessed May 21, 2017).

14. Roger Cohen, "The Inspiration of Ample India." *New York Times*, April 14, 2017, https://www.nytimes.com/2017/04/14/opinion/the-inspiration-of-ample-india.html? (accessed June 14, 2018).

15. A full disclosure is in order here: It is not as if I have been going on a prolonged pilgrimage to these places of worship, and at my expense. Not at all. Whenever I go abroad to give invited guest lectures at universities or deliver keynote/plenary addresses at international conferences, my guests, knowing my interest, have graciously taken me to these places of worship in my spare time.

16. Ramdas Lamb, "Polytheism and Monotheism: A Hindu Perspective," *Huffington Post* (blog), March 3, 2011, http://www.huffingtonpost.com/ramdas-lamb/polytheism-and monotheism_b_841905.html (accessed September 28, 2018).

17. Mpho Tutu, "My Faith is not the Whole Truth of God," Washington Post, Sept. 2008, http://newsweek.washingtonpost.com/onfaith/guestvoices/2008/09/my_faith_is_not_the_whole truth.html (accessed August 7, 2017).

18. Deloitte, "2018 Deloitte Millennial Survey," 2018, https://www2.deloitte.com/content/dam/Deloitte/global/Documents/About-Deloitte/gx-2018-millennial-survey-report.pdf (accessed January 25, 2024).

19. Stephen Bullivant, quoted in Harriet Sherwood, "Christianity as Default Is Gone: The Rise of the Non-Christian Europe," *Guardian*, March 20, 2018, https://www.theguardian.com/world/2018/mar/21/christianity-non-christian-europe-young-people-survey-religion (accessed April 12, 2019).

20. BBC, "Religious Affiliation in Scotland 'Declines Sharply,'" *BBC*, July 1, 2017, http://www.bbc.com/news/uk-scotland-40467084 (accessed August 10, 2018).

21. Alessandra Maldonado, "Poll: Australian Top Choice of Faith Is Now 'No Religion,'" *Salon*, June 27, 2017, http://www.salon.com/2017/06/27/poll-australia-no-religion/ (accessed July 4, 2018).

22. Barna Group, "Atheism Doubles Among Generation Z," *Barna*, January 14, 2018, https://www.barna.com/research/atheism-doubles-among-generation-z/ (accessed February 9, 2019).

23. Pew Research Center, "America's Changing Religious Landscape," May 12, 2015, http://www.pewforum.org/2015/05/12/americas-changing-religious-landscape/ (accessed September 19, 2018).

24. Gregory A. Smith, "About Three-in-Ten U.S. Adults Are Now Religiously Unaffiliated," *Pew Research Center*, December 14, 2021, https://www.pewresearch.org/religion/2021/12/14/about-three-in-ten-u-s-adults-are-now-religiously-unaffiliated/ (accessed January 24, 2024).

25. Robert D. Putnam and David E. Campbell, "Walking Away from Church," *Los Angeles Times*, October 17, 2010, http://www.latimes.com/news/opinion/commentary/la-oe-1017-putnam-religion-20101017,0,6283320.story (accessed December 5, 2019).

26. Kevin Phillips, *American Theocracy: The Peril and Politics of Radical Religion, Oil, and Borrowed Money in the 21st Century* (New York: Viking, Penguin Group, 2006), xv.

27. Michael Gerson, "The Last Temptation," *Atlantic*, April 2018, https://www.theatlantic.com/magazine/archive/2018/04/the-last-temptation/554066/ (accessed May 2, 2019).

28. David Kuo, *Tempting Faith: An Inside Story of Political Seduction* (New York: Free Press, 2006), 213–14.

29. Charles Krauthammer, "An Overdose of Public Piety," *Washington Post*, December 14, 2007, http://www.washingtonpost.com/wp-dyn/content/article/2007/12/13/AR2007121301501.html (accessed January 9, 2018).

30. Wendy Doniger, "The Great Pumpkin Goes to Washington," *Washington Post*, January 30, 2017, http://newsweek.washingtonpost.com/onfaith/wendy_doniger/2007/01/the_great_pumpkin_goes_to_wash.html (accessed March 10, 2018).

31. Kofi Annan, "Embrace Our Differences," February 13, 2007, http://www.tompaine.com/articles/2007/02/13/embrace_our_differences.php (accessed March 10, 2017); now available https://unobserver.net/?folder=item3&pagina=intlaw.php (accessed January 25, 2024).

32. Lerner, *America as a Civilization*, 105.

33. Philip Pullella and Danlela Desantis, "Pope Francis Ends South America Trip by Urging Young People to 'Make A Mess,'" *Huffington Post*, July 12, 2015; updated January 9, 2017. http://www.huffingtonpost.com/entry/pope-francis-ends-south-america-trip-by-urging-young-people-to-make-a-mess_55a3257ee4b0ecec71bc5b65 (accessed May 23, 2018).

CHAPTER 7

1. Ed Pilkington, "Shoes and Insults Hurled at Bush on Iraq Visit," *Guardian*, December 15, 2008, https://www.theguardian.com/world/2008/dec/15/george-bush-shoes-iraq (accessed July 2, 2018).

2. Steve Inskeep, "U.S.'s Cultural Ignorance Fuels Iraq Insurgency," *NPR*, April 28, 2006, https://www.npr.org/2006/04/28/5366677/u-s-s-cultural-ignorance-fuels-iraq-insurgency (accessed January 26, 2024).

3. Raymond Williams, *Keywords: Vocabulary of Culture and Society* (Oxford: Oxford University Press, 1976), 87.

4. Matthew Arnold, *Culture and Anarchy* (1869) (London: Oxford University Press, 2006), 170.

5. Clifford Geertz, *The Interpretation of Cultures* (New York: Basis Books, 1973; 2000), 89.

6. C. N. Trueman, "Pierre Bourdieu," *History Learning Site*, May 22, 2015, https://www.historylearningsite.co.uk/sociology/education-and-sociology/pierre-bourdieu/ (accessed on May 11, 2022).

7. E. D. Hirsh Jr., *Cultural Literacy: What Every American Needs to Know* (New York: Vintage, 1987).

8. Geertz, *Interpretation of Cultures*, 408.

9. Kwame Anthony Appiah, *The Lies That Bind Us: Rethinking Identity* (New York: Liveright Publishing, 2018), 195.

10. Jim Wallis, *God's Politics: Why the Right Gets It Wrong and the Left Doesn't Get It* (San Francisco: Harper, 2018), xxiii. The two Rev. Jerry Falwell Jr. and Rev. Pat Robertson quotes are from this same page.

11. Wallis, *God's Politics*, xxiii.

12. Jerry Falwell Jr., quoted in Kevin Phillips, *American Theocracy: The Peril and Politics of Radical Religion, Oil, and Borrowed Money in the 21st Century* (New York: Viking, Penguin Group, 2006), 215.

13. U.S. Oratory Project, "Patrick Joseph Buchanan, 'Culture War Speech,'" *Voices of Democracy*, August 17, 1992, https://voicesofdemocracy.umd.edu/buchanan -culture-war-speech-speech-text/ (accessed October 14, 2018).

14. Patrick J. Buchanan, *"Death of the West*: An Excerpt from Pat Buchanan's Book," *NBC News*, August 29, 2002, https://www.nbcnews.com/id/wbna3080569 (accessed October 14, 2018).

15. Tim Alberta, "'The Ideas Made It, But I Didn't,' Pat Buchanan Won After All," *Politico*, April 22, 2022, http://www.politico.com/magazine/story/2017/04/22/pat -buchanan-trump-president-history-profile-215042 (accessed May 23, 2017).

16. Patrick J. Buchanan, *Death of the West: How Dying Populations and Immigrant Invasions Imperil Our Country and Civilization* (New York: Thomas Dunne Books, 2002), 137.

17. Buchanan, *Death of the West*, 232.

18. U.S. Census Bureau, "2020 U.S. Population More Racially and Ethnically Diverse than Measured in 2010," August 12, 2021, https://www.census.gov/library /stories/2021/08/2020-united-states-population-more-racially-ethnically-diverse-than -2010.html (accessed January 5, 2022).

19. Patrick J. Buchanan, "Is Secession a Solution to Cultural War?" *Buchanan* (blog), February 24, 2017, http://buchanan.org/blog/secession-solution-cultural-war -126571 (accessed June 5, 2018).

20. Karen Sternheimer, *Celebrity Culture and the American Dream: Stardom and Social Mobility* (New York: Taylor & Francis, 2011), 5.

21. Brian Hiatt, "The Beatles in Spatial Audio: Producer Giles Martin on How It All Works," *Rolling Stone*, July 29, 2021, https://beatles.ncf.ca/archived_news_p26 .html (accessed August 4, 2019).

22. Leah Donnella, "Taylor Swift Is the 21st Century's Most Disorienting Pop Star," *NPR*, September 26, 2018, https://www.npr.org/2018/09/26/646422866/taylor -swift-is-the-21st-centurys-most-disorienting-pop-star (accessed August 19, 2019).

23. Taylor Swift, "30 Things I Learned Before Turning 30," *Elle*, March 6, 2019, https://www.elle.com/culture/celebrities/a26628467/taylor-swift-30th-birthday -lessons/ (accessed August 19, 2019).

24. Brigid Delaney, "'Self-Partnered' Emma Watson Is Right: We Need More Ways to be Single," *Guardian*, November 9, 2019, https://www.theguardian.com/film /2019/nov/06/self-partnered-emma-watson-is-right-we-need-more-ways-to-be-single (accessed January 7, 2020).

25. Gwyneth Paltrow, "From the Archive: Gwyneth Paltrow on Her Conscious Uncoupling Journey," *Vogue* (British), September 27, 2022, https://www.vogue.co.uk /arts-and-lifestyle/article/gwyneth-paltrow-conscious-uncoupling (accessed March 3, 2022).

26. Wenn, "George Clooney Celebrating Brunei's Reversal on Death Sentence for Gay Men and Women," *Hollywood*, May 6, 2019, https://www.hollywood.com/

general/george-clooney-celebrating-bruneis-reversal-on-death-sentence-for-gay-men-and-women-60750312 (accessed March 5, 2022).

27. ESPN, "NFL Commissioner Roger Goodell: I 'Encourage' a Team to Sign Colin Kaepernick," *ABC News*, June 16, 2020, https://abc7news.com/sports/nfl-commissioner-roger-goodell-i-encourage-a-team-to-sign-colin-kaepernick/6249251/ (accessed July 5, 2020).

28. Joseph Margulies, *What Changed When Everything Changed: 9/11 and the Making of National Identity* (New Haven, CT.; Yale University Press, 2013), 145.

29. Putnam, Robert & D. E. Campbell (2010). *American Grace: How Religion Divides and Unites Us*. New York: Simon & Schuster, 542, 545

30. Bruce Stokes, "What It Takes to Truly Be 'One of Us,'" *Pew Research Center*, February 1, 2017, https://www.pewresearch.org/global/2017/02/01/what-it-takes-to-truly-be-one-of-us/ (accessed May 10, 2019).

31. Irene Taviss Thomson, *Culture Wars and Enduring American Dilemmas* (Ann Arbor: University of Michigan Press, 2020). 1.

32. Andrew Hartman, *A War for the Soul of America: A History of the Culture Wars* (Chicago: University of Chicago Press, 2015), 285; emphasis in the original.

33. Rich Lowry, "Why Ron DeSantis Is Going After Disney," *Politico*, April 21, 2022, https://www.politico.com/news/magazine/2022/04/21/ron-desantis-disney-smart-big-business-left-gop-00026886 (accessed January 26, 2024).

34. Claude Lévi-Strauss, *Myth and Meaning* (Toronto: University of Toronto Press, 1978), 93.

35. Hartman, *War for the Soul of America*, 289.

36. Jeremy Safran, quoted in David Forbes, "How Capitalism Captured the Mindfulness Industry," *Guardian*, April 16, 2019, https://www.theguardian.com/lifeandstyle/2019/apr/16/how-capitalism-captured-the-mindfulness-industry (accessed September 5, 2020).

CHAPTER 8

1. Sujata Bhatt, *Brunizem* (Manchester, UK,: Carcanet Press, 1998; 2014). "Search for my Tongue" is part of a collection of poems titled *Brunizem*. Brunizem is the name of the fertile soil found in North America, Europe, and Asia, the three places the poet has lived and experienced.

2. Jacques Derrida, *Monolingualism of the Other, Or, The Prosthesis of Origin*, trans. Patrick Mensah (Stanford, CA: Stanford University Press, 1998), 25.

3. Joshua Fishman, "300-Plus Years of Heritage Language Education in the United States," in *Heritage Languages in America: Preserving a National Resource*, ed. Joy Kreeft Peyton, Donald A. Ranard, and Scott McGinnis (McHenry, IL: Center for Applied Linguistics & Delta Systems, 2001), 82.

4. U.S. Census Bureau, "2015 Press Releases," 2015, https://www.census.gov/newsroom/archives/2015-pr.html (accessed January 26, 2024).

5. Bruce Stokes, "What It Takes to Truly Be 'One of Us,'" *Pew Research Center.* February 1, 2017, https://www.pewresearch.org/global/2017/02/01/what-it-takes-to -truly-be-one-of-us/ (accessed May 10, 2019).

6. U.S. English, "Welcome!" N.d., https://www.usenglish.org/ (accessed November 10, 2019). U.S. English is an umbrella organization that provides online resources concerning the issues of making English the official language of the United States.

7. Carl Hulse, "Senate Votes to Set English as National Language," *New York Times*, May 19, 2006, https://www.nytimes.com/2006/05/19/washington/senate-votes -to-set-english-as-national-language.html (accessed January 3, 2015).

8. Jessica Kwong, "Should English Be the Official Language of the United States? Tucker Carlson Says a 'Core Weakness' of the U.S. Is That It Isn't," *Newsweek*, May 5, 2018, http://www.newsweek.com/should-english-be-official-language-united -states-tucker-carlson-says-core-911959 (accessed May 5, 2018).

9. Charles Krauthammer, "In Plain English: Making It Official," *Time International*, June 12, 2006, no. 74.

10. George F. Will, "A Vote For English." *Washington Post*, May 25, 2006, http: //www.washingtonpost.com/wp-dyn/content/article/2006/05/24/AR2006052402433 .html (accessed August 5, 2017).

11. Carlos Garcia and Loretta E. Bass, "American Identity and Attitudes Toward English Language Policy Initiatives," *Journal of Sociology & Social Welfare* 34, no. 1, (2007): 79.

12. Jennifer F. Samson and Brian A. Collins, "Preparing All Teachers to Meet the Needs of English Language Learners," *Center for American Progress*, April 30, 2012, https://www.americanprogress.org/issues/education-k-12/reports/2012/04/30/11372 /preparing-all-teachers-to-meet-the-needs-of-english-language-learners/ (accessed December 9, 2019).

13. Shirin Hakimzadeh and D'Vera Cohn, "English Usage Among Hispanics in the United States," *Pew Research Center*, November 29, 2007, https://www.pewhispanic .org/2007/11/29/english-usage-among-hispanics-in-the-united-states/ (accessed March 5, 2010).

14. Nuffield Foundation, "Languages: The Next Generation," Report. (London: Nuffield Foundation, 2000), 14, https://www.nuffieldfoundation.org/wp-content /uploads/2019/11/languages_finalreport.pdf (accessed January 26, 2024).

15. Nuffield Foundation, "Languages," 54.

16. American Academy of Arts & Sciences, "America's Languages: Investing in Language Education for the 21st Century," 2017, https://www.amacad.org/language (accessed February 4, 2019).

17. American Academy of Arts & Sciences, "America's Languages."

18. Kathleen Stein Smith, "The Multilingual Advantage: Foreign Language as a Social Skill in a Globalized World," *Language Matters*, May 31, 2017, Mattershttps:// kathleensteinsmith.wordpress.com/2017/05/31/the-multilingual-advantage-foreign- language-as-a-social-skill-in-a-globalized-world-kathys-new-article/ (accessed June 7, 2019).

19. McKinsey Global Institute, "The World at Work: Jobs, Pay, and Skills for 3.5 Billion People," June 2012, https://www.mckinsey.com/~/media

/McKinsey/Featured%20Insights/Employment%20and%20Growth/The%20world%20at%20work/MGI%20Global_labor_Executive_Summary_June _2012.pdf (accessed May 2, 2015).

20. National Immigration Forum, "Immigrants and the Importance of Language Learning for a Global Society," 2016, https://immigrationforum.org/wp-content /uploads/2016/10/Language-Learning-for-a-Global-Society.pdf (accessed May 9, 2019).

21. National Commission on Terrorist Attacks Upon the United States, "Tenth Public Hearing: 9/11 Commission," Washington, DC, April 14, 2004, https://9 -11commission.gov/archive/hearing10/9-11Commission_Hearing_2004-04-14.htm (accessed September 3, 2010).

22. Nataly Kelly, "Ten Years After 9/11, America Still Has a Language Problem." *Huffington Post*, September 12, 2011, updated November 12, 2011, https://www .huffpost.com/entry/ten-years-after-911-ameri_b_956536 (accessed May 9, 2019).

23. U.S. Department of State, Bureau of Education and Cultural Affairs, "Faces of Change," N.d., https://eca.state.gov/files/bureau/fy24_nsli-y_nofo_0.pdf (accessed May 9, 2019).

24. Tina Susman, "Demand Grows for Niche Translators," *Los Angeles Times*, November 19, 2009, https://www.chicagotribune.com/business/careers/sns-jobs-lang -translation-jobs-story.html (accessed October 9, 2010).

25. Amy B. Wang, "Duke Professor Apologizes for Telling Chinese Students to Speak English on Campus," *Washington Post*, January 28, 2019, https://www .washingtonpost.com/education/2019/01/27/duke-professor-warns-chinese-students -speak-english-campus-or-face-unintended-consequences/ (accessed May 4, 2020).

26. American Academy of Arts & Sciences, "America's Languages."

27. Kat Devlin, "Most European Students Are Learning a Foreign Language in School While Americans Lag," *Pew Research Center*, August 6, 2018, https:// www.pewresearch.org/fact-tank/2018/08/06/most-european-students-are-learning-a -foreign-language-in-school-while-americans-lag/ (accessed January 9, 2019).

28. Dennis Looney and Natalia Lusin, "Enrollments in Languages Other Than English in United States Institutions of Higher Education, Summer 2016 and Fall 2016: Preliminary Report," *Modern Language Association*, February 2018, https:// www.mla.org/content/download/83540/2197676/2016-Enrollments-Short-Report.pdf (accessed December 14, 2019).

29. Ellen Bialystok, noted in Claudia Dreifus, "The Bilingual Advantage," *New York Times*, May 30, 2011, http://www.nytimes.com/2011/05/31/science/31conversation .html? (accessed December 14, 2019).

30. Personal communication, May 23, 2019, from Confucius Institute U.S. Center. (Also see, https://www.facebook.com/CIUSCenter/). It must be noted that there have been severe criticisms about the role of Confucius Institutes in the United States, which are seen as Chinese propaganda machines. See, for instance, Rachelle Peterson, "American Universities Are welcoming Chinese Trojan Horse," *Foreign Policy*, May 9, 2017, https://foreignpolicy.com/2017/05/09/american-universities-are-welcoming -chinas-trojan-horse-confucius-institutes/ (accessed November 10, 2019).

31. U.S. Government Accountability Office (GAO), "China: With Nearly All U.S. Confucius Institutes Closed, Some Schools Sought Alternative Language Support," October 30, 2023, https://www.gao.gov/products/gao-24-105981 (accessed November 19, 2020).

32. Samuel P. Huntington, *Who Are We? The Challenges to America's National Identity* (New York: Simon & Schuster, 2004), 231.

33. Theodore Roosevelt, *The Works of Theodore Roosevelt: Memorial Edition* (New York: Charles Scribner, 1919; 1926), vol. 24, 554.

CHAPTER 9

1. See for instance, Daniel Thomas, "Davos 2020: What Is the World Economic Forum and Is It elitist?" *BBC News*, January 17, 2020, https://www.bbc.com/news/technology-51134164 (accessed January 19, 2020).

2. World Economic Forum, "About Us," 2024, https://www.weforum.org/about/world-economic-forum (accessed March 5, 2019).

3. See, for instance, Anand Giridharadas, *Winners Take All: The Elite Charade of Changing the World* (New York: Knopf, 2018). See also, Seth D. Kaplan, "How Do America's Elites Stack Up?" *American Interest*, October 30, 2019, https://www.the-american-interest.com/2019/10/30/how-do-americas-elites-stack-up/ (accessed December 23, 2020).

4. C. [Charles] Wright Mills, *The Power Elite* (Oxford: Oxford University Press, 1956; 2000), 3–4.

5. Gregor Aisch, Larry Buchanan, Amanda Cox, and Kevin Quealy, "Some Colleges Have More Students From the Top 1 Percent Than the Bottom 60. Find Yours," *New York Times*, January 18, 2017, https://www.nytimes.com/interactive/2017/01/18/upshot/some-colleges-have-more-students-from-the-top-1-percent-than-the-bottom-60.html (accessed June 18, 2019).

6. Edward S. Herman and Noam Chomsky, *Manufacturing Consent: The Political Economy of the Mass Media* (New York: Pantheon, 1988; repr. 2002).

7. Rachel Kleinfeld, "Polarization, Democracy, and Political Violence in the United States: What the Research Says," *Carnegie Endowment for International Peace*, September 5, 2023, https://carnegieendowment.org/2023/09/05/polarization-democracy-and-political-violence-in-united-states-what-research-says-pub-90457 (accessed October 2, 2023).

8. Arlie Hochschild, "How the 'Great Paradox' of American Politics Holds the Secret to Trump's Success," *Guardian*, September 7, 2016, https://www.theguardian.com/us-news/2016/sep/07/how-great-paradox-american-politics-holds-secret-trumps-success (accessed April 5, 2019).

9. Andrew Bacevich, *The Age of Illusions: How America Squandered Its Cold War Victory* (New York: Metropolitan Books, 2020), 198.

10. Louis René Beres, "Looking Back at the Trump Presidency: An Informed Retrospective," *Modern Diplomacy*, August 13, 2021, https://moderndiplomacy.eu/2021

/08/13/looking-back-at-the-trump-presidency-an-informed-retrospective/ (accessed January 18, 2022).

11. Tom Brokaw, *Boom! Voices of the Sixties* (New York: Random House, 2007), xiv.

12. Betty Friedan, *The Feminine Mystique* (New York: W. W. Norton, 1963), quoted in Elaine Woo, "Catalyst of Feminist Revolution," *Los Angeles Times*, February 5, 2006, https://www.latimes.com/archives/la-xpm-2006-feb-05-me-friedan5 -story.html (accessed March 7, 2015).

13. Bob Dylan, "The Times They Are A-Changin,'" *The Times They Are A-Changin'* (album) (New York: Columbia Records, 1964).

14. Michael Gerson and Peter Wehner, "How Christians Can Flourish in a Same-Sex-Marriage World," *Christianity Today*, November 2, 2015, http://www .christianitytoday.com/ct/2015/november/how-christians-can-flourish-in-same-sex -marriage-world-cult.htm 1 (accessed November 12, 2019).

15. David Badash, "Watch: Gay People 'Will Die Out Because They Don't Reproduce' Says Pat Robertson," *New Civil Rights Movement (NORM)*, December 17, 2014, https://www.thenewcivilrightsmovement.com/2014/12/watch_gay_people _will_die_out_because_they_don_t_reproduce_says_pat_robertson / (accessed February 1, 2023).

16. PBS, "Jerry Falwell interview with PBS, 'Assault on Gay America,'" *PBS Frontline*, 2000, https://www.pbs.org/wgbh/pages/frontline/shows/assault/interviews /falwell.html (accessed June 9, 2019).

17. John Barrasso, Mary Fallin, and Viginia Foxx, "2016 Republican Party Platform," *American Presidency Project* (UC Santa Barbara), July 18, 2016, https://www .presidency.ucsb.edu/documents/2016-republican-party-platform (accessed Aprril 12, 2018).

18. Patrick Healy, "Hopefuls Differ as They Reject Gay Marriage," *New York Times*, October 31, 2008, https://www.nytimes.com/2008/11/01/us/politics/01marriage.html (accessed March 4, 2023).

19. Pew Research Center, "Attitudes on Same-Sex Marriage," May 14, 2019, https: //www.pewforum.org/fact-sheet/changing-attitudes-on-gay-marriage/ (accessed May 9, 2020).

20. Mackenzie Weinger, "Evolve: Obama Gay Marriage Quotes," *Politico*, May 9, 2012, https://www.politico.com/story/2012/05/evolve-obama-gay-marriage-quotes -076109 (accessed August 7, 2015).

21. Gerhard Peters and John T. Woolley, "2012 Democratic Party Platform," *American Presidency Project* (UC Santa Barbara), September 3, 2012, https://www .presidency.ucsb.edu/documents/2012-democratic-party-platform (accessed August 7, 2015).

22. Anna Tong, Alexandra Ulmer, and Jeffrey Dastin, "Exclusive: Peter Thiel, Republican Megadonor, Won't Fund Candidates in 2024, Sources Say," *Reuters*, April 26, 2023, https://www.reuters.com/world/us/peter-thiel-republican-megadonor -wont-fund-candidates-2024-sources-2023-04-26/ (accessed May 2, 2023).

23. Daniel Burke, "Mormon Church Drops Anti-LGBT Policy from 2015, Saying Children of Same-Sex Couples Now Can Be Baptized," *CNN*, April 4, 2019, https:

//www.cnn.com/2019/04/04/us/mormon-lgbt-policy/index.html (accessed December 6, 2019).

24. Matthew Paul Turner, "Is the Christian Music Industry Softening on Gays?" *Daily Beast*, October 19, 2014, updated April 14, 2017, https://www.thedailybeast.com/is-the-christian-music-industry-softening-on-gays (accessed January 3, 2020).

25. Chris Cillizza, "Rush Limbaugh Doesn't Think America Will Elect a Man Who 'Loves to Kiss His Husband,'" *CNN Politics*, February 13, 2020, https://www.cnn.com/2020/02/13/politics/rush-limbaugh-pete-buttigieg-gay/index.html (accessed February 6, 2021).

26. Nathaniel Frank, *Awakening: How Gays and Lesbians Brought Marriage Equality to America* (New York: Belknap Press, 2017), 10.

CHAPTER 10

1. Barack Obama, "Barack Obama's Speech on Race," *New York Times*, March 18, 2008, https://www.nytimes.com/2008/03/18/us/politics/18text-obama.html (accessed January 3, 2017).

2. Robert D. Putnam and David E. Campbell, *American Grace: How Religion Divides and Unites Us* (New York: Simon & Schuster, 2010), 36.

3. U.S. Census Bureau, "2020 U.S. Population More Racially and Ethnically Diverse than Measured in 2010," August 12, 2021, https://www.census.gov/library/stories/2021/08/2020-united-states-population-more-racially-ethnically-diverse-than-2010.html (accessed January 5 and 10, 2022).

4. William Frey, *Diversity Explosion: How New Racial Demographics Are Remaking America* (Washington, DC: Brookings Institute Press, 2015), 193.

5. Paul Taylor, *The Next America: Boomers, Millennials, and the Looming Generational Showdown* (New York: Public Affairs, 2014), 91

6. A. W. Geiger and Gretchen Livingston, "8 Facts About Love and Marriage in American," *Pew Research Center*, February 13, 2019, https://www.pewresearch.org/fact-tank/2019/02/13/8-facts-about-love-and-marriage/ (accessed May 9, 2020).

7. Pew Research Center, "One-in-Five U.S. Adults Were Raised in Interfaith Homes," October 26, 2016, https://www.pewforum.org/2016/10/26/one-in-five-u-s-adults-were-raised-in-interfaith-homes/ (accessed May 9, 2020).

8. Pew Research Center, "Publications," 1985–2024, https://www.pewsocialtrends.org (accessed October 5, 2020).

9. Thomas L. Friedman, "The American Civil War, Part II," *New York Times*, October 2, 2018, https://www.nytimes.com/2018/10/02/opinion/the-american-civil-war-part-ii.html (accessed November 9, 2019).

10. Pew Research Center, "Americans Have Positive Views About Religion's Role in Society, but Want It Out of Politics," November 15, 2019, https://www.pewforum.org/2019/11/15/americans-have-positive-views-about-religions-role-in-society-but-want-it-out-of-politics/ (accessed October 5, 2020).

11. American Academy of Arts & Sciences, *Our Common Purpose: Reinventing American Democracy for the 21st Century* (New York: American Academy of Arts & Sciences, 2020), 109.

12. Mark Brolin, with Jonathan Haidt, "How to Overcome Tribalism, the Shouty Minority and Facebook Toxicity," *Politico*, November 7, 2021, https://www.politico.com/news/magazine/2021/11/07/social-psychologist-haidt-tribalism-facebook-519720 (accessed April 11, 2022).

13. Pew Research Center, "Beyond Red vs. Blue: The Political Typology," November 9, 2021, https://www.pewresearch.org/politics/2021/11/09/beyond-red-vs-blue-the-political-typology-2/ (accessed January 27, 2024).

14. B. Kumaravadivelu, "Our Prejudices, Our Selves," *San Jose Mercury News*, September 18, 1997, 1, 4; emphasis in the original.

15. Brendan Pearson, "Sorry Still Seems to Be the Hardest Word for Howard," *Financial Review*, June 4, 1999, https://www.afr.com/politics/sorry-still-seems-to-be-the-hardest-word-for-howard-19990604-k8tqp (accessed January 27, 2024). This expression is from the draft version of *The Declaration for Reconciliation*, drafted by the novelist David Malouf and the Aboriginal scholar and activist Jackie Huggins, on behalf of the Australian Council for Aboriginal Reconciliation. The passage mentioning "the gift of one another's presence" was dropped in the final version.

16. Jonathan Sacks, *The Dignity of Difference: How to Avoid the Clash of Civilizations* (New York: Continuum, 2002), 23.

17. Anand Giridharadas, quoted in Yascha Mounk, "It's Time for an Outrage Armistice," *Slate*, May 2, 2018, https://slate.com/news-and-politics/2018/05/how-to-reach-a-truce-in-the-culture-war.html (accessed February 10, 2019).

18. Tim Carman, "How 7 Immigrant Families Transform the Thanksgiving Turkey with Flavors of Their Homeland," *Washington Post*, November 22, 2019, https://www.washingtonpost.com/food/2019/11/22/how immigrant-families-transform-thanksgiving-turkey-with-flavors-their-homelands/ (accessed May 27, 2020).

19. Jeffery Robinson, "Five Truths About Black History," *ACLU*, N.d., https://www.aclu.org/issues/racial-justice/five-truths-about-black-history (accessed December 11, 2018).

20. Ashley Jardina, *White Identity Politics* (Cambridge: Cambridge University Press, 2019), 22.

21. Robert Browning, "Abt Vogler" (1864), in *Rabbi Ben Ezra & Abt Vogler* ([Boston?]: Printed privately, N.d.), https://www.poetryfoundation.org/poems/43743/abt-vogler (accessed January 27, 2024).

22. Olivia Beavers, "Condoleezza Rice Says American Was Born With a Birth Defect: Slavery," *Hill*, May 7, 2017, http://thehill.com/homenews/news/332307-condoleezza-rice-says-america-was-born-with-a-birth-defect-slavery (accessed March 22, 2018).

23. Jim Wallis, *America's Original Sin: Racism, White Privilege, and the Bridge to a New America* (New York: Baker Publishing Group, 2015), 63.

24. Jay Nordlinger, "Thoughts on American," *National Review*, July 19, 2019, https://www.nationalreview.com/corner/thoughts-on-america/ (accessed July 20, 2019).

25. David Crary, "If Barrett Joins, Supreme Court Would Have Six Catholics," *Associated Press*, September 26, 2020, https://apnews.com/article/us-supreme-court -ruth-bader-ginsburg-archive-courts-donald-trump-987e5fb6de8a1a29d1cbb00bf1f1 948c (accessed February 19, 2021).

26. Jeff Diamant, "Faith on the Hill: The Religious Composition of the 118th Congress," *Pew Research Center*, January 3, 2023, https://www.pewresearch.org/religion /2023/01/03/faith-on-the-hill-2023/ (accessed January 27, 2024).

27. Bruce Stokes, "What It Takes to Truly Be 'One of Us,'" *Pew Research Center*, February 1, 2017, https://www.pewresearch.org/global/2017/02/01/what-it-takes-to -truly-be-one-of-us/ (accessed May 10, 2019; February 19, 2021).

28. Jon Meacham, *The Soul of America: The Battle for Our Better Angels* (New York: Random House, 2018), 8.

29. Václav Havel, "The Power of the Powerless" (October 1978; rev. 1985), *HAC Bard*, December 23, 2011, https://hac.bard.edu/amor-mundi/the-power-of-the -powerless-vaclav-havel-2011-12-23 (accessed January 10, 2015). In this powerful essay, Havel writes about totalitarian regimes in Eastern Europe, mainly referring to Soviet-era Czechoslovakia.

30. Israel Zangwill, *The Melting Pot* (play), Columbia Theatre, Washington, DC, October 5, 1908, https://www.gutenberg.org/files/23893/23893-h/23893-h.htm (accessed January 24, 2024).

Bibliography

Abdul-Jabbar, Kareem. "Let Rachel Dolezal Be as Black as She Wants to Be." *Time.* June 16, 2015. https://time.com/3921404/rachel-dolezal-naacp-race-kareem-abdul-jabbar/ (accessed January 16, 2024).

Abdulrahim, Raja. "Punjabi Schools: Language Is the Key." *Sikhchic* (*Los Angeles Times*). May 7, 2011. https://www.sikhchic.com/people/punjabi_schools_language_is_the_key (accessed July 25, 2021).

Aisch, Gregor, Larry Buchanan, Amanda Cox, and Kevin Quealy. "Some Colleges Have More Students From the Top 1 Percent Than the Bottom 60. Find Yours." *New York Times.* January 18, 2017. https://www.nytimes.com/interactive/2017/01/18/upshot/some-colleges-have-more-students-from-the-top-1-percent-than-the-bottom-60.html (accessed June 18, 2019).

Akbar, M. J. "Hear It? Indian Secularism Is Both Enduring & Audible." *Times of India* (blog). December 8, 2014. http://blogs.timesofindia.indiatimes.com/TheSiegeWithin/hear-it-indian-secularism-is-both-enduring-audible/ (accessed May 21, 2017).

Alba, Richard, and Victor Nee. "Rethinking Assimilation Theory for a New Era of Immigration." In *The Handbook of International Migration: The American Experience*, edited by Charles Hirshman, Philip Kasinitz, and Josh DeWind, 137–60. New York: Russell Sage Foundation, 1999.

Alberta, Tim. "'The Ideas Made It, But I Didn't,' Pat Buchanan Won After All." *Politico.* April 22, 2022. http://www.politico.com/magazine/story/2017/04/22/pat-buchanan-trump-president-history-profile-215042 (accessed May 23, 2017).

Alexander, Josh. *Southern Rites.* Directed by Gilliam Laub. Montgomery County, GA: HBO Documentary, 2015.

Allison, Graham. *Destined for War: Can America and China Escape Thucydides's Trap?* New York: Houghton Mifflin Harcourt, 2017.

American Academy of Arts & Sciences. "America's Languages: Investing in Language Education for the 21st Century." 2017. https://www.amacad.org/language (accessed February 4, 2019).

———. *Our Common Purpose: Reinventing American Democracy for the 21st Century.* New York: American Academy of Arts & Sciences, 2020.

Anbinder, Tyler G. *Nativism and Slavery: The Northern Know Nothings and the Politics of the 1850s.* New York: Oxford University Press, 1992.

Annan, Kofi. "Embrace Our Differences." February 13, 2007. http://www.tompaine. com/articles/2007/02/13/embrace_our_differences.php (accessed March 10, 2017); Now available https://unobserver.net/?folder=item3&pagina=intlaw.php (accessed January 25, 2024).

Appiah, Kwame Anthony. "Is the Post- in Postmodernism the Post- in Postcolonial?" *Critical Inquiry* 17, no. 2 (Winter 1991): 336–57, http://www.jstor.org/stable/1343840?origin=JSTOR-pdf.

———. *The Lies That Bind Us: Rethinking Identity.* New York: Liveright Publishing, 2018.

Applebaum, Anne. "Trump's Bizarre and Un-American Visit to Saudi Arabia." *Washington Post.* May 21, 2017. https://www.washingtonpost.com/news/global-opinions/wp/2017/05/21/trumps-bizarre-and-un-american-visit-to-saudi-arabia/ (accessed September 9, 2021).

Arnold, Matthew. *Culture and Anarchy* (1869). London: Oxford University Press, 2006.

Atlantic Monthly Editors. "What is 'the American Idea'?" *Atlantic Monthly.* January/February 2006. https://www.penguinrandomhouse.ca/books/182828/the-american-idea-by-robert-vare/9780307481405 (accessed October 16, 2007).

Bacevich, Andrew. *The Age of Illusions: How America Squandered Its Cold War Victory.* New York: Metropolitan Books, 2020.

Badash, David. "Watch: Gay People 'Will Die Out Because They Don't Reproduce' Says Pat Robertson." *New Civil Rights Movement (NORM).* December 17, 2014. https://www.thenewcivilrightsmovement.com/2014/12/watch_gay_people_will_die_out_because_they_don_t_reproduce_says_pat_robertson / (accessed February 1, 2023).

Balibar, Étienne. *Identity and Difference: John Locke and the Invention of Consciousness.* London: Verso, 1998; 2013.

Barna Group. "Atheism Doubles Among Generation Z." *Barna.* January 14, 2018. https://www.barna.com/research/atheism-doubles-among-generation-z/ (accessed February 9, 2017).

Barrasso, John, Mary Fallin, and Viginia Foxx. "2016 Republican Party Platform." *American Presidency Project* (UC Santa Barbara). July 18, 2016. https://www.presidency.ucsb.edu/documents/2016-republican-party-platform (accessed Aprril 12, 2018).

BBC. "Religious Affiliation in Scotland 'Declines Sharply.'" *BBC.* July 1, 2017. http://www.bbc.com/news/uk-scotland-40467084 (accessed August 10, 2018).

Beavers, Olivia. "Condoleezza Rice Says American Was Born With a Birth Defect: Slavery." *Hill.* May 7, 2017. http://thehill.com/homenews/news/332307-condoleezza-rice-says-america-was-born-with-a-birth-defect-slavery (accessed March 22, 2018).

Bennett Cory, and Bryan Bender. "How China Acquires 'the Crown Jewels' of U.S. Technology." *Politico.* May 22, 2018. https://www.politico.com/

story/2018/05/22/china-us-tech-companies-cfius-572413 (accessed January 10, 2019).

Beres, Louis René. "Looking Back at the Trump Presidency: An Informed Retrospective." *Modern Diplomacy.* August 13, 2021. https://moderndiplomacy.eu/2021/08/13/looking-back-at-the-trump-presidency-an-informed-retrospective/ (accessed January 18, 2022).

Berg, Achim, Harsh Chhaparia, Sadkia Hedrich, and Karl-Hendrik Magus, "What's Next for Bangladesh's Garment Industry, After a Decade of Growth?" *McKinsey & Company.* March 25, 2021. https://www.mckinsey.com/industries/retail/our-insights/whats-next-for-bangladeshs-garment-industry-after-a-decade-of-growth (accessed March 26, 2021).

Bethel, B. J. "I Sent My Dad's Manufacturing Job Overseas. My Own Ended Not Long After." *Washington Post.* November 28, 2018. https://www.washingtonpost.com/outlook/2018/11/28/i-sent-my-dads-manufacturing-job-overseas-my-own-followed-not-long-after/? (accessed October 14, 2019).

Bhatt, Sujata. *Brunizem.* Manchester, UK,: Carcanet Press, 1998; 2014.

Bremmer, Ian. *The End of the Free Market: Who Wins the War Between States and Corporations?* New York: Portfolio, 2010.

Brennen, J. Scott, and Daniel Kreiss. "Digitalization." *Whiley Online Library.* October 23, 2016. https://onlinelibrary.wiley.com/doi/10.1002/9781118766804.wbiect111 (accessed February 22, 2024).

Brodkin, Karen. *How Jews Became White Folks & What That Says About Race in America.* New Brunswick, NJ: Rutgers University Press, 1998; 2004.

Brokaw, Tom. *Boom! Voices of the Sixties.* New York: Random House, 2007.

Brolin, Mark, with Jonathan Haidt. "How to Overcome Tribalism, the Shouty Minority and Facebook Toxicity." *Politico.* November 7, 2021. https://www.politico.com/news/magazine/2021/11/07/social-psychologist-haidt-tribalism-facebook-519720 (accessed April 11, 2022).

Browning, Robert. "Abt Vogler" (1864). In *Rabbi Ben Ezra & Abt Vogler.* [Boston?]: Printed privately, N.d. https://www.poetryfoundation.org/poems/43743/abt-vogler (accessed January 27, 2024).

Buchanan, Patrick J. "*Death of the West*: An Excerpt from Pat Buchanan's Book." *NBC News.* August 29, 2002. https://www.nbcnews.com/id/wbna3080569 (accessed October 14, 2018).

———. *Death of the West: How Dying Populations and Immigrant Invasions Imperil Our Country and Civilization.* New York: Thomas Dunne Books, 2002.

———. "Is not the endless airing of unproven allegations inherently un-American?" (blog, dated February 17, 2018). http://www.wnd.com/2017/05/comey-the-saturday-night-massacre/ (accessed March 19, 2018).

———. "Is Secession a Solution to Cultural War?" *Buchanan* (blog). February 24, 2017. http://buchanan.org/blog/secession-solution-cultural-war-126571 (accessed June 5, 2018).

Burke, Daniel. "Mormon Church Drops Anti-LGBT Policy from 2015, Saying Children of Same-Sex Couples Now Can Be Baptized." *CNN.* April 4, 2019. https://

www.cnn.com/2019/04/04/us/mormon-lgbt-policy/index.html (accessed December 6, 2019).

Campbell, Joseph. *The Hero with a Thousand Faces.* Princeton, NJ: Princeton University Press, 1949; 2nd ed., 1968.

Carman, Tim. "How 7 Immigrant Families Transform the Thanksgiving Turkey with Flavors of Their Homeland." *Washington Post.* November 22, 2019. https://www.washingtonpost.com/food/2019/11/22/how immigrant-families-transform-thanksgiving-turkey-with-flavors-their-homelands/ (accessed May 27, 2020).

Chakravorty, Sanjoy, Devesh Kapur, and Nirvikar Singh. *The Other One Percent: Indians in America.* New York: Oxford University Press, 2017.

Chavda, Janakee. "Immigrants and Children of Immigrants Make Up at Lease 15% of the 118th Congress." *Pew Research Center.* February 28, 2023. https://www.pewresearch.org/short-reads/2023/02/28/immigrants-and-children-of-immigrants-make-up-at-least-15-of-the-118th-congress/ (accessed January 24, 2024).

Cillizza, Chris. "Rush Limbaugh Doesn't Think America Will Elect a Man Who 'Loves to Kiss His Husband.'" *CNN Politics.* February 13, 2020. https://www.cnn.com/2020/02/13/politics/rush-limbaugh-pete-buttigieg-gay/index.html (accessed February 6, 2021).

Cohen, Roger. "The Inspiration of Ample India." *New York Times*, April 14, 2017, https://www.nytimes.com/2017/04/14/opinion/the-inspiration-of-ample-india.html? (accessed June 14, 2018).

Cohen, Shari. "The Lasting Legacy of an American Dilemma." *Carnegie Results.* Fall 2004. https://www.carnegie.org/publications/lasting-legacy-american-dilemma/ (accessed March 3, 2020).

Confucius Institute U.S. Center. https://www.ciuscenter.org.

Crary, David. "If Barrett Joins, Supreme Court Would Have Six Catholics." *Associated Press.* September 26, 2020. https://apnews.com/article/us-supreme-court-ruth-bader-ginsburg-archive-courts-donald-trump-987e5fb6de8a1a29d1cbb0 0bf1f1948c (accessed February 19, 2021).

de Crèvecoeur, Hector St. John. *Letters from an American Farmer.* London: Thomas Davis, 1782.

Delaney, Brigid. "'Self-Partnered' Emma Watson Is Right: We Need More Ways to be Single." *Guardian.* November 9, 2019. https://www.theguardian.com/film/2019/nov/06/self-partnered-emma-watson-is-right-we-need-more-ways-to-be-single (accessed January 7, 2020).

Deloitte. "2018 Deloitte Millennial Survey." 2018. https://www2.deloitte.com/content/dam/Deloitte/global/Documents/About-Deloitte/gx-2018-millennial-survey-report.pdf (accessed January 25, 2024).

Derrida, Jacques. *Monolingualism of the Other, Or, The Prosthesis of Origin.* Translated by Patrick Mensah. Stanford, CA: Stanford University Press, 1998.

de Tocqueville, Alexis. *Democracy in America* (1835). New York: Generic, 2003.

Devlin, Kat. "Most European Students Are Learning a Foreign Language in School While Americans Lag." *Pew Research Center.* August 6, 2018. https://www.pewresearch.org/fact-tank/2018/08/06/most-european-students-are-learning-a-foreign-language-in-school-while-americans-lag/ (accessed January 9, 2019).

Diamant, Jeff. "Faith on the Hill: The Religious Composition of the 118th Congress." *Pew Research Center*. January 3, 2023. https://www.pewresearch.org/religion/2023/01/03/faith-on-the-hill-2023/ (accessed January 27, 2024).

Dispatch Editorial Board. "Patrick J. Buchanan: The Unpardonable Heresy of Tucker Carlson." *Dispatch*. September 17, 2018. https://cdispatch.com/opinions/patrick-j-buchanan-the-unpardonable-heresy-of-tucker-carlson/ (accessed, September 28, 2018).

Doniger, Wendy. "The Great Pumpkin Goes to Washington." *Washington Post*. January 30, 2017. http://newsweek.washingtonpost.com/onfaith/wendy_doniger/2007/01/the_great_pumpkin_goes_to_wash.html (accessed March 10, 2018).

Donnella, Leah. "Taylor Swift Is the 21st Century's Most Disorienting Pop Star." *NPR*. September 26, 2018. https://www.npr.org/2018/09/26/646422866/taylor-swift-is-the-21st-centurys-most-disorienting-pop-star (accessed August 19, 2019).

Dreifus, Claudia. "The Bilingual Advantage." *New York Times*. May 30, 2011. http://www.nytimes.com/2011/05/31/science/31conversation.html? (accessed December 14, 2019).

Du Bois, W. E. B. *The Souls of Black Folk: Essays and Sketches*. Chicago: A. C. McClurg, 1903.

Dylan, Bob. "The Times They Are A-Changin.'" *The Times They Are A-Changin'* (album). New York: Columbia Records, 1964.

Egan, Casey. "Congressman Joe Crowley Defends Irish-American and Other Hyphenated Americans." *Irish Central*. January 30, 2015. http://www.irishcentral.com/news/politics/congressman-joe-crowley-defends-irish-americans-and-other-hyphenated-americans (accessed December 5, 2028).

Elliott, Anthony. "Introduction." In *Self-Identity and Everyday Life*, by Harvie Ferguson, vii-x. London: Routledge, 2009.

Erikson, Erik H. *Identity: Youth and Crisis*. New York: W. W. Norton, 1968.

ESPN. "NFL Commissioner Roger Goodell: I 'Encourage' a Team to Sign Colin Kaepernick." *ABC News*. June 16, 2020. https://abc7news.com/sports/nfl-commissioner-roger-goodell-i-encourage-a-team-to-sign-colin-kaepernick/6249251/ (accessed July 5, 2020).

Ferguson, Harvie. *Self-Identity and Everyday Life*. New York: Routledge, 2009.

Fish, Stanley. *The Trouble with Principle*. Cambridge, MA: Harvard University Press, 1999.

Fishman, Joshua. "300-Plus Years of Heritage Language Education in the United States." In *Heritage Languages in America: Preserving a National Resource*, edited by Joy Kreeft Peyton, Donald A. Ranard, and Scott McGinnis, 81–97. McHenry, IL: Center for Applied Linguistics & Delta Systems, 2001.

Forbes, David. "How Capitalism Captured the Mindfulness Industry." *Guardian*. April 16, 2019. https://www.theguardian.com/lifeandstyle/2019/apr/16/how-capitalism-captured-the-mindfulness-industry (accessed September 5, 2020).

Frank, Nathaniel. *Awakening: How Gays and Lesbians Brought Marriage Equality to America*. New York: Belknab Press, 2017.

Franke-Ruta, Garance. "Is Elizabeth Warren Native American or What?" *Atlantic*. May 12, 2012. https://www.theatlantic.com/politics/archive/2012/05/

is-elizabeth-warren-native-american-or-what/257415/ (accessed November 14, 2017).

Frey, William. *Diversity Explosion: How New Racial Demographics Are Remaking America*. Washington DC: Brookings Institute Press, 2015.

Friedan, Betty. *The Feminine Mystique*. New York: W. W. Norton, 1963.

Friedman, Thomas L. "The American Civil War, Part II." *New York Times*. October 2, 2018. https://www.nytimes.com/2018/10/02/opinion/the-american-civil-war-part-ii.html (accessed November 9, 2019).

Fukuyama, Francis. *Identity: The Demand for Dignity and the Politics of Resentment*. New York: Farrar, Straus, & Giroux, 2018.

———. "Political Consequences of the Protestant Reformation, Part II." *American Interest*. November 2, 2017. https://www.the-american-interest.com/2017/11/02/political-consequences-protestant-reformation-part-ii/ (accessed August 5, 2018).

———. "Trump's a Dictator? He Can't Even Repeal Obamacare." *Politico*. March 27, 2017. http://www.politico.com/magazine/story/2017/03/trumps-a-dictator-he-cant-even-repeal-obamacare-214958 (accessed March 27, 2017).

Gamboa, Suzanne, Sandra Lilley, and Sarah Cahlan. "Young Latinos: Born in the U.S.A., Craving Their Own Identity." *NBC News*. September 14, 2018. https://www.nbcnews.com/news/latino/young-latinos-born-u-s-carving-their-own-identity-n908086 (accessed May 4, 2021).

Gaouette, Nicole, Manu Raju, and Veronica Stracqualursi. "Khashoggi Was Murdered, Saudis Did It, Leading Republican Says." *CNN*. October 11, 2018. https://www.cnn.com/2018/10/11/politics/trump-saudi-arabia-journalist-corker/index.html (accessed February 12, 2019).

Garcia, Carlos, and Loretta E. Bass. "American Identity and Attitudes Toward English Language Policy Initiatives." *Journal of Sociology & Social Welfare* 34, no. 1 (2007): 63–82.

Gates, Henry Louis, Jr., and Kevin M. Burke. *And Still I Rise: Black America Since MLK*. New York: HarperCollins, 2015.

Geertz, Clifford. *The Interpretation of Cultures*. New York: Basis Books, 1973; 2000.

Geiger, A. W., and Gretchen Livingston. "8 Facts About Love and Marriage in American." *Pew Research Center*. February 13, 2019. https://www.pewresearch.org/fact-tank/2019/02/13/8-facts-about-love-and-marriage/ (accessed May 9, 2020).

Gerson, Michael. "The Last Temptation." *Atlantic*. April 2018. https://www.theatlantic.com/magazine/archive/2018/04/the-last-temptation/554066/ (accessed May 2, 2019).

Gerson, Michael, and Peter Wehner. "How Christians Can Flourish in a Same-Sex-Marriage World." *Christianity Today*. November 2, 2015. http://www.christianitytoday.com/ct/2015/november/how-christians-can-flourish-in-same-sex-marriage-world-cult.htm l (accessed November 12, 2019).

Giddens, Anthony. *Modernity and Self-identity: Self and Society in the Late Modern Age*. London: Polity, 1991.

Giridharadas, Anand. *Winners Take All: The Elite Charade of Changing the World*. New York: Knopf, 2018.

Glaude, Eddie S., Jr. *Democracy in Black: How Race Still Enslaves the American Soul.* New York: Broadway Books, 2016.

———. "What is African American Religion?" Oxford University Press (blog). October 17, 2014. https://blog.oup.com/2014/10/african-american-religion/ (assessed May 15, 2017).

Glazer, Nathan. *We Are All Multiculturalists Now.* Cambridge, MA: Harvard University Press, 1997.

Glazer, Nathan, and Daniel P. Moynihan. *Beyond the Melting Pot: The Negroes, Puerto Ricans, Jews, Italians, and Irish of New York City.* Cambridge, MA: MIT Press, 1963.

Gleason, Philip. "American Identity and Americanization." In *Harvard Encyclopedia of American Ethnic Groups,* edited by Stephan Thernstrom, 31–32, 56–57. Cambridge, Mass.: Belknap Press, 1980.

———. "Identifying Identity: A Semantic History." *Journal of American History* 69, no. 4 (1983): 910–31. https://doi.org/10.2307/1901196.

Goldstein, Eric. L. *The Price of Whiteness: Jews, Race, and American Identity.* Princeton, NJ: Princeton University Press, 2006.

Haass, Richard. "How a World Order Ends: And What comes in Its Wake." *Foreign Affairs.* December 11, 2018. Updated January/February 2019. https://www.foreignaffairs.com/articles/2018-12-11/how-world-order-ends? (accessed February 13, 2019).

Hakimzadeh, Shirin, and D'Vera Cohn. "English Usage Among Hispanics in the United States." *Pew Research Center.* November 29, 2007. https://www.pewhispanic.org/2007/11/29/english-usage-among-hispanics-in-the-united-states/ (accessed March 5, 2010).

Hall, Jonah. "Manufacturing Jobs, Identity and Public Sympathy." *Medium.* March 8, 2017. https://medium.com/@darkoindex/manufacturing-jobs-identity-and-public-sympathy-15b737d22f5 (accessed June 23, 2018).

Hamilton, Carol V. "Why Did Jefferson Change 'Property' to the 'Pursuit of Happiness'?" *History New Network.* 2008. https://historynewsnetwork.org/article/46460 (accessed August 7, 2018). Originally published as "The Surprising Origins and Meaning of the 'Pursuit of Happiness.'"

Hamilton, Isobel Asher. "Interview with Alphabet Chairman John Hennessy." *Business Insider.* November 21, 2018. https://www.businessinsider.com/alphabet-john-hennessy-google-returning-to-china-2018-11 (accessed January 10, 2020).

Handlin, Oscar. *Race and Nationality in American Life.* Boston: Atlantic-Little, Brown, 1957.

Hanna, Mary, and Jeanne Batalova. "Indian Immigrants in the United States." *Migration Policy Institute.* October 16, 2020. https://www.migrationpolicy.org/article/indian-immigrants-united-states-2019 (accessed July 25, 2021).

Hartman, Andrew. *A War for the Soul of America: A History of the Culture Wars.* Chicago: University of Chicago Press, 2015.

Hauser, Brooke. *The New Kids: Big Dreams and Brave Journeys at a High School for Immigrant Teens.* New York: Free Press, 2011.

Bibliography

Havel, Václav. "The Power of the Powerless." (October 1978; rev. 1985). *HAC Bard.* December 23, 2011. https://hac.bard.edu/amor-mundi/the-power-of-the-powerless-vaclav-havel-2011-12-23 (accessed January 10, 2015).

Healy, Patrick. "Hopefuls Differ as They Reject Gay Marriage." *New York Times.* October 31, 2008. https://www.nytimes.com/2008/11/01/us/politics/01marriage.html (accessed March 4, 2023).

Helliwell, J. F., Layard, R., Sachs, J. D., De Neve, J.-E., Aknin, L. B., & Wang, S. (Eds.). (2024). *World Happiness Report 2024.* University of Oxford: Wellbeing Research Centre.

Herman, Edward S., and Noam Chomsky. *Manufacturing Consent: The Political Economy of the Mass Media.* New York: Pantheon, 1988; Reprint. 2002.

Hiatt, Brian. "The Beatles in Spatial Audio: Producer Giles Martin on How It All Works." *Rolling Stone.* July 29, 2021. https://beatles.ncf.ca/archived_news_p26.html (accessed August 4, 2019).

Higham, John. *Strangers in the Land: Patterns of American Nativism, 1860–1925.* New York: Rutgers University Press, 1955; New epilogue, 2002.

Hirsh, E. D., Jr. *Cultural Literacy: What Every American Needs to Know.* New York: Vintage, 1987.

Hochschild, Arlie. "How the 'Great Paradox' of American Politics Holds the Secret to Trump's Success." *Guardian.* September 7, 2016. https://www.theguardian.com/us-news/2016/sep/07/how-great-paradox-american-politics-holds-secret-trumps-success (accessed April 5, 2019)

Hollinger, David A. "Identity in the United States." In *Keywords: Identity,* edited by Mahmood Mamdani, 27–45. New York: Other Press, 2004.

Hulse, Carl. "Senate Votes to Set English as National Language." *New York Times.* May 19, 2006. https://www.nytimes.com/2006/05/19/washington/senate-votes-to-set-english-as-national-language.html (accessed January 3, 2015).

Huntington, Samuel P. *Who Are We? The Challenges to America's National Identity.* New York: Simon & Schuster, 2004.

Ignatiev, Noel. *How the Irish Became White.* New York: Routledge, 1995.

Inskeep, Steve. "U.S.'s Cultural Ignorance Fuels Iraq Insurgency." *NPR.* April 28, 2006. https://www.npr.org/2006/04/28/5366677/u-s-s-cultural-ignorance-fuels-iraq-insurgency (accessed January 26, 2024).

Jardina, Ashley. *White Identity Politics.* Cambridge: Cambridge University Press, 2019.

Jenkins, Richard. *Social Identity.* New York: Routledge, 2004.

Jewish Federations of North America (JFNA). "Meeting the Needs of North American Jewish Community." 2023. https://www.jewishfederations.org/about-jfna (accessed October 10, 2023).

Jindal, Bobby. "Speech." Henry Jackson Society (*HJS*). January 16, 2015. http://henryjacksonsociety.org/2015/01/19/a-lecture-by-governor-bobby-jindal-3/ (accessed July 14, 2017).

Johnson, Jerry, and HBU Editors. "Celebrating Diversity & Distinction." *Pillars: Houston Baptist University (HBU)* 56, no. 1 (Spring 2020): 1–72. https://hc.edu/publications/pillars/PillarsSpring2020web.pdf (accessed January 6, 2020).

Judis, John B. "It's the Economy, Stupid." *Washington Post.* November 29, 2018. https://www.washingtonpost.com/news/magazine/wp/2018/11/29/feature/the-key-to-understanding-americas-red-blue-split-isnt-ideology-or-culture-its-economics/? (accessed December 19, 2019).

Kallen, Horace M. *Culture and Democracy in the United States.* New York: Boni and Liveright, 1924.

Kaplan, Seth D. "How Do America's Elites Stack Up?" *American Interest.* October 30, 2019. https://www.the-american-interest.com/2019/10/30/how-do-americas-elites-stack-up/ (accessed December 23, 2020).

Kelly, Nataly. "Ten Years After 9/11, America Still Has a Language Problem." *Huffington Post.* September 12, 2011. Updated November 12, 2011. https://www.huffpost.com/entry/ten-years-after-911-ameri_b_956536 (accessed May 9, 2019).

Khanna, Parag. *Connectography: Mapping the Future of Global Civilization.* New York: Random House, 2016.

———. "These 25 Companies Are More Powerful Than Many Countries." *Foreign Policy.* March 15, 2016. http://foreignpolicy.com/2016/03/15/these-25-companies-are-more-powerful-than-many-countries-multinational-corporate-wealth-power/ (accessed March 10, 2017).

Kim, Soo. "Is the Dreamliner Worth the Hype? Here's 10 Reasons Why It Might Just Be." *Telegraph.* March 28, 2018. https://www.telegraph.co.uk/travel/news/boeing-787-10-dreamliner-features/ (accessed June 5, 2022).

Kleinfeld, Rachel. "Polarization, Democracy, and Political Violence in the United States: What the Research Says." *Carnegie Endowment for International Peace.* September 5, 2023. https://carnegieendowment.org/2023/09/05/polarization-democracy-and-political-violence-in-united-states-what-research-says-pub-90457 (accessed October 2, 2023).

Krauthammer, Charles. "An Overdose of Public Piety." *Washington Post.* December 14, 2007. http://www.washingtonpost.com/wp-dyn/content/article/2007/12/13/AR2007121301501.html (accessed January 9, 2018).

———. "In Plain English: Making It Official." *Time International.* June 12, 2006. no. 74.

Kumaravadivelu, B. *Cultural Globalization and Language Education.* New Haven, CT: Yale University Press, 2008.

———. "Evangelical Zeal Not Matched by Humility, Curiosity." *San Jose Mercury News.* September 13, 2003. http://www.bayarea.com/mld/mercurynews/entertainment/6762441.htm (accessed April 28, 2017); Now available at *Hindu Vivek Kendra,* https://www.hvk.org/2003/0903/154.html (accessed January 25, 2024).

———. "Our Prejudices, Our Selves." *San Jose Mercury News.* September 18, 1997, 1, 4.

Kuo, David. *Tempting Faith: An Inside Story of Political Seduction.* New York: Free Press, 2006.

Kuttner, Robert. "Phillip Roth's 'The Plot Against America' Is Fast Becoming Reality." *Huffpost.* January 15, 2017. Updated January 16, 2018. https://www.

huffpost.com/entry/phillip-roths-the-plot-ag_b_14190564 (accessed February 24, 2018).

Kwong, Jessica. "Should English Be the Official Language of the United States? Tucker Carlson Says a 'Core Weakness' of the U.S. Is That It Isn't." *Newsweek.* May 5, 2018. http://www.newsweek.com/should-english-be-official-language-united-states-tucker-carlson-says-core-911959 (accessed May 5, 2018).

Lamb, Ramdas. "Polytheism and Monotheism: A Hindu Perspective." *Huffington Post* (blog). March 3, 2011. http://www.huffingtonpost.com/ramdas-lamb/polytheism-and monotheism_b_841905.html (accessed September 28, 2018).

Lapham, Lewis H. *Age of Folly: America Abandons Its Democracy.* New York: Verso, 2016.

Laurino, Maria. *The Italian Americans: A History.* New York: W. W. Norton, 2015.

Lerner, Max. *America as a Civilization: Life and Thought in the United States Today.* New York: Simon & Schuster, 1957.

Lévi-Strauss, Claude. *Myth and Meaning.* Toronto: University of Toronto Press, 1978.

Lévy, Bernard-Henri. *American Vertigo: Traveling America in the Footsteps of Tocqueville.* New York: Random House, 2006.

Lewis, George. "An Un-American Introduction." *Journal of American Studies* 47, no. 4 (2013): 871–79. https://www.jstor.org/stable/i24482947 (accessed January 31, 2024).

Lilla, Mark. *The Stillborn God: Religion, Politics, and the Modern West.* New York: Alfred A. Knopf; Toronto: Random House, 2007.

Liu, Eric. *The Accidental Asian: Notes of a Native Speaker.* New York: Vintage Books, 1998.

———. *A Chinaman's Choice: One Family's Journey and the Chinese American Dream.* New York: Public Affairs, 2014.

Looney, Dennis, and Natalia Lusin. "Enrollments in Languages Other Than English in United States Institutions of Higher Education, Summer 2016 and Fall 2016: Preliminary Report." *Modern Language Association.* February 2018. https://www.mla.org/content/download/83540/2197676/2016-Enrollments-Short-Report.pdf (accessed December 14, 2019).

Lopez, Mark Hugo, Ana Gonzalez-Berrera, and Gustavo López. "Hispanic Identity Fades Across Generations as Immigrant Connections Fall Away." *Pew Research Center.* December 20, 2017. http://www.pewhispanic.org/2017/12/20/hispanic-identity-fades-across-generations-as-immigrant-connections-fall-away/ (accessed July 25, 2018).

Lowry, Rich. "Why Ron DeSantis Is Going After Disney." *Politico.* April 21, 2022. https://www.politico.com/news/magazine/2022/04/21/ron-desantis-disney-smart-big-business-left-gop-00026886 (accessed January 26, 2024).

Maalouf, Amin. *On Identity.* London: Harvill Press, 2000.

Maldonado, Alessandra. "Poll: Australian Top Choice of Faith Is Now 'No Religion.'" *Salon.* June 27, 2017. http://www.salon.com/2017/06/27/poll-australia-no-religion/ (accessed July 4, 2018).

Malik, Ashok. "Why India Hates Bobby McJindal." *Deccan Chronicle*. June 28, 2015. http://www.deccanchronicle.com/150628/commentary-columnists/article/why-india-hates-bobby-mcjindal (accessed July 14, 2017).

Manyika, James, and Susan Lund. "Globalization for the Little Guy." *McKinsey & Company*. January 1, 2016. https://www.mckinsey.com/business-functions/globalization-for-the-little-guy (accessed January 23, 2017).

Margulies, Joseph. *What Changed When Everything Changed: 9/11 and the Making of National Identity*. New Haven, CT: Yale University Press, 2013.

McCullough, David. *The American Spirit: Who We Are and What We Stand For*. New York: Simon & Schuster, 2017.

McKinsey Global Institute. "The World at Work: Jobs, Pay, and Skills for 3.5 Billion People." June 2012. https://www.mckinsey.com/~/media/McKinsey/Featured%20Insights/Employment%20and%20Growth/The%20world%20at%20work/MGI%20Global_labor_Executive_Summary_June_2012.pdf (accessed May 2, 2015).

Meacham, Jon. *American Gospel: God, the Founding Fathers, and the Making of a Nation*. New York: Random House, 2007.

———. "A Nation of Christians Is Not a Christian Nation." *New York Times*. October 7, 2007. http://www.nytimes.com/2007/10/07/opinion/07meacham.html (accessed May 28, 2018; October 23, 2018).

———. *The Soul of America: The Battle for Our Better Angels*. New York: Random House, 2018.

Mills, C. [Charles] Wright. *The Power Elite*. Oxford: Oxford University Press, 1956; 2000.

Mounk, Yascha. "It's Time for an Outrage Armistice." *Slate*. May 2, 2018. https://slate.com/news-and-politics/2018/05/how-to-reach-a-truce-in-the-culture-war.html (accessed February 10, 2019).

National Commission on Terrorist Attacks Upon the United States. "Tenth Public Hearing: 9/11 Commission." Washington, DC. April 14, 2004. https://9-11commission.gov/archive/hearing10/9-11Commission_Hearing_2004-04-14.htm (accessed September 3, 2010).

National Immigration Forum. "Immigrants and the Importance of Language Learning for a Global Society." 2016. https://immigrationforum.org/wp-content/uploads/2016/10/Language-Learning-for-a-Global-Society.pdf (accessed May 9, 2019).

New World Encyclopedia Contributors. "House Un-American Activities Committee." *New World Encyclopedia*. Last updated January 14, 2018. ID: 1008788. https://www.newworldencyclopedia.org/entry/House_Un-American_Activities_Committee (accessed July 18, 2021).

Nordlinger, Jay. "Thoughts on American." *National Review*. July 19, 2019. https://www.nationalreview.com/corner/thoughts-on-america/ (accessed July 20, 2019).

Novak, Michael. *The Rise of the Unmeltable Ethnics: Politics and Culture in the Seventies*. New York: McMillan, 1971.

Nuffield Foundation. "Languages: The Next Generation." Report. London: Nuffield Foundation, 2000. https://www.nuffieldfoundation.org/

wp-content/uploads/2019/11/languages_finalreport.pdf (accessed January 26, 2024).

Obama, Barack. "Barack Obama's Speech on Race." *New York Times*. March 18, 2008. https://www.nytimes.com/2008/03/18/us/politics/18text-obama.html (accessed January 3, 2017).

O'Neil, Shannon K. "How to Pandemic-Proof Globalization: Redundancy, Not Reshoring, Is the Key to Supply Chain Security." *Foreign Affairs*. April 1, 2020. https://www.foreignaffairs.com/articles/2020-04-01/how-pandemic-proof-globalization (accessed May 28, 2021).

Ortega, Andrés. "The Deglobalization Virus?" *Globalist*. March 18, 2020. https://www.theglobalist.com/coronavirus-covid19-pandemic-globalization-deglobalization-globalism/ (accessed January 20, 2024).

Paltrow, Gwyneth. "From the Archive: Gwyneth Paltrow on Her Conscious Uncoupling Journey." *Vogue* (British). September 27, 2022. https://www.vogue.co.uk/arts-and-lifestyle/article/gwyneth-paltrow-conscious-uncoupling (accessed March 3, 2022).

Parekh, Bhikhu. *A New Politics of Identity*. London: Palgrave Macmillan, 2008.

Park, Robert E., and Ernest W. Burgess. *Introduction to the Science of Sociology*. Chicago: University of Chicago Press, 1921; 3rd ed., 1969.

PBS. "Jerry Falwell interview with PBS, 'Assault on Gay America.'" *PBS Frontline*. 2000. https://www.pbs.org/wgbh/pages/frontline/shows/assault/interviews/falwell.html (accessed June 9, 2019).

Pearson, Brendan. "Sorry Still Seems to Be the Hardest Word for Howard." *Financial Review*. June 4, 1999. https://www.afr.com/politics/sorry-still-seems-to-be-the-hardest-word-for-howard-19990604-k8tqp (accessed January 27, 2024).

Peters, Gerhard, and John T. Woolley. "2012 Democratic Party Platform." *American Presidency Project* (UC Santa Barbara). September 3, 2012. https://www.presidency.ucsb.edu/documents/2012-democratic-party-platform (accessed August 7, 2015).

Peterson, Rachelle. "American Universities Are welcoming Chinese Trojan Horse." *Foreign Policy*. May 9, 2017. https://foreignpolicy.com/2017/05/09/american-universities-are-welcoming-chinas-trojan-horse-confucius-institutes/ (accessed November 10, 2019).

Pew Research Center. "American Have Positive Views About Religion's Role in Society, but Want It Out of Politics," November 15, 2019, https://www.pewforum.org/2019/11/15/americans-have-positive-views-about-religions-role-in-society-but-want-it-out-of-politics/ (accessed October 5, 2020).

———. "America's Changing Religious Landscape." May 12, 2015. http://www.pewforum.org/2015/05/12/americas-changing-religious-landscape/ (accessed September 19, 2018).

———. "Attitudes on Same-Sex Marriage." May 14, 2019. https://www.pewforum.org/fact-sheet/changing-attitudes-on-gay-marriage/ (accessed May 9, 2020).

———. "Beyond Red vs. Blue: The Political Typology." November 9, 2021. https://www.pewresearch.org/politics/2021/11/09/beyond-red-vs-blue-the-political-typology-2/ (accessed January 27, 2024).

————. "One-in-Five U.S. Adults Were Raised in Interfaith Homes." October 26, 2016. https://www.pewforum.org/2016/10/26/one-in-five-u-s-adults-were-raised-in-interfaith-homes/ (accessed May 9, 2020).

————. "A Portrait of Jewish Americans, Chapter 1: Population Estimates." October 1, 2013. https://www.pewresearch.org/religion/2013/10/01/chapter-1-population-estimates/ (accessed December 7, 2015).

————. "Publications," 1985–2024, https://www.pewsocialtrends.org (accessed October 5, 2020).

Phillips, Kevin. *American Theocracy: The Peril and Politics of Radical Religion, Oil, and Borrowed Money in the 21st Century.* New York: Viking, Penguin Group, 2006.

Pilkington, Ed. "Shoes and Insults Hurled at Bush on Iraq Visit." *Guardian.* December 15, 2008. https://www.theguardian.com/world/2008/dec/15/george-bush-shoes-iraq (accessed July 2, 2018).

Pinkas, Alon. "American Rabbis, Tell your Congregants: The Israel You Knew Is a Relic of the Past." *Haaretz.* September 11, 2023. https://www.haaretz.com/us-news/2023-09-11/ty-article/premium/american-rabbis-tell-your-congregants-the-israel-you-knew-is-a-relic-of-the-past/0000018a-848c-d37d-a19a-e5ac49030000 (accessed October 10, 2023).

Placek, Martin. "Motor Vehicle Production of the United States and Worldwide from 1999 to 2021." *Statista.* 2022. Last updated December 8, 2023. https://www.statista.com/statistics/198488/us-and-global-motor-vehicle-production-since-1999/ (accessed May 14, 2022).

Politico Magazine, Elizabeth F. Ralph, and Contributors. "Was 2017 the Craziest Year in U.S. Political History?" *Politico.* December 29, 2017. https://www.politico.com/magazine/story/2017/12/29/was-2017-the-craziest-year-in-us-political-history-216119 (accessed March 14, 2018).

Pramuk, Jacob. "At Boeing, Trump Touts American Manufacturing, Says He's Looking at 'Big' F-18 Fighter Order." *CNBC.* February 17, 2017. https://www.cnbc.com/2017/02/17/trump-heads-to-boeing-facility-to-talk-jobs.html (accessed on June 5, 2022).

Pullella, Philip, and Danlela Desantis. "Pope Francis Ends South America Trip by Urging Young People to 'Make A Mess.'" *Huffington Post.* July 12, 2015. Last updated January 9, 2017. http://www.huffingtonpost.com/entry/pope-francis-ends-south-america-trip-by-urging-young-people-to-make-a-mess_55a3257ee4b0ecec71bc5b65 (accessed May 23, 2018).

Putnam, Robert [R. D.]. *Bowling Alone: The Collapse and Revival of American Community.* New York: Simon and Schuster, 2000.

Putnam, Robert D., and David E. Campbell. *American Grace: How Religion Divides and Unites Us.* New York: Simon & Schuster, 2010.

————. "Walking Away from Church." *Los Angeles Times.* October 17, 2010. http://www.latimes.com/news/opinion/commentary/la-oe-1017-putnam-religion-20101017,0,6283320.story (accessed December 5, 2019).

Radhakrishnan, R. "Postcoloniality and the Boundaries of Identity." *Callaloo* 16, no. 4 (1993): 750–71.

Radhakrishnan, Sarvepalli. *The Hindu View of Life*. New York: Macmillan, 1927.
Reiss, Fraidy. "Unchained Holds Historic Chain-In to End Forced Marriage." *Unchained At Last*. April 15, 2015. https://www.unchainedatlast.org/3142015-%E2%80%A2-unchained-holds-historic-chain-in-to-end-forced-marriage/ (accessed January 1, 2024).
Robinson, Jeffery. "Five Truths About Black History." *ACLU*. N.d. https://www.aclu.org/issues/racial-justice/five-truths-about-black-history (accessed December 11, 2018).
Rodríguez, Richard. *Brown: The Last Discovery of America*. New York and London: Penguin, 2002.
Rodrik, Dani. "The Trouble with Globalization." *Milken Institute Review*. October 20, 2017. https://www.milkenreview.org/articles/the-trouble-with-globalization (accessed January 20, 2024).
Roediger, David R. *Working Toward Whiteness: How America's Immigrants Became White*. New York: Basic Books, 2005.
Roosevelt, Theodore. *The Works of Theodore Roosevelt: Memorial Edition*. 24 vols. New York: Charles Scribner, 1919; 1926.
Sacks, Jonathan. *The Dignity of Difference: How to Avoid the Clash of Civilizations*. New York: Continuum, 2002.
Safire, William. *Safire's Political Dictionary*. Oxford: Oxford University Press, 2008.
Saltzman, Paul. *Prom Night in Mississippi*. Directed by Paul Saltzman. Charleston, MS: HBO: Return to Mississippi Productions, 2000.
Samson, Jennifer F., and Brian A. Collins. "Preparing All Teachers to Meet the Needs of English Language Learners." *Center for American Progress*. April 30, 2012. https://www.americanprogress.org/issues/education-k-12/reports/2012/04/30/11372/preparing-all-teachers-to-meet-the-needs-of-english-language-learners/ (accessed December 9, 2019).
Sandstrom, Aleksandra. "Half of All Church Fires in the Past 20 Years Were Arsons." *Pew Research Center*. October 26, 2015. http://www.pcwresearch.org/fact-tank/2015/10/26/half-of-all-church-fires-in-past-20-years-were-arsons/ (accessed July 19, 2017).
Schaeffer, Katherine. "U.S. Congress Continues to Grow in Racial, Ethnic Diversity." *Pew Research Center*. January 9, 2023. https://www.pewresearch.org/short-reads/2023/01/09/u-s-congress-continues-to-grow-in-racial-ethnic-diversity/ (accessed February 2, 2024).
Schlesinger, Arthur M., Jr. *The Disuniting of America*. New York: W. W. Norton, 1992.
Seidel, Andrew L. *The Founding Myth: Why Christian Nationalism Is Un-American*. New York: Sterling, 2019.
Sen, Amartya. *Identity and Violence: The Illusion of Destiny*. New York: Penguin Books, 2006.
Sherwood, Harriet. "Christianity as Default Is Gone: The Rise of the Non-Christian Europe." *Guardian*. March 20, 2018. https://www.theguardian.com/world/2018/mar/21/christianity-non-christian-europe-young-people-survey-religion (accessed April 12, 2019).

Slaughter, Anne-Marie. *The Idea That Is America: Keeping Faith With our Values in a Dangerous World*. New York: Basic Books, 2007.

Smith, Gregory A. "About Three-in-Ten U.S. Adults Are Now Religiously Unaffiliated." *Pew Research Center*. December 14, 2021. https://www.pewresearch.org/religion/2021/12/14/about-three-in-ten-u-s-adults-are-now-religiously-unaffiliated/ (accessed January 24, 2024).

Smith, Kathleen Stein. "The Multilingual Advantage: Foreign Language as a Social Skill in a Globalized World." *Language Matters*. May 31, 2017. Mattershttps://kathleensteinsmith.wordpress.com/2017/05/31/the-multilingual-advantage-foreign-language-as-a-social-skill-in-a-globalized-world-kathys-new-article/ (accessed June 7, 2019).

Spano, Shawn J. *Public Dialogue and Participatory Democracy: The Cupertino Community Project*. New York: Hampton Press, 2001.

Steinhardt Social Research Institute (SSRI). "American Jewish Population Project." Brandeis University. 2016. https://www.brandeis.edu/cmjs/constructs/2016/population-estimates.html (accessed February 2017).

Sternheimer, Karen. *Celebrity Culture and the American Dream: Stardom and Social Mobility*. New York: Taylor & Francis, 2011.

Stokes, Bruce. "What It Takes to Truly Be 'One of Us.'" *Pew Research Center*. February 1, 2017. https://www.pewresearch.org/global/2017/02/01/what-it-takes-to-truly-be-one-of-us/ (accessed May 10, 2019; February 19, 2021).

Suarez, Ray. *Latino Americans: The 500-Year Legacy that Shaped a Nation*. New York: Celebra, 2013.

Susman, Tina. "Demand Grows for Niche Translators." *Los Angeles Times*. November 19, 2009. https://www.chicagotribune.com/business/careers/sns-jobs-lang-translation-jobs-story.html (accessed October 9, 2010).

Swift, Taylor. "30 Things I Learned Before Turning 30." *Elle*. March 6, 2019. https://www.elle.com/culture/celebrities/a26628467/taylor-swift-30th-birthday-lessons/ (accessed August 19, 2019).

Taylor, Charles. *Sources of the Self: The Making of the Modern Identity*. Cambridge, MA: Harvard University Press, 1989.

Taylor, Paul. *The Next America: Boomers, Millennials, and the Looming Generational Showdown*. New York: Public Affairs, 2014.

Tharoor, Shashi. "Should We Be Proud of Bobby Jindal?" *Times of India*. October 28, 2007. http://timesofindia.indiatimes.com/shashi-tharoor/shashi-on-sunday/Should-we-be-proud-of-Bobby-Jindal/articleshow/2495846.cms (accessed June 28, 2017).

Thernstrom, Abigail, and Stephan Thernstrom. "Black Progress: How Far We've Come, and How Far We Have to Go." *Brookings*. March 1, 1998. https://www.brookings.edu/articles/black-progress-how-far-weve-come-and-how-far-we-have-to-go/ (accessed January 24, 2024).

Thomas, Daniel. "Davos 2020: What Is the World Economic Forum and Is It elitist?" *BBC News*. January 17, 2020. https://www.bbc.com/news/technology-51134164 (accessed January 19, 2020).

Thomson, Irene Taviss. *Culture Wars and Enduring American Dilemmas*. Ann Arbor: University of Michigan Press, 2020.

Tong, Anna, Alexandra Ulmer, and Jeffrey Dastin, "Exclusive: Peter Thiel, Republican Megadonor, Won't Fund Candidates in 2024, Sources Say." *Reuters*. April 26, 2023. https://www.reuters.com/world/us/peter-thiel-republican-megadonor-wont-fund-candidates-2024-sources-2023-04-26/ (accessed May 2, 2023).

Trueman, C. N. "Pierre Bourdieu." *History Learning Site*. May 22, 2015. https://www.historylearningsite.co.uk/sociology/education-and-sociology/pierre-bourdieu/ (accessed on May 11, 2022).

Tsui, Anjali, Dan Nolan, and Chris Amico. "Child Marriage in America: By the Numbers." *PBS: Frontline*. July 6, 2017. https://www.pbs.org/wgbh/frontline/article/married-young-the-fight-over-child-marriage-in-america/ (accessed January 1, 2024).

Tsui, Bonnie. "Choose Your Own Identity." *New York Times*. December 14, 2015. https://www.nytimes.com/2015/12/14/magazine/choose-your-own-identity.html (accessed January 1, 2024).

Turner, Matthew Paul. "Is the Christian Music Industry Softening on Gays?" *Daily Beast*. October 19, 2014. Updated April 14, 2017. https://www.thedailybeast.com/is-the-christian-music-industry-softening-on-gays (accessed January 3, 2020).

Tutu, Mpho. "My Faith is not the Whole Truth of God." *Washington Post*. September 2008. http://newsweek.washingtonpost.com/onfaith/guestvoices/2008/09/my_faith_is_not_the_whole truth.html (accessed August 7, 2017).

U.S. Census Bureau. "Income, Poverty and Health Insurance Coverage in the United States, 2021." Press Release Number CB22-153. September 13, 2022. https://www.census.gov/newsroom/press-releases/2022/income-poverty-health-insurance-coverage.html (accessed October 19, 2023).

———. "2015 Press Releases." 2015. https://www.census.gov/newsroom/archives/2015-pr.html (accessed January 26, 2024).

———. "2020 Census Results." Last revised September 21, 2023. https://www.census.gov/programs-surveys/decennial-census/decade/2020/2020-census-results.html (accessed November 21, 2022).

———. "2020 Questionnaire." OBM NO. 0607-1006. https://www2.census.gov/programs-surveys/decennial/2020/technical-documentation/questionnaires-and-instructions/questionnaires/2020-informational-questionnaire-english_DI-Q1.pdf (accessed January 1, 2024).

———. "2020 U.S. Population More Racially and Ethnically Diverse than Measured in 2010." August 12, 2021. https://www.census.gov/library/stories/2021/08/2020-united-states-population-more-racially-ethnically-diverse-than-2010.html (accessed January 5, 2022).

———. "Quick Facts: United States." 2023. https://www.census.gov/quickfacts/fact/table/US/RHI225222 (accessed February 1, 2024).

U.S. Citizenship and Immigration Services, https://www.uscis.gov/.

U.S. Department of State. Bureau of Education and Cultural Affairs. "Faces of Change." N.d. https://eca.state.gov/files/bureau/fy24_nsli-y_nofo_0.pdf (accessed May 9, 2019).

U.S. English. "Welcome!" N.d. https://www.usenglish.org/ (accessed November 10, 2019).

U.S. Federal Trade Commission. "IdentityTheft.gov." N.d. OMB CONTROL#: 3084–016. https://www.identitytheft.gov/#/ (accessed January 1, 2024).

U.S. Government Accountability Office (GAO). "China: With Nearly All U.S. Confucius Institutes Closed, Some Schools Sought Alternative Language Support." October 30, 2023. https://www.gao.gov/products/gao-24-105981 (accessed November 19, 2020).

U.S. Oratory Project. "Patrick Joseph Buchanan, 'Culture War Speech.'" *Voices of Democracy*. August 17, 1992. https://voicesofdemocracy.umd.edu/buchanan-culture-war-speech-speech-text/ (accessed October 14, 2018).

Vogelstein, Fred. "The Wired Interview: Facebook's Mark Zuckerberg." *Wired*. June 29, 2009. https://www.wired.com/2009/06/mark-zuckerberg-speaks/ (accessed January 1, 2017).

Waite, C. *The Digital Evolution of an American Identity*. New York: Routledge, 2013.

Wallis, Jim. *America's Original Sin: Racism, White Privilege, and the Bridge to a New America*. New York: Baker Publishing Group, 2015.

———. *God's Politics: Why the Right Gets It Wrong and the Left Doesn't Get It*. San Francisco: Harper, 2018.

Walzer, Michael. *What It Means to Be an American*. New York: Marsilio, 1992.

Wang, Amy B. "Duke Professor Apologizes for Telling Chinese Students to Speak English on Campus." *Washington Post*. January 28, 2019. https://www.washingtonpost.com/education/2019/01/27/duke-professor-warns-chinese-students-speak-english-campus-or-face-unintended-consequences/ (accessed May 4, 2020).

Weinger, Mackenzie. "Evolve: Obama Gay Marriage Quotes." *Politico*. May 9, 2012. https://www.politico.com/story/2012/05/evolve-obama-gay-marriage-quotes-076109 (accessed August 7, 2015).

Wenn. "George Clooney Celebrating Brunei's Reversal on Death Sentence for Gay Men and Women." *Hollywood*. May 6, 2019. https://www.hollywood.com/general/george-clooney-celebrating-bruneis-reversal-on-death-sentence-for-gay-men-and-women-60750312 (accessed March 5, 2022).

Werbner, Pnina. "Introduction: The Dialectics of Cultural Diversity." In *Debating Cultural Hybridity: Multicultural Identities and the Politics of Anti-Racism*, edited by Pnina Werbner and Tariq Modood, 1–26. London: Zed Books, 1997.

Will, George F. "A Vote For English." *Washington Post*. May 25, 2006. http://www.washingtonpost.com/wp-dyn/content/article/2006/05/24/AR2006052402433.html (accessed August 5, 2017).

Williams, Byron. "The U.S. Is Not a Theocracy, Nor Should It Be." *Winston-Salem Journal*. September 3, 2022. https://journalnow.com/opinion/column/byron-williams-the-u-s-is-not-a-theocracy-nor-should-it-be/article_b234298c-294b-11ed-a7b8-f3edfed215c0.html (accessed February 5, 2023).

Williams, Raymond. *Keywords: Vocabulary of Culture and Society*. Oxford: Oxford University Press, 1976.

Wolfe, Alan. "Review Essay: Native Son: Samuel Huntington Defends the Homeland." *Foreign Affairs* 83, no. 3 (May–June 2004): 120–25. https://doi.org/10.2307/20033980.

Woo, Elaine. "Catalyst of Feminist Revolution." *Los Angeles Times.* February 5, 2006. https://www.latimes.com/archives/la-xpm-2006-feb-05-me-friedan5-story. html (accessed March 7, 2015).

World Economic Forum. "About Us." 2024. https://www.weforum.org/about/world-economic-forum (accessed March 5, 2019).

Zangwill, Israel. *The Melting Pot* (play). Columbia Theatre. Washington, DC. October 5, 1908. https://www.gutenberg.org/files/23893/23893-h/23893-h.htm (accessed January 24, 2024).

Index

About the Author

B. **Kumaravadivelu**, PhD, is professor emeritus at San José State University, California. He was educated at the Universities of Madras in India, Lancaster in England, and Michigan in the United States. He has published four scholarly books, and several research articles in refereed journals. He has served on the Editorial Board of reputed journals. Popular in international conference circuits, he has delivered keynote/plenary addresses in more than twenty countries. His book *Cultural Globalization and Language Education* (Yale University Press, 2008) was awarded the Kenneth W. Mildenberger Prize for Outstanding Research Publication by Modern Language Association, USA. Another book, *Language Teacher Education for a Global Society* (Routledge, 2012), was short-listed for a similar award by the British Association of Applied Linguists, United Kingdom. He lives in Cupertino, California with his wife and children.